CW01022012

On Paul Erasmus

'During apartheid, the security police hunted down, tortured and murdered political activists at the behest of the cabinet, government and judiciary. In this remarkable confession to his son, Paul Erasmus exposes the psychopaths, and the incompetents, who ordered and executed these grave crimes against humanity.'

– REHANA ROSSOUW

'Why is it that since the end of the TRC the only former Security Branch policeman who has voluntarily offered to tell the truth about the horrors of the 1980s and early 1990s at John Vorster Square is Paul Erasmus? In the Ahmed Timol Inquest we heard Neville Els and Seth Sons claim that they had never been involved in the torture of detainees, but that they had only heard rumours of such things. Meantime the ANC ranks are full of activists who claim that they suffered brutal interrogation at the hands of these men. Even at the TRC the security police only offered enough information to satisfy their amnesty claims and nothing more. Why are the foot soldiers of the apartheid security apparatus so intent on maintaining their laager mentality, and not breaking their conspiracy of silence?

'Had Mama Winnie Mandela been alive today there is no doubt that she would have been sitting in the Aggett Inquest, as she was one of the few people who appreciated Erasmus's honesty about the past, and was determined for the truth to come out. [...]

'Mama Winnie had been the target of Erasmus's Stratcom dirty tricks in the early 1990s, and his entire job had become about discrediting her as a human being and freedom fighter. One day in 1997 Erasmus came clean and admitted to Winnie over the course of three hours everything he had done to her, which left her sobbing and in great pain. [...] What was most surprising, even to her ANC comrades, was that she took forgiveness to another dimension, and in 1997 presented Erasmus's daughter with her wedding ring from Madiba.'

– SHANNON EBRAHIM

'My experiences with Paul were confined to testimony and evidence at the Timol and Aggett Inquiries, where he made a significant contribution. He opened up the window on the culture of the Security Branch and enlightened two courts as to how the State operated.

'During his Timol testimony, together with his statement, his significant contribution makes him one of the very few honest Security Branch policemen not to perpetuate the cover up.

'Erasmus helped to open the door to have these cases examined and to question the unholy agreement to suppress these cases soon after the TRC. I have written to President Ramaphosa to set up an inquiry into why there has been no prosecution of these cases, and to tell us how this decision was reached and if it was a matter of policy.'

– ADVOCATE HOWARD VARNEY

'Paul Erasmus swam against the tide of avoidance and denial that was the prevalent code of South Africa's security police establishment on the subject of criminality and human rights violations within its ranks. In my experience, Paul felt he was obliged to shed light on the dark underbelly of apartheid-era policing and did so repeatedly over a period of over 25 years. It is a great shame that so many others failed to follow his example.'

– PIERS PIGOU

Confessions of a Stratcom Hitman

Paul Erasmus

There are descriptions in this book that are violent, which may upset the reader, particularly those, or the family of those, who were targeted by Paul Erasmus.

First published by Jacana Media (Pty) Ltd in 2021

10 Orange Street
Sunnyside
Auckland Park 2092
South Africa
+2711 628 3200
www.jacana.co.za

© Paul Erasmus, 2021

All rights reserved.

All royalties from this book's sales will be donated to the
Teddy Bear Clinic For Abused Children.

ISBN 978-1-4314-2962-2

Cover design by publicide
All photos are from the author's collection unless otherwise stated.
Editing by Glenda Younge
Proofreading by Russell Martin
Set inEhrhardt MT Std 10.5/14pt
Printed by CTP Printers, Cape Town
Job no. 003847

See a complete list of Jacana titles at www.jacana.co.za

Contents

Prologue

Mossel Bay, 1993

FIVE SHOTS OUGHT TO DO it and, if I were lucky, I might be able to get off another two. Maybe three. I glanced down at the rifle magazine on the seat beside me, while Pink Floyd's 'Dark Side of the Moon' blasted out of the car speakers.

There was no hi-tech hospital trauma unit here. This was Mossel Bay, a small town not geared to handle the damage I had in mind. He would have to be transferred to George, some 50 kilometres away.

In my imagination, I saw him in the ambulance, suffering and screaming the whole way, each jolt of the speeding vehicle producing another cry of agony. Hopefully, the swine would have already consumed his daily quota of J&B – double with two blocks of ice and soda in a tall glass. It would make him an easier target. I thought of the hundreds of drinks I had poured for him and laughed as I wondered how he would experience the lead cocktail I was about to serve him now.

I took a long swig of beer before turning off the national road to Cape Town and slowly made my way through the outskirts of town. Lights began to flicker as dusk settled. I stopped in a quiet spot where I screwed the silencer onto the rifle and loaded the magazine. I also checked and double-checked my other weapons – a service-issue 9 mm Beretta and an R3 assault rifle, which I placed beside me. Then I cracked open another beer.

My wife Linda was a shell of her former self. My children, Candice and Dylan, were damaged. The bank was about to foreclose on our home and my life was essentially over. I had no career. I had nothing left to lose.

I raised the rifle and aimed its telescope at a distant light moving in and out of the crosshairs.

Dammit to hell!

I tossed back another pill, lit a cigarette and started the engine, the sudden boom from the speakers startling me. I pulled a blanket over the weapons and headed into town, considering my options.

There was little chance of me getting away. Everyone knew my car. A description would be circulated within minutes and the few exit roads would be quickly blocked off.

What would jail be like?

Maybe I was actually mad, just as that bastard had said. But I didn't give a damn. As long as I could do what I had set out to do, nothing else mattered.

I had considered that the light 22 rounds might not drop the target, but I was ready for that. The heavier-calibre 9 mm and the assault rifle would do the job just as well.

I cruised past the house in Maroela Street; a child was playing on the lawn. There was no sign of my target's car in the driveway. I stopped about 20 metres away, pushed my seat back and eased the barrel of the rifle through the half-open passenger window. The child's form jumped into focus as I raised my forearm. My hands were shaking, even on the dead rest of the window, so I lowered the rifle again, swallowed another pill and opened another beer, willing myself to relax.

This was my plan. When the target finally arrived, I would call him or flash my lights – catch his attention somehow. Then, as he climbed out of his car and made his way to the safety of his home, I would let him have it.

There was no excitement, no fear. I was emotionally drained. I settled down to wait, a dull ache expanding in my head and my stomach burning. The child finally went inside and I brought the rifle up again, aiming at various points on the house.

My target, Colonel Herbert Rommel van der Merwe, divisional commander of the Security Branch (SB) and the Crime Intelligence Service (CIS) of the South African Police (SAP), Southern Cape, had destroyed what was left of my life. I hated him.

As I waited, my thoughts drifted to where it had all started; with an ideological vetting and a red pen.

It was December 1975. I was at the door to the office of Lieutenant Colonel Johan Viviers, better known as 'Feef', senior staff officer of the SB, John Vorster Square (aka John Vorster), Johannesburg. Giving me the once-over, he motioned for me to enter. I came to attention in front of his desk and presented my most polished Police College salute. He stared at me through thick frames.

'Constable Paul Erasmus.' It was a statement.

'Yes, sir,' I replied.

'English or Afrikaans?'

'English-speaking, preferably, sir.' I didn't want to ruin my chances before the interview had even started.

'Very well, Erasmus,' he said. 'Why do you want to join the Security Branch?' I had prepared the answer weeks earlier, when I had been given the heads-up that this would happen.

'Sir, I have a deep interest in politics. And secondly, I find the Uniform Branch is not very intellectually stimulating.'

Feef reflected on this for a moment. 'So,' he responded, 'you wish to tell me that there are no intellectuals in the Uniform Branch?'

I suppose I could have debated the issue with him, but he interrupted when I tried to answer. 'Let me tell *you* something, young man. Without the Uniform Branch, there would be *no* Security Branch. Most of our members are drawn from the Uniform Branch, and without their excellent cooperation, we would have an extremely difficult job.' He paused. 'Where is your loyalty that you can tell me that there are no intellectuals in the Uniform Branch? Aren't you proud to wear your uniform?'

I began to explain, but the colonel silenced me by standing up and walking over to a filing cabinet from which he pulled an SB application form and questionnaire – in Afrikaans, of course.

'Fill this in,' he instructed. 'If you want to write in English, I won't mind. One has to be bilingual in this country, you know.'

I'd blown it. All my bullshit preparation had been for nothing. I would be left to rot at the Cleveland SAP with bobby-on-the-beat policing.

Maybe I could resign and find an office job like so many of my friends.

I took the forms from Feef, trying to hide my anxiety. He showed me to an adjoining office where there was a small desk and little else. I took off my cap, sat down and began to answer questions about my family background, previous convictions (if any), service history and sporting interests. Then, to my horror, my pen ran dry. I patted my pockets, searching frantically, but found nothing. I glanced around the office. Nothing.

I was doomed! I knocked on Feef's door.

'Finished so soon?' he enquired.

'No, sir. I have a problem.'

'What?' he raised his voice slightly. 'You, an Erasmus, an Afrikaner, don't understand Afrikaans?'

'Sir, I'm sorry, but could I borrow a pen?' It had been drummed into our heads in Police College that *'n polisieman sonder 'n pen is soos 'n man sonder 'n piel.*

'And you have the cheek to suggest that uniformed police are stupid,' he snorted. 'What sort of stupid uniformed policeman are you anyway?'

I was too unnerved to look him in the eye. I focused on a spot above his balding head, where a black-and-white portrait of Prime Minister John Vorster hung – authorised by standing orders as acceptable office decoration – gazing balefully from the confines of an appropriately heavy, black picture frame. The photograph, I noted, must have been taken in Vorster's youth, before the threat of what he considered the *'swart gevaar'* – or was it the brandy and Coke? – took its toll on him.

Feef gestured across his desk to a box of pens marked RSA. Government issue.

'Take one of those,' he said, but immobilised by fear, I stayed still, leaving him to lean across the desk, select a pen and toss it to me.

'Thank you, sir. I apologise ...'

'Just hurry up with the form,' he grunted.

When I was done writing all my answers – in red ink – I returned to his desk. He stared at me for a while before he asked whether I had heard of Margaret Thatcher.

I had, I said. 'She's a member of the Conservative Party in Britain, sir.'

'Lenin? Who was Lenin?'

'One of the fathers of communism, sir.'

'What does MPLA stand for?'

'Popular Movement for the Liberation of Angola, sir.'

That one seemed to impress him because there was a brief intake of breath before he asked: 'Who was prime minister when we became a republic?'

'Verwoerd, sir,' I replied, and almost before the words had left my mouth, he raised his voice: '*Doctor* Verwoerd to you, young man. What was his full name?'

'Hendrik Frensch Verwoerd, sir.'

The questions went on and on, lightened only by 'Who's the Springbok rugby captain?', the game being an SAP priority. The answer was Morné du Plessis, although he wasn't everyone's favourite, being a touch too 'liberal' for many conservative South Africans.

The final question was put forward in a lowered voice: 'What do you know and understand by communism, especially communism in South Africa?'

I'd rehearsed this one. I was ready.

'Communism is a dictatorship by the proletariat.'

Feef gaped at me and, for a moment, I thought I had made another blunder, so I hurried on to answer the second part of his question.

'Advocate Bram Fischer was a leading communist in South Africa, sir, and communists were responsible for the 1976 riots, sir. A lot of people are communist sympathisers, like Helen Suzman.'

'Helen Suzman?' he responded in surprise. 'Young man! Helen Suzman is a member of parliament, an MP. How can you say she is a communist?'

'Well, sir, she's always attacking the National Party and she supports blacks.'

He didn't hesitate: 'She gives us a lot of trouble, yes, but I'm not sure she's a communist.'

I felt slightly uneasy. Was this more than a knowledge test?

'As you know, there are lots of people and groups against us – the Anglican Church, for example,' Feef sat forward in his chair. My stomach twisted into a knot. I was a Methodist now, but I had been christened in the Anglican Church and that's what I'd written on my questionnaire.

'Where were you raised, young man?'

'Bedfordview, sir.'

'Nice area, lots of nice homes. What does your father do for a living?'

I felt on safer ground here. My father had recently retired after some 40 years in the civil service, having started during the Jan Smuts administration that ended in 1948 and running through much of the Second World War. Not that anyone knew he was a soldier or, more specifically, a South African Air Force pilot. It was as though there had been an oath of secrecy around that. As children, we were never able to ask him what it was like being in a war. He was closed to everything but a man's daily life: work, home, eat, sleep, wake up, work. An endless cycle of drudgery.

I came to hate that. I asked endless questions, always challenging values and norms. I needed the story behind the story – the stuff that was hidden and not on the daily news.

At the end of his working life, my dad was an under-secretary at Bantu Affairs, the government department that administered all aspects of the daily lives of black South Africans.

When I told Feef that, the expression on his face changed completely.

'Your mother's name is Daphne? Hell, your parents got married in 1940.' He became quite animated. 'Your father came to Johannesburg in 1933 from the Eastern Cape, a pilot in the South African Air Force.'

I was shocked.

Had the SB been checking me out in the six weeks since I had applied to join? My heart raced. They must know then that I'd been expelled from Queens High School in Kensington. Did they also know that I had smoked zol? A list of sins flashed through my mind.

But Feef was smiling, explaining that, by coincidence, he'd known my parents since the 1930s – he had even attended their wedding. He had met them through his friendship with my uncle Kobus, who was in the Police College – or depot, as it was known then.

What luck! Feef spoke warmly of my parents and 'the old days', ordered us coffee and chatted at length about his own career in the SAP, mentioning that he was soon to retire. All that was left after that was for Feef to discuss my application with the Johannesburg SB commanding officer (CO), Colonel H.C. 'Hennie' Muller.

Their offices were interleading and I overheard their conversation in Afrikaans. Feef told the CO that I had an exceptional knowledge of politics, that I had given brilliant answers to the myriad questions and that my English-speaking background would be an advantage because most 'enemies of the state' were English too. Most importantly, he could 'vouch' for me as he knew my family well. This was of cardinal importance to SB selection. If an applicant's parents were 'ideologically sound', it was safe to assume their children were at a 'lower risk' of turning on the system.

Feef then summoned me to Muller's office, and once again I came smartly to attention, saluted and moved forward to greet the CO, a small, neat man with an engaging grin. He stood up behind his enormous desk and leaned forward to shake my hand.

He asked a few questions about my personal life, then said that although my application still had to 'go to Pretoria', he was sure that wouldn't be a problem.

Right there, at that moment, began the story of my undoing.

No one put it better than the acting CO at SAP Cleveland, Captain Hartman. After my SB interview, I returned to the station, my head in the clouds, and Hartman immediately told me I was 'bloody mad'. The moment would come, he quipped, when I would regret it.

I hit back, figuring he was envious of the security police who had immense powers. Hartman, in turn, couldn't resist a comeback, tired as it was: 'So one of these days you'll be writing your name with an eraser, hey? *Lekker windgat* in your fancy car and fancy suit!'

Then his tone turned, switched to seriousness. He believed I was making a 'big fuck-up' going 'to work with the spies'. That the SB was 'nothing but glory-hunters and arse-creepers'.

YEARS LATER, WHEN DYLAN and I are picking our way through stacks of photographs from my days at the Security Branch Ovamboland and then as a security policeman in Johannesburg, I vacillate between those two descriptions of myself.

Two pictures stand out.

One is a desert scene taken in 1980. There are dark patches that make no sense until I provide context. Those were people. How many? I don't know. There was a landmine, or two, and I'm standing near an armoured police Casspir vehicle, taking a snapshot of the unthinkable cruelty. I'm 24, and many of the men in the vehicle with me – whom you can't see in the picture – are today dead or crawling around their gardens, *bosbevok*, riddled with and doomed by post-traumatic stress disorder (PTSD).

The other is of men in suits, a few of them – including me – laughing and pulling faces for the camera. We're in an office at John Vorster Square, appearing to have the time of our lives. The expressions on a couple of faces are less jocular, some even looking away from the camera. But not me. I'm the guy right in the front, the one with the widest grin.

Dylan, who is in his early thirties, is quiet as we sort these pictures into piles of (1) cannot be used because they're abominations; (2) might be of historical interest; and (3) have to be seen to be believed. The highest pile is (1). That goes back into a box.

There's an understated humour in my son. We've been living together since he was 11 years old, for more than 20 years now. Mostly, we've been making art, or tending animals, or running a bed-and-breakfast at our farmhouse just outside George. It's a plot of land where the driveway requires you to keep to a fenced-in track.

No one's tried to kill me lately, but I've had threats and insults. Poisoned viennas in my driveway meant for my other 'children' – my Great Danes; swoops by local cops who had been informed that I was dealing in drugs; further searches for unlicensed firearms; or encounters with the local Afrikaner Weerstandsbeweging (AWB).

On the darkest winter nights, when the power sometimes fails, or when there's no water supply from the municipality, it can be grim. When it's a summer afternoon and there are calves in the fields, there's no other place we would rather be.

It's been rough for Dylan. He's heard every second of my life told and retold and told again, and knows every character and every scene. He's helped painstakingly sort and file every document, notebook, scrap of paper and picture, and vicariously experienced my years of misanthropy.

He's been everywhere with me. When I wasn't there, he would try to fight his way back into my space. I would have done anything then to have him with me, and I did. But I was, obviously, persona non grata. A torturer. A racist. An apartheid foot soldier. A political scumbag. And I was – I was all of that. So who'd have trusted a man like me with a son with disabilities? Not many.

Dylan's been through a lot. It's never quite stopped. Just as we thought the pendulum was swinging more calmly, his back was seriously injured in a car accident we had on the way to the Ahmed Timol hearing in the North Gauteng High Court in Johannesburg in 2017; I suffered internal bleeding and organ damage. Maybe this is my punishment.

The reasons we live together have nothing to do with either of us being weird or lonely, even if it may seem that way when we climb onto our motorbikes and go riding along the coastline with only our own minds and the wind for company. It's at times like these, with the wind in my face and the roar of a powerful engine in my ears, that I find some kind of solace and succour.

Hell, I'm not a good-news story. I know that. This son of mine is sometimes like propaganda for me, as if I had been someone else the whole time. He's a decent and gentle soul, the antithesis of the man his father once was.

I'll tell you the story of how he tended the bar for Winnie Mandela at the age of ten, pouring generous tots of whisky and vodka for a busload of African dignitaries who'd showed up to visit her at her house in Soweto, on a day in particular when she sought solitude. Dylan did it the same way he'd do it now – quietly, with a slight smile.

Time to watch my back again.

The devil never sleeps.

Chapter One

The Silver Coffins

January 1977

DYLAN WAS JUST A youngster during the first two decades of the twenty-first century. I talk to him about what this means in terms of freedom. After all, just 15 years earlier, until as late as the early 1990s, there was still conscription. Boys weren't men until they'd gone to the army.

I worry about my son. I'm a tough guy. I gave up trying to prove something and just learned to do things my own way, accepting my own past. I've grown my hair, added to my tattoos and will no longer shut up and be ignored. If someone wants to pick a fight, I'll take them on.

My issue is that Dylan can be like a protective shadow in these situations. If someone headbutts me for my political views, I'll get stuck in – and so will Dylan. We're not even drinkers, but living on an isolated farm can drive you stone-cold crazy at times, and sometimes we just want to get away, get out and go into town. Occasionally, we find ourselves getting rough-housed at the pizza place, but it's safer than the pub.

To some extent, our biker jackets – and the reputation that comes with these – offer some protection. In fact, it's been a while since I've worn a suit.

When I started working at the SB in January 1977, my parents lent me R100 to buy new suits. Security policemen prided themselves on their two-piece and, even flashier, three-piece suits and ties. We were known for our suits and dark glasses, and our targets recognised us by them. They knew that, once we'd placed our lounge jackets – usually brown, sometimes grey – neatly on the back of a chair and loosened our neckwear, they were in for it. Suits notwithstanding, we never held back. It was usually brutal.

I couldn't wait to get out of my SAP uniform, boots, cap and all. A suit was a symbol of being a man. I was 20 years old, and even relatives who had written me off as a delinquent schoolboy called to congratulate me on my new status. Becoming a security policeman meant success.

Initially I worked under the command of Major J.H.L. Jordaan, section head of 'Blanke Personeel' – a label that referred not to the race of the staff, but to those being monitored and the organisations being infiltrated: predominantly white suspects. The other section was 'Nie-blanke Personeel', which had the highest number of staff on the SB. There was also a coloured and Indian section, commanded by one of the very few black officers in the SAP at the time, Lieutenant Seth Sons.

Our two sections were on the ninth floor of John Vorster Square, while the tenth was occupied by Major Arthur Benoni Cronwright and the Investigation Branch, which received information from us and prepared cases for prosecution.

This sounds professional, within the bounds of a secret service – at the very least, straightforward – but this would be far from the truth. If there was a location that could serve as a backdrop for a horror movie, the tenth floor was it. In my sixties now, I'm still triggered by the memory of it, and I wasn't even a victim, taken there against my will to be tortured.

No suit was required 40 years later when I appeared in the North Gauteng High Court to testify in the second sitting of the reopened inquest into the death of activist Ahmed Timol. I was still at school when Timol was reported to have committed suicide by jumping to his death from the tenth floor of John Vorster Square in 1971, so I never really knew much about the teacher and activist until I started working in that building six years after he was killed. In 2017, I wore a leather jacket and tie rather than a suit when I testified in support of the Timol family, who had been trying for nearly four decades to have the Timol inquest reopened.

My task at court was simple: to recount my time on the ninth floor, when I was an eager protagonist with a special talent for forgery, harassment and dangerous, devious schemes. At first, the government paid me to plan and commit sabotage, but, before long, the fieldwork turned into full-scale persecution.

I witnessed torture multiple times. I perpetrated physical torture more often when I was part of the Security Branch and its infamous offshoot, Operation K or Koevoet, in Ovamboland, than I ever did at John Vorster. Torture was the business of the Investigation Branch. Over the years, I came to accept that twisted psychological operations, which were also our domain on the ninth floor, can cause shifts in a person that can never be fixed.

When Feef was interviewing me that day, I had no idea of the requirement to strip away your own defences if you were to become a security policeman. If you were compassionate in any way, you simply failed to fit the brief. If you second-guessed any officially sanctioned act, you'd probably not make it.

There was something wicked in all those acts of power. I gave an example of one such act to the court in 2017. During the 1980s, an American philanthropist had written to Archbishop Desmond Tutu, stating that she wanted to make a monetary contribution to the liberation cause. Since the SB monitored every piece of incoming and outgoing international post that passed through the Jeppe Post Office, not far from John Vorster Square, we picked up her letter. I immediately forged a sneering response that rebuffed her: 'We resent you, a white capitalist, interfering in our internal affairs. Thank you very much but we don't need your money.' She never again made any contact with left-wing groups in South Africa.

But this was minor in comparison to what would come. As soon as I stepped into John Vorster Square as a member of the SB, I realised that the SB operated, to some degree, under cover of charges that were brought by the Uniform Branch, and there was a huge range of charges from which to choose. SB suspects were usually brought in and held under particular security legislation, such as the Internal Security Act, the Riotous Assemblies Act, the Terrorism Act, the Suppression of Communism Act, and other weapons in the apartheid statutory armoury. These were aside from common-law crimes such as high treason, sedition and murder.

Although we were often co-opted to assist, it was Major Cronwright and his cronies who made the arrests and handled interrogations. The major was dangerous as an enemy. He was a legend in the SB – crazily anti-communist, anti-Semitic, anti-Freemasons, anti-black, anti-gay, anti-anything other than what supremacists hold dear. He was best avoided, but the question was, how was one supposed to do this? Not knowing how, he and I were to have a date in hell.

SB logistics was made up of a small administrative section – which kept track of personnel, vehicles, claims, equipment and firearms, and paid out the salaries of informers – and a technical section, which offered back-up to operatives in the field. The latter were the guys who did the photography and the bugging, and it was their records that I was so determined to get my hands on after I left the SB – evidence is everything when you're fighting for your life.

Also important were the WH10 and WH11 sections, which carried out the interception of mail, such as that letter to Archbishop Tutu, and phone monitoring. These operations were conducted under the Post Office Act, and formed the backbone of the SB. Without WH10 and WH11, we wouldn't have been able to do nearly as much as we did. If operatives needed these services – to bug a hotel room, take a photograph that would serve to jog someone's memory, or rig a parcel at the Head Office in Pretoria that could maim or murder – we had to apply for authorisation from the Minister of Police under the Post Office Act. Applications required written motivation and were usually good for three to six months, if we had solid corroboration that our efforts were in the interests of the national security of the Republic – the primary function of all policemen in South Africa.

On day one at the SB, Major Jordaan gave me a pep talk about discipline and then handed me a casebook, in which I recorded all my fieldwork and activities – even before I was introduced to the 15 or so colleagues, whom I would come to either like or despise. New members were broken in by having to learn the filing system. I've never regretted that initiation.

Naturally there were files on activists such as the Reverend Beyers Naudé, Nadine Gordimer, Helen Joseph, Peter Wellman, Horst and Ilona Kleinschmidt and Jeanette Schoon. But there were thousands of files on people now dead and some forgotten, all sitting in rooms full of chaotic cabinets.

I absorbed as much as I could from the files on the African National Congress (ANC), the Pan Africanist Congress (PAC) and the South African Communist Party (SACP). I wanted to know everything about banned organisations, and there was plenty for me to learn. They were the radicals and we, the SB, had to crush them one by one, or they would crush us.

It was through these files as much as through my fieldwork later on that I saw first-hand how powerful apartheid's monitoring capacity was in the 1970s. A decade later, the regime had gained a reputation as one of the most dreaded information-gathering machines in the world, and I was part of this. However, although it knew how to use violence, force and the most subversive methods of intimidation to extract and gather information, this didn't mean that the SB's actual intelligence mechanisms were that impressive.

I read the files voraciously, and soon became immersed in apartheid thinking – right up until that day in Maroela Avenue, Mossel Bay, when I lifted the rifle. It was only many years later that I accepted that this kind of thinking was unsophisticated and narrow. It was fascistic. Because South Africans had been denied information on any banned organisations and their leaders, I was fascinated by the history I thought these files held. We had no knowledge, and I wanted to know it all.

As for drilling down, the actual clandestine grit, the SB had very little with which to trade, and that's why we, as SB members, spent so much time playing deadly games, gambling with people's lives. We didn't understand so much or so deeply, which meant that there was no real planning with proper intent. More often than not, we just shook the tree to see what would fall out.

Most of the source information at the time came from agents operating on the periphery, the main users of WH12 – those who planted 'tomatoes' or bugging devices. These were installed, sometimes on a permanent basis, in venues where anti-state activities were held, such as the Wits Great Hall, St Mary's Cathedral, the Johannesburg City Hall and the Regina Mundi Church in Soweto. This set-up was emulated across the country.

When B.J. Vorster resigned following the Info Scandal,[1] even the incoming prime minister, P.W. Botha, found a 'tomato' in his office. Such was the paranoid South African psyche: everybody was watching and trying to find something on everyone else. The 'tomato' in Botha's office had in fact been planted by National Intelligence (NI). It was no secret that Botha relied almost entirely on Military Intelligence (MI), placing his faith in the army's espionage, rather than that of the SB or the NI – an important indicator of the extent of the dissension, distrust and disunity in the inner sanctum of the regime.

I once drew a file on the Broederbond, the secret Afrikaner brotherhood that had dominated the upper strata of South African life since 1948. It was a significant factor in securing the positions of the fascist elite, who clung on even after 1994. There is still a brotherhood, but it is no longer secret.

In contrast to the others, the Broederbond file contained only one report, in which some lunatic alleged that the brotherhood had been infiltrated by the KGB. I suppose they had to file that type of information somewhere.

The Broederbond was certainly not an organisation that would have been of interest to the SB. Spying on the Broederbond would have been tantamount to investigating the Afrikaner elite – in other words, the government. No. Far too dangerous. This was left to the journalists whom we, in turn, watched. The SB had staff devoted entirely to damaging journalists at all possible levels. This was what I did in one of my many roles in the system. Chasing the Broederbond was not in the SB's interests at all. The National Party was permeated and controlled by the Broederbond. The whole of South Africa was manipulated by it to some extent. This was the 'state capture' of the time. We English-speakers in the civil service were raised to be apprehensive about even mentioning the Broederbond because we were entirely excluded from it.

I also read files on the Ku Klux Klan (KKK), which contained mainly newspaper reports about its activities in South Africa. Of course, we had also files on the United States' Central Intelligence Agency (CIA) and Britain's MI5, the United Kingdom's counter-intelligence and security agency, but much of what was in these was little more than a collection of disjointed clippings.

On enquiring why the files on the CIA and MI5 were so thin on content, I was told that external organisations and foreign counter-intelligence operations were the exclusive domain of the Bureau for State Security, BOSS, which would later become the National Intelligence Agency (NIA) – an agency that is probably as deeply politicised today as BOSS ever was.

The SB office at John Vorster Square was the largest in the country, with 185 000 personal and organisational files. At one point, there was genuine concern that the floor housing the filing rooms would collapse under the weight of all the steel cabinets.

Shortly after joining the SB, I was among the fieldworkers instructed to concentrate on the Reverend Beyers Naudé, then director of the Christian Institute of Southern Africa. He had become the focus of much hatred in the Afrikaner establishment and was regarded as a heretic after he turned his back on the all-powerful Nederduitse Gereformeerde Kerk (NGK) at the Cottesloe Consultation in 1960. It was here that he had taken a brave and bold stand against the church's biblical justification for apartheid. Naudé was the first major target on whom I was to focus as a young SB agent, with work also being done on other staff members of the Christian Institute.

At the time, the government was obsessed with Black Consciousness, and Naudé, the Christian Institute and the South African Council of Churches (SACC) were believed to be major players behind what we termed the 'rioting' that swept the country in June 1976. Hundreds of people were killed by the SAP, and thousands of others were injured, also mostly by the police. The uprising had cost the country and further tarnished the image of the apartheid state under John Vorster. As a result, our instructions were that those who had orchestrated this – meaning the liberals or 'communist whites' – had to be dealt with efficiently and ruthlessly.

Much time was devoted to gathering technical and human intelligence (HUMINT) on the people and organisations perceived to be behind the revolutionary mayhem, and we were driven to prove that it was all spearheaded by the individual considered to be the country's greatest traitor: Naudé. Some securocrats even believed that he had taken on the role of heading the underground SACP.

Efforts were made to plant a 'tomato' in Naudé's home, but that was unsuccessful – all because of the incompetence of the technical department of WH12 and its lack of planning, imagination and outdated equipment. The small technical complement was headed by Warrant Officer Potgieter, who regarded the equipment as his personal property. His dubious reputation within the SB wasn't helped by his having taken hundreds of useless, out-of-focus, undercover photographs, sometimes even failing to load the camera. For the SB and, in fact, the SAP, he was a square peg hammered into a round hole and was ill qualified to fill a key position. He was finally sidelined in 1981 when a new wind blew through the SB and, under a different command structure, incompetence was less tolerated.

The Beyers Naudé situation came to a head on 19 October 1977 – a day popularly known as Black Wednesday among opponents of the state – when the Christian Institute was banned, along with 17 other organisations, as well as *The World* newspaper, under ruthless security legislation. This was just before I was initiated into the field.

Attempts to show that Naudé was running the banned SACP, or that he was a surrogate of Bram Fischer,[2] or that he was in the leadership of the underground ANC within the country's borders, were all bungled. And, in the end, of course, there was nothing to prove – Naudé had no formal association with any of it. There was no truth in this whatsoever. At the time, however, Naudé remained a painful thorn in the apartheid flesh, and one that had to be excised at all costs. Should be easy, we thought; this timid old man should be a pushover.

Chapter Two

The Moscow Radio

Mossel Bay Again, 1993

I SPENT TWO WEEKS IN training at SAP Maleoskop, the counter-insurgency unit based in the farming town of Groblersdal, about two-and-a-half hours north of Johannesburg. The course was shortened for SB members. Instead of the eight weeks completed by regular policemen, we did only a fortnight covering the anti-terrorism 'bush course'.

I went to Maleoskop to prepare for where I really wanted to be at the time: Ovamboland in what was then South West Africa. I couldn't wait. That was my heart's desire. To be a real policeman, I felt, I had to have this notch in my belt. At Maleoskop, SB members were expected to sail through the training because we were supposed to be more disciplined than other SAP members. The punishing regimen of endless running and route marches wasn't part of our course. Instead, our training was in combat theory, map reading, handling mortars, machine guns, hand grenades and rifle grenades and mines and developing wilderness survival skills. The presentation was professional, but nothing could prepare me for the savagery to come.

We flew in a regular Hercules C130, designed to carry combat troops to the South African Air Force (SAAF) base at Ondangwa, South West Africa. I found the rapid descent from 30 000 feet – standard anti-missile procedure and a necessary operational demand – terrifying and a few men vomited into their helmets or caps.

But what nauseated me more than the rapid descent was that the woman sitting next to me spent the entire flight relating to the woman next to her the gruesome events that her husband had seen at the military hospital in Oshakati where he worked. Injured South African Defence Force (SADF) personnel were described in soft tones, sympathetically, but her morbid case histories were punctuated by accounts of dying 'terries'. Her demeanour, however, shifted to glee when she described injuries to 'the k-----s. Her husband had apparently been awarded several medals.

The SB operations headquarters were in Ovamboland, which is precisely why I wanted to be there. Operation K or Koevoet – which held a special status in the SAP – used it as an operations centre and we worked in partnership there. The SB's primary function was to collect and evaluate intelligence gathered from rural communities and uniformed SB staff at different bases in that vast area, and to coordinate the information. Sometimes we supplemented Koevoet as a *gevegsgroep*.[3]

I was seconded to the Central Group, commanded by a Captain Smit, a thick-set and rather dim individual known as '*koning van die bosse*'. Smit was a caricature of Nazi general Rommel. He was seldom without his silvered Schirmmützen-style field service cap, neck protector all neatly rolled up, and powerful binoculars around his neck. Out on patrol, his visor was set at a rakish angle – without seeing the irony, I suspect that Smit fancied himself as Richard Burton in *Raid on Rommel*. He saw himself as a feared combatant in the war against the South West African People's Organisation (SWAPO), and he liked to lead from the front.

We had three armoured personnel carriers (APMs) in our fighting group: a Hippo, a Ribbok and a Swerver. The Hippo, which became notorious during township incursions by the SADF in the 1980s, can carry ten soldiers plus two drivers, with mounting for two machine guns. The problem is that while it is mine-resistant, it doesn't do well under fire. Instructions were that we were to be strapped in when expecting incoming fire, but these directives were ignored for the most part by our fearless leader, who would act the hero and stand straight up in the hatch next to the driver, arms outstretched and head moving slowly from side to side as he scanned the tops of trees.

Every so often, Smit would slowly raise his right hand – a signal to decrease speed or stop – before snapping his binoculars to his eyes. Then the hand would swiftly drop, indicating a change of direction, and we would head off, gears grating and engines revving in the soft sand. That was how our dauntless leader would relieve the endless boredom, demanding we proceed with caution, despite the deafening noise of the engine, announcing on the ICS (intravehicular communication system) that we should prepare for contact with the enemy: '*Maak ... gereed ... vir ... kontak.*'

We never did spot the enemy, however, and after three weeks of this aimless riding around, members of our unit became disgruntled. This was especially after spending two days following a track that the Ovambo men in our unit quietly, out of fear of Smit, assured us was at least two weeks old and a waste of time to follow.

One night at Omungwelume, a camp operated by the SAP at the time, SB Sergeant Eugene Fourie – who had considerable experience in Ovamboland – informed Smit that he wanted to be transferred to another group because he couldn't work under a commander who never communicated his intentions. Fourie was right.

Earlier, I had had a similar encounter with Smit when he told us that he had developed what he called 'a great anti-ambush concept'. He planned to tie M18 Claymore mines down both sides of the Hippo, his idea being that if we drove into an ambush, we would be able to detonate the mines, which fire steel balls out to about 100 metres, and thus flatten everything within a 60-degree arc. I asked him whether he was aware that the blast of a Claymore was not only confined to the direction in which it faced, but that there was something like 10 to 15 per cent blowback. In my layman's opinion, I said, the combined effect of this blowback of several Claymores would roll up the Hippo's relatively thin skin like a tin can – with its occupants inside. Firefights with terrorists were one thing, but I, for one, had no intention of ending up a mashed sardine.

What followed was something of a mini-revolt in the unit and the following day we were all made to appear before the SB commanding officer. Colonel 'Flip' Meyer tended to treat every member of his staff with respect, and so Smit was immediately reassigned, and Senior Sergeant 'Tubby' Campbell and I were given control of a unit to lead in the Central Region.

We immediately set about doing precisely what we were supposed to do: gathering and evaluating intelligence and expanding our contact with community leaders, usually headmen, most of whom were living in 'protected villages' with a contingent of 'buddies' – in reality, Ovambo members of the SAP living in their villages or kraals.

Protected villages, or PVs, were regularly pounced on by SWAPO. One attack involved a group of about 50 fighters. On that occasion, they launched a brace of mortars and, shortly before the first landed and exploded, they opened fire with AK47s – the ruse being to drive the villagers to run for cover. At the moment of the people's greatest exposure, the bullets rained down on them in a deadly storm. The headman survived but several of the villagers did not. Bodies lay scattered everywhere and the centre of the kraal was completely burnt out. The sparse vegetable fields and kraal fencing posts were little more than smouldering patches of hot ash.

When we ventured in to investigate – my boots began smouldering too – I made my way into the headman's hut, which had taken a direct mortar hit. There lay the burned remains of the headman's mother, who had been about 90 years old. It having been a pre-dawn raid, she had been in bed when the mortar struck. I later photographed the ruins of the kraal and still have the pictures taken that day. Dylan and I have spoken about them many times. There's one of the dead woman's sister that holds a strange, sickening power over me, something that I've tried to convey to my son.

But how do I do this? I couldn't expect Dylan to grasp, in any real way, the horror of that day. Nevertheless, because of the promise I made to myself that when I became a father I would not confine all my experiences to my own head and then expect my children to interpret my silence, I try to describe what I encountered by means of the weather, the geographical textures and the sounds, and the terrible emotions that drift to the surface.

That day I asked our translator, Johannes, to convey my sympathy to the sister, an arrogance I can reflect on now but that at the time was little more than a feeble attempt on my part to absolve us from blame. The SAP, I told him, were there in that village that day, not as perpetrators but 'on the side of the people'. Despicable, of course, but we all firmly believed it then. The woman cried, and then she sobbed, but no tears flowed down her cheeks. That feels impossible to explain now.

At the same time, as I've admitted to Dylan, there was another side to all of this, another side of me, one that I struggle to come to grips with. I'd no sooner had this exchange with Johannes and the woman than I berated myself. What the fuck are you sympathising for? We may rule by day but SWAPO ruled by night. So let these bastards realise whom they're supporting – terrorists who wouldn't think twice about massacring them all before the sun comes up.

Sometimes I battled with this conflicted thinking, but on other occasions it was all too clear to me. Perhaps it had something to do with what Johannes revealed to me: that the woman killed by that mortar, the headman's mother, was 110 years old; she had memories of the Dorsland trekkers, Afrikaners who'd travelled with their wagons and oxen and slaves into northern Namibia in the late 1800s.

In the follow-up operation spearheaded by Koevoet, seven SWAPO men were killed. A man was decapitated through a direct hit from a rifle grenade, and two were captured alive – one was injured by a bullet to his upper thigh.

He was interrogated by Koevoet at the scene, although tortured would be a more accurate verb here: a bayonet was jabbed into his wound until he answered specific questions. Finally, responding to the intelligence they'd coerced from the prisoner, Koevoet followed the spoor while our group drove the two SWAPO members back to Oshakati, dropping the wounded man at the hospital and the other at the SB cells for further interrogation, which was set for the following day.

Base days in Oshakati began punctually at 7.30 am, with a relatively informal parade around the veranda of the austere SAP post at the entrance to the town. A Captain Spannenberg opened the morning conference with an impassioned exhortation to the Almighty to 'protect us, our country, our families at home and to preserve us through the coming days' in our noble God-given mission to destroy the satanic, communist enemies of our beloved Republic. This was the usual practice in the SAP. I recall wondering at the time whether the Almighty was receiving similar pleas from a SWAPO member to preserve him in his fight against the 'satanic white oppressors' of his motherland.

The interrogation of the suspect began immediately after the morning conference. He was about 17 or 18 years old, and claimed he had been forced into joining SWAPO, which had trained him to use an AK47. He insisted, too, that he didn't know or couldn't remember the names or histories of other members of the unit to which he was attached. He said everyone used *noms de guerre* and were careful not to divulge incriminating details, such as where they came from. So we beat the hell out of him.

By teatime, the beatings hadn't yielded any success, so we resorted to the use of 'Radio Moscow', a generator from an old-style telephone that produced an electric current via two wires strategically placed on the body. This form of interrogation was used widely in South Africa by SAP detectives and the SB to extract confessions or gather information. Using 'Radio Moscow' back in Johannesburg, I would allow the electrodes to just touch the skin, while a colleague spun the handle to produce the current. This usually induced the desired effect but without the telltale marks.

By lunchtime, he was still holding out. So over lunch, we discussed what to do. Consensus was that the young soldier was highly trained, which is why he was able to withstand the torture. This was a problem. We were aware that the Koevoet strike force was hot on the trail of the SWAPO unit involved, and that the onus was on us to relay to them as much additional information as possible. So, at five minutes past two, the suspect was once again delivered to us by Johannes.

We kicked off by attaching electrodes to him, taping these in place with Elastoplast from the medic kit. Still he held out; his only response, apart from some screams and moans, was laughter.

So we went for broke. And the results were instant and dramatic.

I haven't told Dylan this.

Chapter Three

More of a Hooligan

Johannesburg

SHORTLY AFTER I STARTED at the SB, my section head, Major Jordaan, sounded me out about what he called 'putting pressure' on subjects as part of the monitoring process. This, my colleagues had already told me, could and would happen beyond the confines of the law – an aspect of our jobs that was not only tolerated, but encouraged.

'You know, Paul, the youngsters go out a lot at night and sometimes they make a bit of *kak*,' said Jordaan. 'I must warn you, though, that if you ever go with them, you must never get caught.'

It was a simple but clear warning. We, the SB, had to be extra careful of the Uniformed Branch because nailing a security policeman was a coup for people like Captain Hartman at Uniform and other 'backstabbers', as we called them.

The 'bit of *kak*' to which Jordaan referred included ordering unwanted supplies for suspects, killing their pets, tossing bricks through their windows and vandalising their cars – all relatively straightforward compared with what was yet to develop – and acts that Jordaan considered to be 'morale boosters' for his staff.

At the time, the official mindset of Head Office, which took its instructions from government, was that the country was better off without the likes of Beyers Naudé and other white traitors, so every effort was made to goad them into leaving South Africa on a one-way ticket. How this was achieved, even if it included our own acts of terror against them, was merely a secondary consideration. This was all part of the laager mentality: get them out of our midst so we can carry on and win the battle against the '*swart gevaar*'.

The perception that the struggle for liberation was being orchestrated by white liberals and communists, and the left-wing English-speaking media, was entrenched in us, and was behind everything we did in the 1970s. We were taught that white English-speaking activists (and a handful of Afrikaner 'traitors' such as Beyers Naudé) were puppets in the hands of Soviet masters.

Each of us was given a group of suspects to monitor and my priority was Gavin Andersson, a prominent trade unionist who had been banned. My instructions were to harass him in every way possible, so I started by visiting him regularly at his home in Auckland Park, night after night after night. I'd knock on his door at all hours and ask him questions: 'Are you alone, Gavin?' Or smile and say, 'I'm just popping in to make certain that you haven't run away yet.' And it seemed to be working. On one of these visits, the powerfully built Andersson – fair-headed, muscular and fit – lost it. He was so livid that I was convinced he was going to take a swing at me.

Contrary to our method of getting the white liberals and communists to flee, and thus eliminating the 'nuisance factors' as we called them, a warrant was issued for Andersson's arrest. We never caught him and, later, when he had gone to ground, we attempted to use him as a lever, as justification for the illegal search of Dr Neil Aggett's parents' home after Aggett was murdered in detention in 1982.

One of the first acts in which I participated as an SB agent was at the Kleinschmidt home in Fifth Avenue, Melville. Dr Horst Kleinschmidt was one of the directors of the Christian Institute and an associate of Beyers Naudé. His wife, Ilona, was a well-known activist. In the early hours of the morning, my colleagues and I, having scrounged leftover paint from our parents' garages, poured the paint into plastic bags and tossed them at Ilona Kleinschmidt's car and over the front of the house. Just for fun, we painted a hammer and sickle on the wall. We were rewarded the next day when one of the Afrikaans dailies headlined the incident with photographs.

The Kleinschmidts were not an easy target, though; in a previous SB attack on their house, a neighbour had opened fire on policemen with a high-powered rifle and nearly shot one of our section officers. However, most of our narrow escapes involved avoiding the patrolling Uniform Branch, as they liked nothing better than nabbing us. There was mutual hostility, which was compounded by our sense of superiority.

Our activities were not for the faint-hearted. The more of a hooligan you were, the better. And anecdotes about these exploits were always well received at the ubiquitous police braais where the liquor flowed very freely.

Helen Joseph didn't have a neighbour like the Kleinschmidts. As a listed person under the Suppression of Communism Act, Joseph lived alone in the quiet tree-lined suburb of Norwood, and was already in her sixties by the time my generation of SB operatives started homing in on her. She was just too tempting for us. We had a theory that she was inured to the harassment anyway. Joseph had first been put under house arrest under the Sabotage Act[4] of 1962 and we figured that she should have become accustomed to having shots fired outside her home and once through her bedroom windows. An explosive had even been connected to her gate. Two decades later, I'd talk about how we persecuted Helen Joseph when I made my amnesty submission to the Truth and Reconciliation Commission (TRC).

We vandalised her property many times, and once even damaged a car belonging to a friend of hers. We fired shots to unsettle her. We called her relentlessly on her home phone. We placed obscure orders of goods to be delivered to her house. We did this over a period of at least three years, and she was more frequently a victim after we had gone out for a couple of drinks or needed to lift the tedium of endless surveillance. Jordaan called her an '*ou teef*' and 'the mother of all troubles'. He instructed us to keep up the pressure on her until she 'cracked'. She never did.

In March 1978, we pelted her house with rocks and followed that up with numerous death threats, at least one of which I made while a *Rand Daily Mail* reporter was in her home, photographing the damage we had caused. On another occasion, I sent the SAP mortuary van to collect her body and she nearly collapsed when the cops arrived and told her why they were there.

After that appalling incident, the Commissioner of Police, General Mike Geldenhuys, made a public statement that 'every effort' would be made to 'protect' Joseph, and communication received at John Vorster was that 'this nonsense must stop' because it was now 'embarrassing' the police. Despite the public pronouncements, however, behind closed doors congratulations were dished out and new strategies were already being formulated against her. Helen Joseph received more attacks from the SB than just about anyone else in the white left.

She was, simply put, the epitome of what we regarded as an evil communist and a threat to our South African way of life. This seemingly innocent, granny-like figure had spearheaded a march of 20,000 women on 9 August 1956 to the Union Buildings in Pretoria to protest against pass laws.

We were led to believe that she was one of the driving forces behind the ANC moving from passive resistance to the armed struggle. It was easy then to hate her and I was assured by our seniors, the day they put 'Tannie Helen' in the ground, it would be a huge blow to the communist forces.

As field operatives, we often acted above the law. We would take our chances when they presented themselves: an unlocked door or an open window were golden opportunities for quick searches to lay our hands on useful information, or to plant evidence and compromise an enemy of the state.

I received my first commendation in June 1977 as a result of the illegal search of student activist Diana McLaren's flat in Hillbrow. The SB Head Office was impressed with the quality and detail of the information, and the letter complimenting me was even mentioned at our morning staff and coffee meeting. This irritated some of my colleagues who considered this type of thing to be brown-nosing, but I was not to be deterred – my talents were being noticed where it really mattered, at the SB Head Office in Pretoria.

I followed up this success with another illegal entry, this time into the flat of a *Christian Science Monitor* journalist, June Goodwin, in Joubert Park. I gained entry using a laminated police ID to unlatch the front door. This time I wasn't so lucky, however. I couldn't even begin the search because of the mass of printed material in her home. I decided to leave, some sense of relief washing over me as I made my way out – but then Goodwin and I almost walked into each other in the lobby and I had to cover my face as best as I could. Despite the close shave, I didn't give up.

A week later, I called her and told her a long story about wanting to study journalism and wishing that I could meet with a journalist of her stature. To my surprise, she invited me around to her flat on a Saturday afternoon. I wore a suit, was scrubbed and shaved, looking nothing like an aspiring leftie journalist. I was also punctual, which seemed to surprise her.

Goodwin's opening words, 'Haven't I seen you somewhere before?', unnerved me, as did the realisation that we were to be joined by a man she had invited for tea. I was so thrown that I forgot his name the instant we were introduced. In the ensuing 10 or 15 minutes, which felt interminable, Goodwin dominated the conversation, asking me about the 'border' where I hadn't yet been. I was hardly able to respond.

The man never said a word. He just sat there and checked me out with a look that told me, 'I know you're a cop, so fuck you,' and every time I gave another faltering answer to one of Goodwin's questions, she would give him a knowing glance. I eventually stood up to leave, offering some feeble excuse.

Jordaan and my colleagues laughed when I reported back, but shortly afterwards we were instructed to lay off Goodwin. The reason, we heard, was that there was an awkward situation involving her that was being handled from the very top.

Apparently, WH11 – telephone tapping – had found out that she was receiving information to further her cause from a senior policeman stationed in Soweto.

When all of that happened, Goodwin was fair game again, only this time she fell into my hands inadvertently and, on my part, reluctantly. She had once interviewed Major Cronwright, labelling him in print as a 'mad fanatic' and 'raving' supremacist, among other choice descriptions. So, motivated by vengeance, Cronwright now took a personal interest in her. He made no secret of his hatred of Goodwin and Visser, and one night, after a particularly hectic SB social event at the police canteen, Cronwright cornered me. He was very drunk.

'I've been hearing good things about you, Erasmus,' he stuttered. 'You're the sort of person we need on the Branch. You are not scared of those fuckers.'

I was transfixed by Cronwright's black eyes. I sensed something was coming that I wasn't going to like, and it did.

'You know that commie bitch Goodwin?'

I knew I had to reply. He paused, waiting.

'Yes, sir. I know who she is.'

'Well,' he started to slur and sway a little more, 'tonight's the night we fuck her up good and solid.'

I started to get really anxious, as I knew this meant trouble. He said this would involve only him and me – and June Goodwin. I didn't have a choice. I knew it, and he knew it. In the SB, juniors were at the mercy of managers like this madman.

On the way to the flat, Cronwright – driving at a terrifying speed – ranted, mumbled and shouted as if he was possessed.

'The fucking bitch. You don't kill her. You maim her. Break her fucking legs! She must suffer. You understand?'

Tossing stones through windows, emptying bags of paint over cars, breaking and entering to destabilise activists, calling them at all hours – this was the stuff to which I had been privy until then. Smashing a woman's body on the instruction of a drunk and narcissistic policeman – no matter what his rank – was something new for me, at least at that point.

We parked around the corner from Goodwin's flat near the Johannesburg Art Gallery, where the Noord Street taxi rank is today. In the late 1970s, Joubert Park was already down at heel; the number of discos was climbing, which meant more noise, drugs and police. It wasn't a good place to live, although not nearly as suffocating and oppressive as it is today for the thousands of people living in its broken buildings. Back then, however, you could risk parking your car in the street without being hustled or, worse, held up by men with guns. Murders were rare. Hijackings were unheard of. So Cronwright got out and staggered to the boot, from which he produced a small but solid baseball bat. He handed it to me and assured me he would provide me with the requisite back-up.

He then climbed back into the car, to wait, and I stepped quickly into the foyer of the block of flats where Goodwin lived, hiding what I could of the bat under my jacket. I was still green, with very limited experience of this sort of thing, and I was afraid.

I paced up and down the passage, passing her flat several times. I'd decided from the start to tell the maniac in the car that she wasn't answering her doorbell. In those days, when you didn't answer a knock, you were either expecting the cops or you were not at home. So I gave it about ten minutes and then headed out of the building, straight into a group of uniformed policemen on patrol. It was a brightly lit area, and I was more than conscious of the bat concealed under my clothes. But we just greeted each other, and I kept on moving. My heart skipped a beat. Thank god for uniformed cops on the beat. Fortunately, Cronwright had spotted them too, so I was off the hook that night.

By 1978, when I'd been a member of the SB at John Vorster for about a year, members of the clergy were becoming regular targets for me, even more so than the media people or trade unionists. One of my disguises was as a member of the Young Christian Workers (YCW), which provided me with the cover to have tea with a Catholic nun named Sister Marie Waspe. The SB Head Office was anxious to find a way to 'neutralise' her because it was becoming apparent that she was turning many young Catholics into aspirant freedom fighters.

Sister Marie was more gullible than Goodwin, and I was better prepared. I wore a wig – a leftover from a temporary secondment to the drug squad – and Sister Waspe talked enough to enable me to compile a thorough report, which I forwarded to the SB Church Desk.

It wasn't long afterwards that I received a further commendation from Head Office, this time with the instruction to search – illegally, of course – the home of former SACP members Julius and Tamara Baker. This was to prove a particularly good harvest of useful information on especially the older generation of communists.

Despite the intrigue I may have enjoyed as a youngster at the SB, much of what we did was mind-numbing. Our work was dominated by security clearances – vetting people for government work, especially for the SAP, the Atomic Energy Board, the Council for Scientific and Industrial Research (CSIR), the South African Broadcasting Corporation (SABC) and El Al Airlines, Israel's national carrier (Israel being a great friend of the apartheid state). Israeli interests in South Africa were regarded as sacrosanct.

But the SB rank and file quickly grew weary of surveillance work, and so did many of our targets, particularly those who had not experienced any kind of violence at the hands of the police and were thus perhaps less intimidated. A colleague once had coffee sent out by a target to the vehicle in which he had been sitting, patiently recording registration numbers for hours on end in the blistering cold – which he accepted with gratitude. On another occasion, two colleagues watching trade unionist Taffy Adler's house were invited inside, and Adler poured them so many drinks that he had to help them back to their car.

At times we wondered what the point was in watching activists' houses. Phone tapping and mail interception offered a far more accurate picture of their activities, and of course we all enjoyed actual searches. That was addictive – it gave us some sense of power. And raids were something else entirely. The open monitoring, however, was another way of keeping up the pressure on those opposed to the policies of the state.

From time to time, we'd also head out in the dead of night to apprehend 'terrorists'. The first time I was part of such a raid, we bundled the target back to John Vorster, and in the early hours he was immediately rumbled up to the tenth floor where Cronwright and a lieutenant gave him a severe beating. The lieutenant crushed the guy's testicles, his unheard screams echoing down the passage outside Room 1026, the so-called Truth Room, where Ahmed Timol was interrogated.

Cronwright was a man to avoid. We were all well aware of his explosive fanaticism, and it was not long before he and I would clash dramatically, soon after the Goodwin incident. The fight happened at just the right moment for me – when I'd finally exceeded my appetite for what I saw at the time as being little more than an irrelevant SB 'prankster'.

I don't expect Dylan to be able to picture me as that grinning guy in a suit portrayed in a photograph – the man I was at the time Cronwright and I reached our crossroads. Dylan was born in 1987, a few years after I'd joined and then departed from and then rejoined the SB. By the time Dylan came into my life, I'd already completed the tour in Ovamboland, which had left me broken, with my mind in tatters. I'd already satisfied my appetite for the SB by 1979, when I made my way to South West Africa, after only two years in the game. I'd had 18 months with the Uniform Branch before that.

Although I had met and married the love of my life, Linda, who had given me a different perspective on my potential, I was really in bad shape – emotionally, spiritually and psychologically – by the time Dylan was born. Neither he nor his sister Candice would ever experience the close and loving presence of a dad who came home at the end of the day and played with them until supper time.

Dylan has let me off lightly. Whether this is because he would rather not hear a different truth, or because I resist any attempt by shying away from sinking into that dark and terrible place I've struggled to recover from, I don't know. All I know for certain is that I wasted 15 years of my time with my son before I was able to see the light: inasmuch as I can, that is.

Chapter Four

The Gathering of Losers

Soweto, 1976, and Germiston, 1979

WE DIDN'T HAVE ENOUGH SHOTGUNS on June 16. Instead, we were packing the potent R1 (7.62 mm) battle weapon, which can penetrate body armour, and the 9 mm sidearm, which was standard issue for every policeman. There was an assortment of supplementary weapons, shotguns and hand-machine carbines. Shotguns, which discharge numerous small pellets widely at short range, can reduce the mortality rate in riot situations but there was a serious shortage of them in 1976. At the same time, a bullet from the powerful R1 (South Africa's first military assault rifle) could kill more than one person at a time.

Of course, it wasn't only about how we were armed as policemen sent out to quell the most serious rebellion against National Party supremacy since Sharpeville in 1960. The SAP was also wholly unprepared for that terrible day. Nothing readied us for that kind of bloodshed and how out of control all of us were, from constables to senior officers. It was a nightmare, the stench of which I've never quite been able to wash out of my being.

Winnie Mandela's banning order had been lifted a few days before what white South Africans, and most of the media, called 'the 76 riots'. The Black Parents' Association (BPA), which Winnie had helped found, was accused by government media of driving the uprising to create propaganda for the ANC, while we were told that *The World* and the *Rand Daily Mail* newspapers had further inflamed the people.

On the morning of 16 June, though, we knew none of this. I went to work as usual, attended the morning parade, got coffee and I went to buy sandwiches for this fat guy I was working with. He used to eat a cake tin full of sandwiches. I'd go back to the station and do some work, and by 9 am I was finished. Then I'd go and see the girls. That day I went to see Maria – she'd been my girlfriend since standard 6. The radio was on and she said that I'd have to go back to work, that there was violence in Soweto. So I got on my motorbike and raced to Cleveland station. I was amazed when I turned into the back gate and saw everyone lined up, even the reservists. They'd opened the strongroom and we took out R1 assault rifles – Fabrique National, made in Belgium – and as much ammo as we could fit in our tunic pockets. It was a cold day, and that afternoon we were taken to Soweto. On the highway I noticed people gathering, and eventually we were dropped off. We formed three 'D' formations: the flat part of the 'D' facing the protestors. Most of the protestors, it seemed to me, were women, and they were shouting and ululating and giving the Black Power salute. I'd never been so scared in all my life. The people moved slowly towards us, and we shuffled backwards a couple of steps.

I was in the second 'D' formation, and I saw a woman lifting up her dress. It's difficult to remember it all, such was the horror. And on top of it all, we had to deal with the tear gas. We'd gassed ourselves. Our commander that day, Colonel Van Noordwyk, was plastered. We could smell it on his breath on the way into Soweto. He hadn't figured out that the wind was blowing in our faces. Luckily it began to change direction, and holding my R1, I went forward and knelt with the other guys in the shotgun and rifle section.

The group shifted again towards us, and we fired. We fired as they ran back, and a friend of mine, Kloppers, shot the woman who had been holding up her dress, point-blank, and killed her instantly.

I heard the call 'All sections forward' and then there was a lot of sporadic shooting as the crowd ran back. I remember the stones lying all over the place, and bodies everywhere. I remember the sound of crying coming from the injured.

As the gas cleared, I felt this incredible excitement. I felt as though I'd passed a test, and it was at that moment that I decided not to leave the police. I was affected so positively and at the same time horribly negatively.

I later heard that within minutes of the first schoolchildren moving out of Morris Isaacson High School at the start of their march (there were other marches happening as planned), ten members of the SAP had been injured, two police dogs were dead and 29 police vehicles had been damaged. Naturally, we had great compassion for the dogs and sympathised with one another about the pile of paperwork that would have to be attached to the claims for the damaged official cars. At no point, however, did we ask why the security forces, especially the intelligence component, could not predict the series of events that followed. Not once did we question why our colleagues seemed oblivious to the writing on the wall *before* a meeting about June 16 was held at the Donaldson Community Hall in Orlando East. Instead, we, the ordinary SAP members, seemed to simply accept that marches happened on an ad hoc basis. That's how we understood life in South Africa.

Prime Minister John Vorster and Deputy Minister of Education Andries Treurnicht must have known long before June 1976 that the township was at breaking point, and that the people needed neither Winnie Mandela nor the BPA, nor the left-wing media, to push them into rising up. I found out later, too, that the SB had submitted reports to Head Office about high levels of 'intimidation' – an apartheid euphemism for anti-apartheid protest action – in Soweto. Archbishop Desmond Tutu, in his capacity as a prominent cleric, had also written to Vorster, warning the government that he was fearful of what could erupt as black people struggled under the oppressive yoke of apartheid. But Vorster not only dismissed the appeal from Archbishop Tutu, as a ploy devised by the Progressive Federal Party (PFP), the liberal opposition, but he also ignored the SB, which had been taking ever more violent action against the burgeoning Black Consciousness Movement. Even Brigadier Hennie Muller warned the Minister of Police, Jimmy Kruger, to back down on the issue of language.

By 1975 the apartheid leaders had been digging in their heels, forcing Afrikaans on black children as a medium of instruction in subjects such as Arithmetic and Mathematics, thus furthering the aims of the Bantu Education Act of 1953. As Dr Hendrik Verwoerd, then Minister of Native Affairs, argued in 1953, 'there is no place for [the Bantu] in the European community above the level of certain forms of labour … What is the use of teaching the Bantu child mathematics …? Education must train people in accordance with their opportunities in life, according to the sphere in which they live.'[5]

Four years later, when the state-appointed Cillié Commission of Inquiry into the Soweto Uprisings published its statistics – 575 people dead, 451 as a result of shooting by the SAP, 3 907 people injured, at least 2 389 of these by the SAP, and 5 980 people arrested – many white South Africans were doubtful, even disparaging, of the commission's report, which reflected their blinkered worldview. Most black people and white activists, however, said the numbers were too low, that there were far more deaths and injuries, and that the figures had been manipulated.

At an SB course sometime later, we were encouraged to recount our own roles as members of the SAP during the '76 disturbances', and we came to the unanimous conclusion that we should have killed more people and thus sent out the message that this sort of dissent would never be tolerated and would never succeed.

It was at this course that I recounted my own experience in which I, like dozens of other ordinary cops, was cold and hungry for three days, during which we couldn't change our clothes, bath, sleep or eat, or have access to proper toilet facilities. We, too, were tear-gassed, we pointed out, and panicked and ran because we had no gas masks. We had been among the cops on duty on the third day, when Colonel Van Noordwyk issued the order to fire tear gas into the crowd of about 10 000 people.

At one point, there was a moment of terrifying silence, swiftly followed by an incoming wave of gas and then ululating and a roar from the growing crowds in front of us as the tear gas burned our eyes, throats, armpits and crotches before we fled.

I told my colleagues on that SB course about being inside the Johannesburg mortuary on Monday, 21 June 1976, when bodies were still piled up in the ante-room between the freezer units. There had been a fog of death hanging in the air that day, and even after I had been able to go home, strip off the uniform I'd had on for nearly a week, and bath after five days on the streets, that indescribable, unspeakable smell still clung to me. I felt unhinged.

No one who was listening to me flinched. Some even laughed.

Then another cop told a story he had heard about notorious Brigadier T.J. 'Rooi Rus' Swanepoel, who had apparently killed 'six or seven people' with his private hunting rifle fitted with a night scope. Swanepoel was said to have slipped away from Soweto to fetch his rifle from his home as darkness fell on the first day.

No one was surprised at that, either.

It was, however, unusual for a member of the SAP to be in the thick of ongoing violence like that. By this time, the apartheid government had managed, for the most part, to squeeze the banned ANC to the point where it was barely operating. The SADF and the SAP were ruthless and seemed unstoppable in crushing every sign of the liberation movement inside the country.

The ANC's doldrums, and the vacuum left by it in the wake of its persecution by the regime, allowed the Black Consciousness Movement (BCM) to flourish, although, of course, it was only a matter of time before prime ministers Vorster and Botha became even more vicious and set their sights on it too. The ANC was small change compared to the Black Consciousness zeitgeist, an ideology that could fire up people anywhere, at any time, without a known leader's fist in the air on a podium or in a jail cell.

Not only that, but the BCM was taking shape in other parts of the world, especially in the United States, where President Gerald Ford and the Republican Party were trying to deal with their own problems with the rise of the Black Panthers. So, it seems to me that June 1976 was not an ANC-created moment, but one that blew up out of the powerhouse that was the BCM.

Not that we, in the SAP, knew anything about it – we were entirely oblivious, and so caught up in our own ideology that we didn't have a clue. It was only when I was preparing to write the test to join the SB that I uncovered some fragments of information on Black Consciousness, the literature around it having been banned. In fact, it was only on later SB courses, which would eventually lead us to practise proper strategic communications (under Stratcom)[6] as a final desperate battle for the National Party to maintain power, that I – and others – actually grasped the intricacies of the BCM.

When we collapsed amid the clouds of tear gas on the streets of Soweto on June 16, we thought we were facing an enemy we knew: the godless, satanic communists and, naturally, its surrogate arm, the ANC. The SAP Head Office was comfortable, when it launched its security forces, that we were ignorant about the extent of the anti-apartheid struggle. It made far more sense for the government to propagandise that the crowds we were facing were just savage, stupid black people who wanted to help the USSR steal our land – white people's land – our gold and our oranges and turn our churches into badminton courts.

'*Vaderland, volk en vlag ... voorwaarts!*' thundered Brigadier Neels du Plooy, senior lecturer on the security course, spit flying in all directions as he worked the class up into a frenzy of emotion and hatred.

But once I was working for the SB, I saw other sides to this unfolding. I saw torture, but this time it was not taking place in a desert region, far away from prying eyes, as it had been in Ovamboland. This torture was happening in Johannesburg in a ten-storey-high building, around which people strolled, ate their lunch and drove their cars, as if nothing was happening.

Cronwright would later claim in court that he had 'never personally' seen a suspect assaulted at John Vorster Square. Perhaps this was true: he never *saw* it – he *did* it himself. He directed it.

Cronwright unwittingly became an SB target himself in January 1979 when Greg Deegan, whose brother John had been together with me in Ovamboland, and I were instructed to investigate the recently formed National

Front of South Africa (NFSA), a far-right movement that claimed roots in and association with Enoch Powell's National Front in the United Kingdom. The SB Head Office wanted details of those involved and an assessment of whether it posed any kind of threat to the state.

It was our luck that, just as we were given the assignment, the NFSA advertised a cocktail party at a low-budget Johannesburg hotel. Naturally, we showed up at what we thought was a gathering of losers. Apart from its expat founder, a Brit by the name of Jack Noble, and his sidekick, a no-hoper named Raymond Hill, the turnout was an assortment of reprobates and down-and-outs attracted by the free liquor and snacks. Some prostitutes also turned up for the refreshments.

Greg and I settled on a few whiskies and were getting stuck into the eats when the meeting was called to order. Noble was introduced and delivered a rousing 20-minute speech announcing the NFSA's intention to remove the National Party government. It was, he said, 'selling out to the Communists, Zionists and Internationalists' under the leadership of Vorster and Botha, who were giving in 'daily' to the Illuminati while the 'Jews' controlled the country, Harry Oppenheimer being cited as an example of this secret power. The National Party, he said, was going to usher in a new era, compromising with 'the blacks' and overseeing the disintegration of white rule until it allowed the ANC to take over the country within 10 to 15 years.

He said educating 'the blacks' was a fatal mistake, one that would lead to the downfall of white Christian South Africa as we knew it. The NFSA would, instead, accommodate all those disenchanted by what was rapidly unfolding. In this vein, Noble invited whites from neighbouring countries, such as Rhodesia, to sign up to the party, stating that Salisbury had also been 'sold out' to the Internationalists. The National Front, he said, intended to build a mighty power bloc by unifying the right wing, which would fight to the end for a white subcontinent and the continuation of white Christian rule. These were supremacists through and through.

Noble's rhetoric was punctuated by applause from the audience, but as soon as he finished, everyone once again raced for the bar.

An old drunk came up to me and Greg and asked what we thought of Noble and the NFSA. We gave him some noncommittal reply. Then he asked whether we thought the SB should be told about the meeting. We asked him why.

'Well, son,' he replied with some disdain, 'this man's obviously a k-----r-loving communist.'

We burst out laughing at the demented irony of what this guy said. But, to facilitate further contact and involvement, Noble needed to be spun a story of sorts, so when he approached us in a convivial spirit, we told him outright that we were policemen. He was immediately impressed – of course we neglected to mention that we were SB – and, hoping that the SAP would be fertile recruiting ground for the National Front, he invited us to his home.

Greg and I were thus able to send a colourful report to the Head Office about the NFSA. What we didn't know, though, was that we'd incurred the wrath of certain colleagues – especially in Cronwright's Investigation Branch – who were supporters of a National Front-style pushback.

Cronwright and I met in the lift not long after that report was filed, and he directed his most aggressive pose – reserved for blacks, Jewish people, Wits students and detainees, I imagined – at me. I said a cheery 'Good morning, sir', but there was no reply from him as his eyes locked with mine for that long minute or two as we rode up together in the lift. I remember telling my girlfriend that it was like trying to outstare a crocodile, and I was so entranced by the intensity of it that I forgot to push the button for the ninth floor.

The lift moved off and, when I realised that I hadn't entered my destination, I unlocked my eyes and raised them to his forehead. There was a black line a couple of centimetres below his receding hairline. He'd obviously underestimated the strength of his hair dye because his scalp, forehead and the tips of his ears were stained black.

Since childhood, I have laughed out of nervousness, and that's exactly what happened. I had to stare back into his little black eyes to stop myself.

'I think you're getting too big for your fucking boots, Erasmus,' he said. Then he disarmed me with a broad smile before hitting back: 'We don't laugh on the tenth floor, Erasmus – and don't ever think about fucking with me.'

I wouldn't have a choice, as it turned out.

Shortly afterwards, Greg and I got wind of an NFSA 'executive committee' meeting at the home of Raymond Hill, in Primrose, a suburb of Germiston outside Johannesburg. I told Greg that I'd pop past on my way home to Bedfordview, which was in the same area, take the registration numbers of the cars outside and file a report before I left for a security course the following week. And I was as good as my word. At around five that evening I drove slowly past the house, and there was a large green Toyota – Cronwright's police vehicle. I turned around at the end of the road to take another drive past so that I could make sure. And that's when I saw that there were cars belonging to several members of the Investigation Branch – and not only that, but two of my SB colleagues, Roy Baker and Piet Seyfert, were standing in the garden.

I stopped my car. Perhaps, I'd got it wrong, I thought. Maybe the Investigation Branch was staging a raid on the meeting.

At the sight of me, Piet disappeared into the house and a moment later returned to tell me that the boss wanted to see me inside. Flanked by the subservient Roy and Piet, I made my way into the lounge where Cronwright, glass in hand, held sway, centre floor. Sweat pouring from his forehead, he advanced on me with his head cocked slightly to one side.

'Come here, you!'

He grabbed my tie at the knot, yanked my head down, and began to parade me, shocked and embarrassed, in front of the National Front 'executive'.

'This, ladies and gentlemen,' he shouted, 'is a spy and a traitor! Paul Erasmus of the Security Branch is investigating the National Front, the future of this country!'

There was applause from the 30-odd people standing around him, and I was terrified. A senior policeman had just physically assaulted me, with members of his own staff looking on. He'd also divulged my identity during an investigation sanctioned by the SB Head Office.

'Who sent you here, you bastard?' he screamed. I stammered a reply that it had been my section head, Jordaan. Cronwright staggered slightly as he raised his voice again.

'Ladies and gentlemen, Major Jordaan is also – if you'll pardon my language – a fucking traitor. These are the fucking tools of the National Party that are giving our country to the k-----s and Jews.' He tugged harder on my tie, yanking my face down to meet his beady eyes. 'You, my friend,' his spit sprayed over my face, 'I'll break you into a million fucking pieces. You fucking bastard!'

Then Cronwright let go of my tie and grabbed the lapels of the jacket of my three-piece suit. I was speechless when Raymond Hill intervened, stepping between Cronwright and me.

'Arthur,' he said, calmly, 'let me speak to Paul. Let's just carry on with the meeting.'

Cronwright released me and Hill steered me towards the kitchen where I downed two double-whiskies in quick succession. Roy and Piet joined us. Roy went for the soft approach, but Piet laid into me as if I was just another detainee. Another colleague, Jorrie, also appeared, blind drunk. He started pinching me on my shoulder and my neck. Then Piet – equally inebriated – snatched at my lapels while Roy, whom I regarded as a friend, patted me on my left shoulder.

'You're in the shit now,' Roy said. 'We have members throughout the force.'

Jorrie was less worried about me than he was about himself. He tightened his grip on my neck: 'Are you going to mention our names?'

I immediately saw an opportunity, so I quickly insisted that I had no intention of ever sending a report. Besides, I said, I didn't have time because I was due to attend a course at the Police College in Pretoria.

At that moment, Cronwright stepped into the kitchen. He dismissed everyone else with a wave of his hand and then grabbed me again.

'Now you listen to me, you fucking fool. I can make or break you. You can join us and fight the k-----s or you can go and tell Jordaan what you've seen here.'

He pushed me out of the kitchen, and I headed back to my car in a state of terror. I nearly struck the pavement as I shot away.

Later, I met up with Greg and relayed to him what had happened. He was shocked but insisted that we had no choice but to ride out the storm.

The next day Cronwright summoned me to his office and instructed me to close the door behind me. He then told me that I had to report to him before anyone else if I had information about the National Front. I kept quiet.

'From now on,' he hissed, 'I control you and your career, and if you cross me, I will destroy you. You'll never pass another exam and I will finish you in the SB and beyond. Don't underestimate me.' Then he told me to get out, to leave his office, but just as I reached the door, he called me back. 'Cross me, my friend, and you're dead.'

Of the many stories about Cronwright, the one that held the most terror was that he, along with some of his colleagues, had thrown Timol out of that window on the tenth floor in 1971. Lieutenant Robbie Bouwer, on Cronwright's staff, was alleged to have been among those who knew what really happened to Timol. The extreme interrogations that took place there were nothing new to us, and we knew and believed that there were people who had met their deaths while being tortured in their 'offices'. We all knew about the abuse that had taken place when members had fallen foul of Cronwright – members whose careers in the force had taken a turn for the worse.

If, indeed, there had been an ANC death list, Cronwright would surely have been in the top three of the marked men, along with 'Rooi Rus' and Colonel Andries 'Dries' Struwig.

I was a junior constable in the SB system at the time Cronwright threatened me. I found myself caught between three factions – a National Party apartheid 'mainstream'; comparative moderates represented by my section head Major Jordaan and Brigadier Hennie Muller; and neo-Nazis like Cronwright, Struwig and Swanepoel.

45

The last-mentioned were fanatics and theirs was the faction to which many young security policemen, who had been ideologically desensitised even more than I had been, would gravitate. I realised the extent of this when we as SB operatives started to watch the right wing, and organisations such as the Wit Kommando and the more notorious Afrikaner Weerstandsbeweging (AWB) began to emerge. The AWB was a prime example of police involvement in far-right activity. Its leader, Eugene Terre'Blanche, was a former policeman, as was the bulk of the organisation's elite.

I had my future to think about. I had to at least consider resigning, try to find employment in a bank, like so many of my friends. Or I could sell cars. Or typewriters. Or insurance policies. Or die of sheer boredom. I decided to pull myself together.

However, I thrived on the thrill of being a security policeman. I liked the status it held within the force and within white society. I couldn't just give all of this up because of Cronwright and degenerate, as I saw it, into a humdrum existence – either inside or outside the police.

So I decided to tell Jordaan the whole story. He listened attentively to my blow-by-blow account, with no visible expression. I stressed the fact that Cronwright had warned me he would ruin my career, that he had threatened my life.

When I finished, Jordaan made only one comment. 'Cronwright's arse.'

That's all. No words of reassurance regarding my position, not a hint of gratitude for my loyalty. In fact, I detected some hostility, probably for even involving him in the first place. He then simply dismissed me from his office, telling me that I was to carry on as before, and not discuss the situation with anyone else.

Two weeks later, while I was on the security course in Pretoria, I was taken to the infamous SB Head Office in the Wachthuis Building in Pretoria, where I was required to make a lengthy statement about what had happened. Again, there was no reassurance regarding my job or my personal safety. I was required to provide only a clinical rendition of the facts, and upon completion of this, there was the usual master–servant dismissal.

I returned from the course at the end of March 1979 and resumed my duties at John Vorster Square, but I perceived a change in attitude towards me from several officers – notably, my section head, Jordaan.

I avoided Cronwright and his staff, but I heard via the grapevine that I wasn't to be trusted, that I was a backstabber. And that I was gay – regarded in SB culture as worse than being a communist.

I also heard that Cronwright and the colleagues I had seen at that

National Front meeting in Primrose had been taken under guard to Pretoria for questioning, but had extricated themselves by claiming that they were merely investigating the NFSA, that the best way to get to the heart of the organisation was to join it.

Questions were asked in Parliament, and my name, as well as Greg Deegan's, came up as members of the SAP actively involved in, and as secret members of, the National Front. That affected me deeply. I was scarred by it, even if a part of me saw through it all, that this was what had made Cronwright a master of the game.

By 1979, the NFSA's radical anti-Semitism and rising anger among Jewish youth led to pressure on the government by PFP MPs Harry Schwarz and Alf Widman to do something about the organisation itself. Helen Suzman described the National Front as an English equivalent of the Herstigte Nasionale Party and said South Africa had enough trouble without them. As a result, the police raided Hill's home and, within six months, the National Front had ceased all activities.

It then came to light that Jack Noble's wife had been convicted of child battery in the United Kingdom, and Noble's contention that he was a person of stature in his home country and a close friend of Enoch Powell was rendered laughable when it was established that he had been a London bus conductor. Hill subsequently fled South Africa after defrauding a local charity.

The entrails of the National Front lingered on, however. They continued to operate underground, a fact attested to by the arrest and conviction of members of the militant Wit Kommando.

This was, nevertheless, still a painful episode for me. Although I had been proven right, I had had to endure the humiliation of a public betrayal in Parliament, which had in turn dealt a devastating blow to my reputation. Even when investigations into those organisations were concluded successfully, using my and Greg's input as evidence, I was excluded from the list of medal recipients. Despite the shutdown of the NFSA and the Wit Kommando, the right wing had hardly been cowed and in fact went on to establish itself as a force to be reckoned with. And, as I'd warned Jordaan and others, there was no sphere more important to it in terms of recruitment than the SAP, yet they allowed it to spread for eight years. Its entrenchment in the force was so profound that it would be almost impossible to uproot it.

It was only in 1987 that we at the SB were given instructions to investigate the right wing and I was given the responsibility to probe into the AWB. It took me only three days and not much effort to identify two senior police officers as members of the organisation. One was a colonel from Uniform

Branch Head Office and the other, a district commandant. Not only were both active supporters of the AWB, but they were also recruiting new members from police staff under their command.

It was clear to me that there was serious division in the ranks at John Vorster Square regarding the AWB, in fact a rift that was reflective of divisions in the SAP in general at the time. So much so that I took the unusual step of submitting a three-page memorandum to then CO Brigadier Gerrit 'Sterk Gert' Erasmus, setting out the reasons why I wanted to withdraw from the investigation to which I'd been assigned. I had no wish to complicate my life any further and feared a repetition of the Cronwright/National Front affair.

I was, nevertheless, subsequently involved in the arrests of right-wingers Leonard Veenendaal and Darryl Stopforth, both wanted for murder in Namibia. They were identified and arrested after an incident in Hillbrow when they attempted to prevent black people from using the indoor public swimming pool.

Their story didn't end there, however.

Instructions were later issued by the SB Head Office that the AWB files were to be moved from the conventional filing system to the CO's safe. Agents attached to this investigation were also to report directly and only to the CO. Minister of Police Adriaan Vlok further issued an order to the effect that no policeman was allowed to hold membership of the AWB, but to the best of my knowledge, even if they remained within the AWB's ranks, no member of the SAP was ever charged in accordance with the Vlok directive.

At the first-ever armed confrontation between the SAP and the AWB in Ventersdorp, a couple of hours' drive from Johannesburg, many policemen disobeyed a direct order to open fire on the AWB. On the other hand, an English-speaking member of the riot squad – who is said to have reacted overzealously, firing the most shots – was so ostracised by colleagues that he was forced to transfer to another unit.

Ultimately, those SB members who were investigating the AWB faced complete rejection by their colleagues, and some resigned, including a close friend, a respected young policeman named Constable Ryno Goosen.

Despite steps taken – on paper, anyway – to facilitate the probe into the AWB and to prevent the recruitment of SAP members, the number of cops who secretly joined flourished. As late, and at such a pivotal time, as 1990 and 1991, senior police officers and SB members were privately reported to be attending AWB meetings in Johannesburg.

The most notorious police connection with the supremacists was undoubtedly Barend Strydom, self-styled leader of the Wit Wolwe and an ex-policeman, who in 1988 massacred eight black people, and wounded sixteen more, on a public square in Pretoria. Earlier he had murdered a black woman and injured another in an informal settlement outside Johannesburg. He maintained that this was a practice run to see if he was capable of killing people. Strydom was released from prison in mid-1992 by President F.W. de Klerk, in an ANC and National Party prisoner exchange. In 1994 he was granted amnesty by the Truth and Reconciliation Commission on the grounds that the attack was politically motivated.

Chapter Five

The Kill Rate

Ovamboland, 1979

I DECIDED ONE DAY TO talk to my son about the interrogation of a SWAPO teenager in Ovamboland. It was a conversation I had never really been able to have with John Deegan and the other two men in that cell with me when we tortured the boy.

I knew John a little better than the others, and he was what we called a 'regular' – someone with a permanent posting to the border. He was not a camper or 'short-termer' like me.

'What happens if you, if *we*, kill someone?' I once asked, tentatively.

They were dismissive of my query, insisting instead that since Ovamboland was a war zone – an operational area – there were no inspectors of detainees or magistrates to 'fuck you around' with questions. This wasn't the tenth floor where Cronwright and his staff engaged in 'civilised' interrogations.

'Here,' said my colleagues, 'we just go for it.'

'But what if the person dies?' I asked again. I was still thinking about the SWAPO attack on the village and the old woman. The guys admitted they had felt the same way when they arrived but that I 'would get used to it'.

The regimen of war was a relentless three to seven days on patrol out in the bush, following up information and recruiting sources, then two or three days in base camp at Oshakati for admin, resupplying and rest. But the horror of what we saw out on patrol and what we did when we were 'following up on information' punctuated our every day. Nearly everyone drank as if the devil itself was driving us on.

Civilians – or the 'local pops' (local population), as we referred to them – were often caught in the inevitable crossfire. By day, the security forces – the SADF and the SAP – ruled as kings of the bush, and mostly the local pops' attitude to us was one of resignation or apathy, and sometimes even full cooperation – or so it seemed.

After the dusk-to-dawn curfew had settled under the Ovambo sunset, SWAPO would emerge, moving from village to village and kraal to kraal, laying landmines, setting ambushes, intimidating and sometimes committing heinous crimes not all that different from the ones that we, as the security forces, were committing on civilians. Throughout all of this, we were repeatedly reminded of our soldierly education: that the enemy was spreading satanic communist ideals. This was so ingrained that we were unable to see another side – that SWAPO was being welcomed by the local pops as liberating heroes.

Invariably, once our alcohol-driven euphoria was replaced by the growing darkness, a deep sombreness would set in. We were young, in our late teens and early twenties, and some – not all, and certainly not openly – would wonder what the hell we were doing 1 800 kilometres from home in what was a pretty twisted situation.

But such negative thoughts were usually dispelled when the enemy mirrored our deplorable behaviour. One incident comes to mind: it involves a family that was blown to pieces in their Ford F250 van by a landmine placed indiscriminately by SWAPO. I have an image of body parts strewn across a stretch of sand, which plays havoc with my psyche, and that's the photograph Dylan and I have paused over more than once. It's in the box of pictures that we never intend to publish.

Dylan finds it depressing to examine an image like that. His response has as much to do with how it affects me as it does with what is in the picture. I used to express a mix of shock – as if I hadn't really been there, even though I was the one who took the photograph – and confusion. How did that happen? Again, as if I weren't there. Lately, it makes me take a deep breath. Is there anything I can say that will adequately explain all of this to him? He has never got as angry with me as his sister, Candice, aged 11, once did when I showed up at her school in the pit of despair while her mother and I were in the throes of divorce.

She threw agonising rhetorical questions at me in front of a group of parents and other children, pointing out how despicable my past had been. This was when South Africa was on the cusp of a new democratic order, and Candice had not been ideologically damaged. She wanted to be a part of the 'new South Africa', and I was a bloodstain on that. She was very, very hurt, ashamed and furious.

By this time, Candice was battling her own terrible fears. Not only had she lacked the constant presence of a father and force of good in her life, because I'd been spending every waking hour on the job and was suffering from severe stress as a result, but we'd also been relocated as part of a witness protection programme – first to London, and then to Denmark, and then back to London, and, finally, home to South Africa, where it was almost worse.

We'd received multiple death threats. Candice had missed months of school. There was no 'normal' for us. She then had to tolerate children at her school in KwaZulu-Natal asking questions about why we were on a witness protection programme, when no one was supposed to know.

She'd seen her mother and me fight, wail, and shout at each other. We were lost and broken. This alone would have been rough on any child, but add to this the constant state of flux under which we were all living. I imagined her asking, 'What name or surname will we be using today, Daddy?'

Then again, Candice had also witnessed, first-hand, the attacks from virtually everyone – the SB, the SAP, the government, the media, ex-colleagues and former friends. It went on and on. I was in and out of hospital, my mind crashing repeatedly. It was as though we were entirely isolated and the hate projected onto me would stick to her forever.

She and I have since come to terms with things. I'm not even sure how, but we have. We found each other sometime ago, and are now able to be together as a family. I have wondered, though, if Dylan had not been there as a link, a non-judgemental force between us, whether it would have been as uncomplicated, as it ultimately was, to make peace.

In terms of the photograph of the bodies after the detonation of the SWAPO landmine, I have had to tell myself that the security forces were well trained. This kind of image enabled us to torture, even if we were having second thoughts. Our minds had been so severely manhandled by the state and the church that it made it much easier to be fuelled by hatred once we closed the cell door and got stuck in.

We had plenty of help in forgetting what we saw and experienced from South African Breweries (SAB), who quenched the dry throats of soldiers during the Border War, and made a lot of money in the process. The army canteen at Oshakati was especially well stocked. SAB sent its trucks in week after week, loaded with distractions for the psychopathic imagination. Many are the times I personally crashed headlong into Castle Lager.

In a prominent position in the canteen was a scoreboard with two columns

– 'Ours' and 'Theirs' – reflecting the 'kill' rate. One could sit in the comfort of that pub, get thoroughly inebriated and reflect on the scoreboard. If you'd killed someone during the day, you could run in there at 4 pm, which was opening time, and excitedly summon the barmen to chalk up another one. That could even get you a free drink – celebrating the taking of another life with an ice-cold Castle Lager.

The SB received regular updates on the reality unfolding beyond the confines of the camp. This would include how many local people had been killed, many through crossfire, as well as the numbers of reported abductions of civilians by SWAPO. We also had to know how many SADF members had been killed – most as young as or younger than us – and SWAPO members killed, confirmed and unconfirmed.

The SAP, specifically Koevoet, was a vital part of that war machine, which carried out hundreds of search-and-destroy missions. Its methods were controversial and it was accused of many atrocities against civilians, some of which would be incorrectly attributed to the SADF. All kills from Koevoet, and for that matter from the SA Police, were recorded and every effort was made to identify the person killed, to record their details and to establish if the person was previously known as a suspect. The SADF didn't have these forensic and intelligence-based skills, and many civilians caught in crossfire were identified as terrorists. This is an agonising history for Namibians, and for the families of the many soldiers and policemen who were killed or injured, physically and mentally, during the so-called Border War.

How we tallied our 'successes' had a tremendous psychological impact on us. In the SB's case, we were highly motivated by kills – confirmed by photographs and other evidence – carried out by Koevoet. We noted, however, that the SADF often inflated its kill rate in an attempt to improve its morale and probably its budget allocation, and to justify its massive human deployment, which was about 15 or more to our 1 in the SAP.

There was another key difference between the SAP and the SADF too, one that was not readily recognised and was detrimental to us when we tried to have our mental health issues taken seriously later. This was that the army dispatched conscripts – usually reluctant young men forced into war – to the border, while policemen like me went willingly.

We wanted to be there, or so we thought.

Koevoet fell under the leadership of Brigadier Hans 'Sterk' Dreyer, someone who dispensed with military etiquette and convention, and engaged the enemy in highly unconventional ways. He would probably describe his approach as having been the 'pragmatic' response.

Koevoet members considered themselves to be dedicated professionals, and there is no doubt that many military analysts have categorised them as a hugely effective force in terms of counter-insurgency – probably one of the most effective anywhere in the world. The SADF and the SAP were also tasked with promoting the policy of WHAM (winning hearts and minds), a tactic with which I became more familiar a decade later.

The aim of the security forces – the SAP and the SADF – in Ovamboland was to neutralise and eliminate SWAPO as a military entity, and to win an ideological war among the local population. Our psyches were built with the ideology that we, the white race, were the Chosen Ones, and that we had a God-ordained destiny to destroy the satanic communism that was seeking to destroy us.

In 1981, this bloodthirsty madness was an exercise costing about R1 million a day. Even 'psych ops' – the propaganda effort at that time – could not offset the exigencies of that. The reality is that three decades ago, the regime spent a million bucks a day on promoting death and torture to prop up an Afrikaner elite, although at the time we didn't see it like this at all.

The war effort had to be maintained at all costs, and the relentless campaign to do so – widespread and covering the broadest spectrum – gathered supporters from every corner of society. These included the likes of Elizabeth Albrecht of the Southern Cross Fund – who supplied us with sewing kits, mock-leather folders embossed with the SAP badge, and writing pads and envelopes – and rugby hero Naas Botha.

Another supporter was 'Die Silwer Sluiper' (the Silver Sneaker), Colonel Leon Mellet, a former news journalist and actor in photo-comic epics such as *Rocco de Wet: Grensvegter*, which was hugely popular in white South African society at the time. Mellet was appointed to head the SAP's fledgling public relations department, tasked with improving morale and promoting a positive image of the SAP back home. Hence, he was all over *Servamus*, the monthly SAP magazine, pictured 'in action' with policemen on the border. Mellet sported a non-regulation wide-brimmed hat that reminded me of the khaki felt hat worn by Sir Robert Baden-Powell of the Boy Scouts movement.

To obfuscate and prevent any compromising of information regarding the war situation, the wearing of uniforms was strictly taboo for all units at the guest house in Oshakati. It was there that politicians, non-security-force visitors and officially sanctioned journalists were housed on excursions to the operational area. The SAP and the SADF didn't want foreign or local journalists to hear things that they shouldn't and be able to trace the source to Oshakati.

I remember once being given the luxury of going there, and ended up having a quiet round of tequilas with Eugene de Kock from Koevoet. I was there with SAP members John Adams and Willie Nortjé, and we'd just returned from a hard ten days in the bush where we didn't even have water to wash.

We were discussing rugby, the national obsession, when in walked Colonel Mellet, whom we called the 'plastic' colonel, in other words, an entirely fabricated colonel, owing to what they called his 'lateral inversion' into the SA Police. He joined as a colonel and didn't have to go through what we normal members had to endure -- training and climbing the ladder of ranks. Mellet arrived, resplendent in tailored camouflage police fatigues and his trademark hat, accompanied by a civilian. The two sauntered up to the bar and ordered drinks, our conversation silenced in astonishment at this flagrant flouting of the ban on uniform.

'Now SWAPO is going to shit!' burst out John Adams. 'The main man is here!' We all laughed. De Kock had only one word for Mellet: '*Kont!*'

The only available seats in the lounge were at our table, and a while later Mellet and his sidekick wandered over and asked whether we would mind if they joined us. Mellet introduced himself and his companion from Head Office. We didn't reciprocate in terms of introductions and simply carried on with our conversation. Finally, I turned to Mellet and asked him to explain how Naas Botha – then a top Springbok rugby player – had been promoted so rapidly within the SAP. I also asked him why, as a policeman, Botha was allowed to sport long hair when the Police Commissioner was personally enforcing the provisions of the relevant standing order for regulation short back and sides.

'Naas Botha has been appointed at the discretion of the Commissioner, who has the unquestionable right to appoint anyone to the SAP and to whatever rank,' Mellet replied. Undeterred, I asked whether this was fair to other members, many of whom had a generation of experience and hadn't been compensated for their efforts, either through promotion or remuneration.

'Naas', inhaled Mellet, 'is the idol of the South African youth and it's a great public relations boost to have him in the Force.'

De Kock repeated his judgement of Mellet under his breath.

This must have been something of a sore point for Mellet. Without any prompting, he proceeded to tell us that he, Mellet, had a military background and had been 'operational' for years, while working as a journalist for the *Natal Mercury*. All the while, he said, he had worked as an undercover Bureau for State Security (BOSS) agent in the neighbouring states. We were taken aback by his revelation.

'You guys don't know anything!' he became animated. 'I also burgled premises to obtain documents, and was involved in organising hits, so I'm not exactly new to the business.'

'Colonel,' I felt I had to interject. 'With respect. Do you know who I am and who we are?' He said he did not. 'Then how can you tell us things like this? Do you know anyone sitting at this table?' He shook his head.

'Well, Colonel, again with respect,' I said, 'I regard what you're saying as a breach of national security and I no longer want to be a part of this conversation.'

I pushed back my chair, stood up and headed for the bar.

'Fuck him, Porky,' said John Adams, using my nickname.

But De Kock wasn't going to leave it there, and an argument rapidly ensued between him and Mellet. When I turned around towards the table again, Mellet was disappearing into the bathroom, followed by De Kock and John Adams, and they in turn were being followed by the person from the SB Head Office, who was trying to prevent what appeared to be the imminent demolition of the colonel.

I decided to go in, only to find De Kock and John holding Mellet by the throat, the colonel pressed up against the basins. The situation was spiralling out of control, but fortunately, after some tense moments, Mellet beat a retreat. We later heard that he'd quickly returned to Pretoria, cutting short his tour of duty on the border.

The next morning I was summoned to the Koevoet base, where all hell had apparently broken loose. Police Commissioner Geldenhuys had called Brigadier Dreyer and demanded to know the identity of 'Porky', the 'bliksem who had started all the shit', and the two lieutenants De Kock and Adams.

Geldenhuys wanted answers as to why officers and non-commissioned officers were socialising together – it was said to be bad for discipline – and, indeed, standing orders had sufficiently Victorian provisions to sort one of us out forever. If Geldenhuys had had his way, and if 'Sterk' Hans had been less enthusiastic in defence of his staff, we would probably have been demoted or worse.

Both De Kock and John Adams made impassioned pleas for my survival, and Dreyer refused to divulge the identity of Porky. He apparently encouraged the Commissioner to remove Mellet from Ovamboland, because not only was the presence of the 'plastic' colonel bad for morale, but he also could not guarantee that similar incidents would not recur.

A year or so later, after Neil Aggett's death in detention and the crisis of his inquest, the SB at John Vorster Square was visited by Mellet and the

Minister of Justice, Police and Prisons, Louis le Grange. They were to host a cheese and wine party to try, once again, to bolster morale. I was already back by then, having served my time in Ovamboland, and avoided all contact with Mellet until, at the end of the function, we had to line up to be personally thanked by Le Grange who, we were told, had 'each of our best interests at heart'. After the perfunctory handshakes, I looked up at the ceiling as Mellet approached, sticking out my hand and hoping that a lack of eye contact would somehow keep me incognito.

'And this is Sergeant Erasmus,' said my CO. Mellet shook hands and moved on. I could hardly believe it! I was safe. But within moments he stopped, turned on his heel and looked me straight in the eye.

'Haven't we met before, Sergeant?'

'No, sir. I don't recall.'

'But I know you,' he said firmly. 'You're Porky. You were at the guest house in Ovamboland with De Kock.'

I remained silent.

'Well, now at least I know who you are,' Mellet smirked. 'Sergeant Paul Erasmus.'

I wanted to spit at him.

Chapter Six

The Chance to Breathe

Mossel Bay, 1996, and Johannesburg, 1998

ALTHOUGH MY WIFE LINDA was falling apart, taking extreme strain both from all my years of brutalising and being brutalised, and from the cracks in our marriage, she helped me to draw up a document detailing some 500 instances in which I could have been criminally prosecuted had I been a civilian. There were about 80 specific events, ranging from the theft of pot plants to sabotage, from attempted murder to the killing of a man in Ovamboland.

This condensed form of the horrors I had been involved in or had perpetrated was a prerequisite for what I had to do in order to apply for amnesty to the Truth and Reconciliation Commission (TRC) in 1996. We were entirely focused on that, to the exclusion of virtually everything else. I was obsessed with getting it all down on paper – somehow it seemed that if it were on paper and being dealt with, I could get it off my chest. However, I couldn't escape the sense that my life appeared to be fading away and it seemed inevitable that I would flirt with suicide, as did so many of my colleagues before and after.

I was already nothing. All my senses had collapsed. I was lifeless – so damaged that I was being held together only by medication. The same was true of Linda. The tentacles in my world had touched her too, and it had been devastating. She knew a lot, not only because she had been married to and lived with me, but also because of the evidence I had given to the Goldstone Inquiry prior to the TRC submission, and from which I had hoped to get amnesty. If seeing it all in a condensed form shocked me, the horror it visited on her all but destroyed her.

I had been hospitalised repeatedly with depression, insomnia and other symptoms of post-traumatic stress syndrome (PTSD), all of which brought me crashing down. And this brought even more uncertainty into our marriage and family life, the relocations in particular killing Linda's spirit. To top it all, Dylan's remedial situation weighed heavily on us both. Of everything, this was the issue Linda was least able to handle. She was a mother, and she was shattered.

I had, of course, fallen apart long before 1996, but in those earlier years I didn't think there was anything I could do about it. You just carried on. I was sure that if I spoke about it, I would lose my job. In the meantime, the PTSD rapidly intensified. Each visit to the psychiatrist in Mossel Bay, not far from where we were living in George, triggered fears, and resurrected the ghosts that had emerged after so much death and torture. Eventually, just to stay somewhat together, I began tossing back handfuls of tablets.

The despair I was feeling was all-consuming, and there seemed to be no remedy. No psychotherapy or anti-depressants, and certainly no amount of prayer, could prevent me from looking every day into the eyes of the man I'd killed in Ovamboland, or seeing the image of that old woman's remains in the village hut. A visit by Linda and me to a local minister of a charismatic church in George felt as destructive as anything I'd been through before; he was adamant that I would pay the price by going to jail and, behind my back, his wife convinced Linda that she should divorce me – 'for the sake of the children,' she said.

Love and hate are a hair's breadth apart, but if the turmoil of divorce is too terrible to even contemplate, the prospect of losing custody of one's children is much more terrifying. Even in 1996, as we were working closely together to try to save my skin, we knew what was coming further down the line. Dylan was not yet ten years old, but we silently knew that there was no chance that our marriage would survive. We were not going to be able to carry on trying to parent our son together.

Although the Attorney-General's office had advised me to apply for amnesty, and that for a brief moment felt like a burst of hope, it failed to bring about enough of a change in our relationship to give us that final chance. The new Promotion of National Unity and Reconciliation Act of 1995 had come into effect, and I could technically unleash myself from my past if the TRC agreed that I had met its demands. But the emotional and psychological hammering, which both the apartheid state and I had meted out on myself, was too great for us to overcome as a couple.

In preparation for a hearing to decide the fate of the children, therapists decided that nine-year-old Dylan should stay with me. He wanted that. The very astute 11-year-old Candice refused to choose between her mother and me, but insisted that she didn't want to leave her home town of George. This meant she would stay in my preserve anyway.

Despite the reassurances, Linda nonetheless relocated the children to Johannesburg, which drove an insurmountable wedge between us that has never really been bridged. In the eight months in which I neither spoke to nor saw my children, the stress was so overwhelming that I lost 49 kilograms. I was forced to move to Johannesburg too, and hire a lawyer in order to gain limited access to my children.

There are many who believed that I had been certified a psychopath, which meant that I was a threat even to my own children. Eventually, a court order allowed me to attend an end-of-year prize-giving function at Candice's school. That was the moment she lashed out at me.

Heart beating wildly, I saw her afterwards and ran up to greet her where she was standing with some of her friends and their parents. But she pushed away from me, and after a brief silence, under the glare of perfect strangers, Candice launched into a tirade that left me reeling.

'How many children did you shoot in Soweto, Dad? Why did you go into the police when you left school? If you are so clever, why didn't you go to university? Why didn't you leave the police?'

The blows rained down on me, and with my heart pounding, I tried to answer my daughter's questions. A darkness descended. It was clear that no one wanted me there. Even the headmistress had been told I was a danger to my daughter, and on an earlier occasion, when I arrived at the school, she had called the police.

The hell of fighting for the right to see Dylan and Candice, having no money, being unable to work and preparing for the looming TRC took a heavy toll. There were only two places of serenity to which I could retreat, two islands in my lost world that were special to me: St Mary's Cathedral in Johannesburg's CBD and the Cathedral Church of Christ the King in Saratoga Avenue, Hillbrow. When I was unable to navigate my feelings around my useless life, it gave me some solace to sit in those pews. The irony was not lost on me that I had once firebombed St Mary's and Cronwright had ordered us to destroy Christ the King during one of his insane rages against the Catholics and the world in general.

One Sunday morning, when I honestly believed that I was not going to survive another week of this kind of pressure, I received a life-changing phone call, which continues to linger in my memory.

'You have one hour to fetch Dylan,' Linda said. 'He can stay with you for the time being.'

I was stunned. Up until then she had been relentless in her efforts to secure custody. We had been fighting a no-holds-barred battle.

But my joy was short-lived because it wasn't long before Linda wanted Dylan back and I had no resources to legally object. It was only after a man was assaulted in Linda's home, in front of Dylan, that I got the courage and decided that it was time he was allowed to speak for himself.

I took him, in his school uniform, to the Supreme Court, and demanded to see a judge. My son's rights had been violated. An emergency hearing was scheduled with the family advocate, with counsel appointed to represent him at no cost.

Advocate Maharaj was at her desk when Linda and I presented ourselves. As soon as I laid eyes on her, I knew we had met before. She instantly recognised me too, and it was quite clear during the proceedings that she didn't like me. She gave Linda and her lawyers plenty of leeway to destroy my credibility.

Among Linda's accusations was that, as a security policeman, I had had experiences that affected my capacity to parent. Linda referred to my TRC amnesty application as 'a horror story' and suggested that when I stopped drinking, South African Breweries 'nearly went out of business'.

Then, with all the accusations flying through the air, and my stress levels at an all-time high, it came to me suddenly how I knew Maharaj. I had arrested her during the State of Emergency back in 1987, and I could still picture her standing in front of me with other Wits students, among the thousands detained during that time. I remembered being infuriated by her then – she was full of confidence, so sure of her support for the ANC. This had incensed me, so I had signed a detention reception order and she was taken away to the cells.

But now I was so anxious at the thought of losing Dylan, so convinced that Maharaj would be determined to deny me because of her experience back then, that I told the counsel appointed to me about the episode. He immediately suggested we apply for a new hearing before a different advocate, but we finally agreed to proceed as planned. After all, all that was left was for me to put forward my presentation. I was exhausted.

At the end of it, we were advised only that Maharaj would give her findings 'soon'.

That was the lowest point in my life. I had nothing left. It was the end. I sat on the wooden bench at the court thinking about my boy. Declared deaf as an infant, Dylan had since gained some hearing, but still had to attend schools for children disabled in different ways. He was perpetually unsettled, and his behaviour was erratic. I felt, however, that I could give him the attention he needed in order to finally feel loved by me, to feel secure. Fortunately, Candice was academically gifted and to her great credit, almost unbelievably, came across to the court as emotionally stable and calm.

We received a summons to attend a meeting in chambers a week later. I was drained, frightened beyond anything I had ever experienced, so it came as a shock to hear that Maharaj had ruled in my favour and had awarded me permanent custody of Dylan. My counsel was highly uncomfortable – he'd fully prepared me to lose. He asked whether there had been any impropriety, any pressure that I may have been able to exert on Maharaj, considering that I had once been her tormentor. He demanded to know whether I had blackmailed her in some way, warning me that the consequences would be irreversible.

Naturally I denied this, so he called Maharaj and asked, on a speaker phone, why she had come to make such an unexpected decision. He told her that he knew I had once detained her.

Maharaj remained serene. She said that she had seen how Linda and her lawyers had tried to use my past to demonise me, but remained unconvinced that those events had turned me into a poor parent. She said that she had given Linda every opportunity to present anything that would detract from my ability to be a good father to Dylan and this had not been forthcoming. Counsel told me afterwards that he had never felt such a sense of respect for another advocate, and that her objectivity was firmly situated in jurisprudence.

Maharaj's decision gave Dylan and me a chance to build a father–son relationship and I was in tears. After a few days I decided to call Maharaj to thank her. She wasn't friendly. She said the memory of my thuggish behaviour at John Vorster Square had not left her, and she hadn't forgotten how I had called her 'a coolie bitch'.

I felt her briefly soften at the end of our short conversation when she asked me to ensure that Dylan never walked in those footsteps, that I wouldn't even allow him to carry a gun and that I would raise him to be a decent citizen. I cried when she told me that she was entrusting me with my son's future. Such decency and care and forgiveness were beyond the realm of my experience and I resolved to honour her expectations and trust in me, whatever it took.

I cried again a few months later when I heard that Maharaj had died, apparently as a result of a brain aneurism. She had been sitting at her desk when she suddenly slumped forward. Few people had ever shown me such decency and objectivity, and after Maharaj's transformative intervention it became very clear in my mind where I had been. A poison had filtered through my consciousness for two decades, and it was Maharaj – and only Maharaj – who had released that toxic fog and given me a chance to breathe.

Chapter Seven

Ripping off the Grilles

Pretoria and Johannesburg, 1979

USUALLY, SAP STAFF WERE treated only fractionally better than the police horses, stabled at the Police College (Polkol) in Pretoria West. So when two colleagues from John Vorster Square – Johan 'Doc' du Plooy and Paul van Coller – and I joined 80-odd SB members from around the country on a security course, we were surprised to find that we'd been invited to a five-star lunch in the mess.

There were decorations on the tables and second helpings, the meal starting not long after we'd arrived late one Sunday morning. Just as we were lighting up smokes after dessert and looking forward to another five weeks of hotel-class treatment, the horrified master of the mess stormed in, sweat streaming down his face.

'There's been a terrible mistake! You guys are eating in the wrong place!'

Fortunately, it was too late.

We'd just ploughed our way through a lunch that had been set out for a team of international gymnasts being hosted by the SAP, and those poor sods had been subjected to the usual Polkol slop served to them in the spartan conditions of the adjoining mess.

We all had a good laugh, but there was nothing funny about the course that followed. This was 1979. I'd been in the SB for a couple of years, but I was growing weary and bored with the incessant surveillance and the tedium of the hours and days on the job. I felt I had to feed the adrenalin monster eating away at my soul, especially given that a renewed ANC wind was blowing over the country.

The previous year, Prime Minister Vorster had resigned under a heavy cloud of corruption as the Information Scandal swept across the political landscape and he had been replaced by the hardline militarist P.W. Botha. The uprisings of 1976 had also injected a certain heat and energy back into the ANC, and its uMkhonto we Sizwe (MK) guerrillas were now being sighted returning to South Africa from the camps and safe houses in Angola, Mozambique, Swaziland, Botswana and Zambia, or from operating underground in South Africa. And then, as if to warn other guerrillas intending to come home and cause chaos, the state hanged Solomon Mahlangu, the young MK operative, in April that year.

But still things did not quieten down. This was a time when bombs were being detonated and explosives were being found on the tracks or close to railway stations around the country. It was clear that infrastructure was being targeted. There were also increasing numbers of incidents of MK operatives opening fire on or hurling hand grenades into police stations or the homes of police officers in the townships.

When a bomb exploded at the Sasol oil refinery causing significant structural damage, government decided it needed to beef up its intelligence component. We were told that the ANC had established a special operations unit and that the SADF would thus be intensifying its cross-border attacks.

As an example, brutal as it was, the South African Air Force destroyed the ANC's Nova Catengue Training Camp in Angola by means of a devastating aerial bombardment. And while we in the security forces celebrated, I was becoming edgy about wanting that experience of being on the border too. Life in Johannesburg was just too tame. People in the suburbs were becoming complacent, their greatest excitement being Jody Scheckter becoming the Formula One world champion, and the F1 Grand Prix being held at Kyalami.

I craved the adrenalin rush I had only heard about from other SAP operatives who'd been to Ovamboland. I wanted that. Besides, the patriotic one-upmanship that played out on the security course only spurred me on. If I was going to amount to anything, I reckoned, I would have to go through that rite of passage; I had to fully embrace the national values described by the course coordinator, Brigadier Neels du Plooy.

'Sagmoedige' Neels, as he was 'affectionately' known in SB circles, where he was considered meek and gentle, was a senior member of the Afrikaner Broederbond and was said to be the confidant of some powerful people. We were told that he had contributed to the formulation of the National Party government's Total Onslaught campaign. Du Plooy delivered the opening lecture with an emphasis on how the SB was committed to the 'national values of honesty and mercy' to our opponents. He emphasised that we should understand, and perfect, crisis management and maintain independence of thought. Most importantly, we had to hold Christian values paramount and know that empires collapse when immorality, greed, corruption and the ignorance of virtue begin to dominate.

'Duty to one's country is one's anchor in life,' said Neels. 'Patriotism and love of our mother country is our strength.' He instructed us, with tear-filled conviction, that 'the implementation of apartheid was our only salvation'. The essence of our struggle was 'moral preparedness', he said, and the will to wage war against 'satanic and demonic communism'.

The ANC, especially, had to be fought with 'God, gun, conscience and duty'. And yet, he continued with a straight face, 'not one person' had ever been sentenced to death under South African security legislation, demonstrating the 'Christian decency' and benevolence of our nationalism. By this time, of course, there had already been at least 50 deaths of detainees being held and interrogated by SB members alone, not to mention all the hangings at Pretoria Central Prison.

Moving along, Brigadier Du Plooy demonstrated how security legislation was based on biblical precepts. House arrest, for example, was justified by the Bible in 1 Kings 2: 36: 'The king ... told him, "Build a house here in Jerusalem and don't step outside the city on pain of death."' Of course, when the rest of us discussed this privately afterwards, there was a lot of laughter, but our lecturer had, nevertheless, held us spellbound with his oratory, spit flying in all directions as his eyes filled with tears.

One of his favourites was: 'En ek sê vir jou, 'n polisieman wie sy vrou verraai, verraai sy land!', suggesting that marital infidelity was akin to treason. Infidelity was, in their eyes, immoral and immorality was, after all, a tool of the satanic communists. Lectures were even punctuated with vitriolic attacks on *Scope*, a popular girlie magazine, and we were warned that those who read it were betraying their country.

We studied banned organisations, old and new, as well as anti-apartheid propaganda, with Du Plooy advising us to heed the message of *Servamus*, *Paratus* (the official magazine of the SADF) and propaganda from the SABC. What he didn't know, of course, was that in private *Servamus* was a source of entertainment for us. We mocked senior members of the SAP whose sons and daughters were featured in pictures in the magazine for having achieved excellent academic results at university. Small wonder. They were, in many instances, being provided with free higher education by means of the corrupt use of the so-called RS Programme (Republic Security) – as spies at universities, whose studies were paid in full by the SB.[7] We also laughed at the intoxicated grins of members of the military hierarchy pictured at functions. With booze in hand, the captions described how they were 'in 'n gesellige luim'.

Yet I was drawn to Du Plooy's lectures about the anti-apartheid disinformation machinery aimed at what he called 'breaking down the fibre of people'. This was not only evident in the cloak-and-dagger stuff of secret radio messages, banned magazines and flyers, but also in mainstream movies, live music and theatre shows. In fact, so well versed was the apartheid state in these methods that it used similar methods to fight the Total Onslaught and break down the resistance – or so we were taught.

We were also taught about Black Consciousness and black theology, which, Du Plooy explained, was a 'Red' or 'socialist' gospel practised by the English churches and Afrikaner traitors like Beyers Naudé to encourage black South Africans to overthrow the state. This topic clearly affected and agitated Du Plooy, and a rainstorm of spittle cascaded on the poor sods in the front row during his vitriolic tirades. A spin-off of this evil, insisted Du Plooy, was conscientious objection to national service.

After lectures, Doc and I took refuge in the bar at Keevy House, which was usually out of bounds to students and other plebs. We walked across the Polkol parade ground, where many drops of sweat had fallen from so many brows, and passed the musketry section where we had done bayonet drill as recruits wearing Nazi-style helmets. Years later, trading stories with police officers from the United Kingdom and Denmark, when my family and I were relocated under witness protection, they couldn't believe that we had used bayonets during training for civilian policing duties.

When we finally returned to John Vorster Square from Polkol, the animosity towards me, as well as towards other SB members who were involved in exposing the prevalence of right-wingers in the force, had increased. Greg Deegan, who was never at a loss for words, wasn't too perturbed about it, and gave back as good as he got. I was not quite as bold as that.

Cronwright had apparently issued an 'edict' banning us from the tenth floor, and on the odd occasion that we bumped into him, I had to suffer Greg's whispered barbs and hisses about Cronwright being Little Hitler. That's what we called him – behind his back, of course. However, we taunted him to his face from time to time.

One morning, Greg and I got into the lift with Little Hitler and I muttered a greeting to a grunt of acknowledgement, but Greg piped up in his loudest voice: 'Good morning, Major! How are you today, sir? Nice day today, sir!'

Cronwright, slightly taken aback, delivered another grunt: 'Uh … fine, Deegan.'

'Lovely day today, sir,' Greg continued cheerily. 'And how's the family?' This was a something of a sore point, as we all knew that Cronwright was in the process of getting divorced and was not handling the break-up of his family very well. The little man stared at Greg with something between surprise and anger. This time there was no reply.

The lift door opened and we got out.

'Jesus, Greg, you're really pushing it,' I said.

'Aw, fuck him,' Greg bellowed. 'What's he in our lives anyway?'

In another incident, a detainee had been beaten up during interrogation and demanded to see a doctor, so Greg was dressed up in a white safari suit, with white socks and shoes, and handed a medical bag, a stethoscope and an assortment of medicines. 'Dr' Deegan proceeded to thoroughly examine the detainee, after which he heavily berated Cronwright about the man's health, in front of the detainee. Cronwright became red-faced and was spitting with rage at Greg's antics as the 'district surgeon'. In a sick kind of way, Greg won the day, however – the detainee was happy with the 'excellent medical care' provided by the SB and withdrew his complaint.

It was clear that Cronwright was not going to let go of the National Front incident. On the other hand, our boss, Jordaan, who was now a colonel, only once brought up the subject, quipping: 'I hear you've made some enemies, Paul.'

'And how, sir!' I responded, but not quite ready for his next remark: 'What's this nonsense about you being queer?'

'There's no substance in it, sir.' I played it cool. 'As you know, I have a girlfriend.'

'Well,' mumbled Jordaan, 'that whole thing's been sorted out now with Major Cronwright. Just do your job.' I decided to let his comment go.

I was making a lot of progress with my informants at the time. I had infiltrated Youth For Peace (YFP) as well as a non-violence group headed by the Reverend Rob Robertson, head of the division of Justice and Reconciliation in the South African Council of Churches (SACC). I was also making steady headway within an organisation known as the Forty Percenters, who claimed to represent the 40 per cent of white South Africans who were English speakers.

At one of their first meetings, the Forty Percenters talked about setting up their organisation along the lines of the Broederbond in order to publicly contradict it in every way possible to promote the cause of the English speakers.

I faithfully reported this to the SB Head Office and was surprised – or, as it turns out, very naive – at the extraordinary interest in this organisation, which I imagined was only on the periphery of anti-state activity.

Demands were immediately made for full identification of everyone involved, photographs of the suspects and any technical coverage in the form of tape recordings and transcriptions of Forty Percenters' meetings. At the time, this being 1979, I didn't quite understand the intricacies of the white political scene, but during one of their meetings the Forty Percenters had referred to a recently published book, *The Super-Afrikaners*. It was all about the Broederbond, and I thought this could help me get to grips with what the hell was going on in my own community. So I bought a copy and read it with great interest.

I was especially taken with a list of Broederbond members (known as Broeders), their membership numbers and even addresses. The book also contained some tantalising information: my boss, Major Jordaan, and Brigadier Du Plooy were among the many names included from the SAP and the SADF hierarchy.

The Broederbond contended it was merely the Afrikaner equivalent of the Freemasons – the most notable distinction being that the Broederbond had a political agenda, whereas the Freemasons apparently did not. This I established from, among others, my dad, who was a Master Mason.

I discovered, too, that there was considerable friction between the two organisations, my father maintaining that he had been overlooked for promotion in the civil service because he had not been a member of the Broederbond. He believed that the bureaucracy's neglect of him also had something to do with a revelation about his Freemasonry.

Thus, even when the Forty Percenters started to taper off – as did many fringe organisations investigated by the SB – I was curious enough to continue to concentrate on the issues that had been raised. In my naivety, I believed that the old English–Afrikaans rivalry had been consigned to the dustbin of history – where I thought it belonged. After all, there were more pressing matters at hand, and weren't we, the whites, 'one nation' and standing united?

Black politics and aspirations were neither here nor there for me at the time. My energies, attention and unbridled hatred as an SB operative were focused on the white left, which, we were taught, was using black people – whom, we believed, were basically ignorant and harmless – as tools to achieve their own political objectives. Remembering the heap of bodies at Braamfontein mortuary following the 1976 riots somehow made it easier for me to hate, with unrestrained intensity, the people said to be the brains behind this carnage.

While all of this was fomenting in my mind, Jordaan strode into my office and spotted *The Super-Afrikaners* on my desk.

'I see you have some interesting reading,' he said.

'Yes, sir,' I nodded.

He picked up the book, put it down again and headed for the door. Then he stopped and turned around. 'I'm not in the Broederbond, you know!'

This unexpected statement shook me: first, because he was lying and, second, if he had read the book, he would have known that I knew he was lying. After that, Jordaan's attitude towards me changed perceptibly, and I was more than relieved when he eventually retired.

Greg didn't have my – albeit meagre – sense of boundaries. He specialised in overstepping the mark.

Notorious pamphlet bomber and 'white terrorist' (as propaganda of the time had it), Stephen Lee had been arrested and an ID parade was thus scheduled on the tenth floor. A 'witness' was going to point out Lee (who later escaped with comrades Tim Jenkin and Alex Moumbaris from Pretoria Central Prison).

At the appointed time on the scheduled day, Lee's leg-irons and handcuffs were removed, and he took up his position among 15 of us who had been assembled for the parade. In came the torturers, and Cronwright read out the formalities.

'I am Colonel Arthur Benoni Cronwright,' he said. We all knew he had a chip on his shoulder about his second name, which was also the name of a town on the East Rand, and set his initials at A.B.C. – another sore point for Little Hitler. Immediately, there were sniggers from Greg, standing in the line-up next to me.

Cronwright then moved down the line, the legal requirement being that all initials and full names were to be recorded. He stopped in front of me.

'Name?'

'Erasmus, P.F.: Paul Francis.'

'Name?'

'Deegan, C.G.: Charles Germiston.' (Germiston is another town on the East Rand.)

Greg's second name was actually Gregory. The entire ID parade, including Lee, erupted into uncontrollable laughter.

Cronwright turned crimson, eyes blazing, his pen hovering over the page where I noticed he had entered 'Germiston'. I now had tears streaming down my face.

The line-up continued, but this time with a different tension playing out as everyone pretended to be serious. Shortly afterwards, Jordaan found out that, in protest at not having a state vehicle, Greg hadn't done any real work for a month and, as punishment, transferred him to the tenth floor to serve under Cronwright.

This would surely be the end of Greg, we thought. But Greg was irrepressible.

Office-bound and with not much else to do, Greg wrote a long letter to his brother in which he described Cronwright as a 'little Hitler clone' who 'resorted to self-flagellation as the [SB's] prisoners were tortured'. To illustrate his letter, he drew a caricature of Cronwright in a Gestapo uniform, Hitler moustache and hairstyle, with an oversized erection and a whip, towering over a handcuffed and manacled detainee.

At teatime that day, Greg left the office and the letter lying on his desk. When he returned, it was gone. He searched for it, hoping that someone other than Cronwright had found it. He began to believe that this might be the case when Cronwright initially behaved in his usual way. About a week later, however, Cronwright summoned Greg into his office, and asked him to sit down.

'So ... how do you find working here under my command, Greg?'

Cronwright's friendliness disarmed Greg so completely that he relaxed, just managing to hide his surprise at this sudden warmth from Little Hitler.

'Well, sir, it's the best thing that's ever happened to me.'

Greg took the opportunity for a bit of arse-creeping, with a view to having his confinement to the tenth floor lifted.

'I'm really happy here, sir. I would like to get more involved, though ... Probably get out a bit, you know, with the other chaps.'

'And how do you find working under a section head like me?'

Greg was in top form.

'It's great, sir! You know you're a tremendous commander and, if I may say so, sir, I don't think people have enough respect for you and for your capabilities.'

'Really, Greg?'

'Yes, sir, and I just want to ...'

'You really think I'm a great guy?'

'Yes, sir, and ...'

'Then what is this all about, you fucking liar?' Out came the missing letter and picture. Unsettling him, Cronwright then commended him on the artwork. Such was the trickery of Cronwright.

We had times like this at John Vorster. The deviousness and toxicity of the

72

place were intense: it was a form of mind control. It was power. Our infantile reactions to our superiors and their demonstrations of power, our power over suspects, being part of a fascist organisation and calling Cronwright 'Little Hitler', all went over our damaged heads.

I tried to concentrate on infiltrating target organisations, but it was tough. There were many internal distractions, but then in 1980 I was given a major task as the alternative handler of an agent at the *Rand Daily Mail*, who was a goldmine of information. I had to keep my eye on the ball.

At the same time as keeping our moles in the print media happy – which was a priority – I was also growing my pool of agents in left student communes and organisations. Some might have seemed peripheral, but there were often links to our white left target groups there.

The Quakers, for example, were of concern to the Head Office – specifically senior member Vernon Baker, who had become 'a little too involved' with the Reverend Rob Robertson and the SACC. The Head Office didn't like the united stand they were taking on conscientious objection, especially when Robertson set up the Conscientious Objector Support Group (COSG), an alliance of the various groups around the End Conscription Campaign (ECC). We intercepted thousands of ECC stickers and other material. We even put the Hell's Angels onto them.

But I liked my job most when it compelled me to sit in on live music or theatre shows, and one of special importance took place in June 1980 at His Majesty's Theatre, a fancy spot in the centre of Johannesburg. Surrounded by sophisticated apartments and smart restaurants and shops opening onto well-kept pavements, His Majesty's was a real drawcard.

The show featured a new personality on the South African music scene: Roger Lucey and his band, the Zub Zub Marauders. They were making waves, not only among young white liberals, but also at the SB Head Office. A set of Lucey's music and a recording of him airing his anti-apartheid views had been monitored by Military Intelligence during transmission to Voice of America, the US government-funded radio network. I was told to open a file on him and his girlfriend, Sue Cullinan.

Not long after I started monitoring Lucey, I was summoned to a meeting with senior security policemen at the office of Brigadier J. 'Kalfie' Broodryk. Lucey's file was on the brigadier's desk, alongside a tape recorder with a recording of Lucey singing, unbelievably, about the SB torturing people. I was instructed to prioritise the full personal identification of this individual who was clearly highly dangerous, and also 'see what could be done about stopping this filth'.

So I got to attend Lucey's shows and record his evocative ballads about deaths in detention and state oppression, faithfully transcribe them and forward the lot to Head Office. I reported to Broodryk on a daily basis.

My bosses were enraged by Lucey's first LP, *The Road Is Much Longer* – it included now-classics like 'Lungile Tabalaza'[8] and 'You Only Need Say Nothing', which I submitted to the Publications Control Board (PCB) for consideration. It was, however, becoming clear that the kind of rote monitoring I had been doing until then was not going to be enough to satisfy Head Office. Remember, white activists were our 'real' enemies, and Lucey was an A-grade target.

I was regularly summoned to the brigadier's office where, more often than not, his sidekick, Colonel Hans Gloy – believed by us to be one of the torturers in the Ahmed Timol case – would gaze at me with hooded eyes. Lucey was persistent in his attacks on the SB, and every time we heard these songs, it was as if each of us was being repeatedly punched in the stomach. We were accustomed to the hatred. That was part of the job. But somehow Lucey stuck in the craw. This had to be stopped. Soonest!

I contacted WEA Records and 3rd Ear Productions, which were publishing and distributing Lucey's music, and threatened the director, David Marks. I told him the record was banned and demanded to know how many presses had been made and where they'd been delivered. I also planted the seed that Lucey was connected with either the ANC or the SACP, or both, and dropped the hint that Marks was facing imminent arrest and detention under security legislation.

WEA Records seemed aghast. The SB could destroy a person or a business and the record company's directors went to great lengths to assure me that they didn't want trouble. I then went to Hillbrow Records – South Africa's legendary music shop – and confiscated all the LPs and cassettes of Lucey's music.

Lucey's house in Crown Mines was duly searched, and we started to monitor his family and the musicians who featured with him on his album. One of the high points for us in the victimisation of Lucey was when we sabotaged Mangles, a popular Braamfontein music spot, by pouring tear-gas powder into the air conditioner while he was playing. We watched the evacuation from across the road, howling with laughter. We followed this up with a series of phone calls threatening to blow the place up if it continued to host Lucey there. Using WH11, I was able to establish which other venues he'd be playing at to give them the same treatment, using Mangles as a compelling example of what could happen.

It didn't take long before Lucey's contracts and gigs screeched to a halt. That was a rare moment, however, when I paused for reflection. I'd actually started to become a fan of his music, but still I thought he was wasting his talent on anti-apartheid songs, simply because they'd only be banned. I was convinced he'd have done better to write songs that slipped under the SB's radar, but of course that would never have been an option for Roger Lucey. He may have been a pacifist, but he was also a revolutionary spirit, and he taunted us specifically, knowing that there was no way we'd ever let go.

The success of the tear-gas incident at Mangles essentially gave us the go-ahead to use the same method at other clubs and venues where 'lefties' gathered. We had an abundant supply of the CS powder and it became a favourite in our arsenal of dirty tricks for a while. All of this was to be recounted in a remarkable documentary, *Stopping the Music: A Story of Censorship in South Africa*, which was broadcast in a number of countries but not here in South Africa. Going public eventually with what happened with Roger, and how his career came to an end, was as much a shock to him as it was to me when, meeting him during the filming of *Stopping the Music*, I found he bore no malice and chose to forgive me and even defended me to many who criticised him for this benevolence.

I've never experienced such decency anywhere in my life and have had the privilege of joining this gracious person in many forums, including, many Freemuse-sponsored events, locally and abroad, where we've shared the stage and spoken of our experiences. As one of his greatest fans, I can never forgive myself for what I did to this wonderful person.

We got our kicks blowing tear gas into the air vents of our enemies' cars too, leaving them with burning eyes as the powder reacted with moisture on their bodies. Our inventiveness was on the increase and we often supplemented the CS treatment by letting down tyres or tying fenders and grilles together. We took pleasure when a target drove off, ripping the grilles or bumpers off other cars in the process.

Quasi-religious groups were a quarry for us. As per instructions from the Head Office, one of the groups I focused on was the Reformational Africa Studies Programme (RASP), led by Anthony John 'Tony' Russell. RASP operated out of an old mine house in a commune in Germiston, and although it seemed harmless enough, it attracted the SB's attention because of Russell's radical views on religion and history. Information from agents suggested that he and RASP were influencing sections within the SACC, especially its Justice and Reconciliation division, and Robertson's COSG, which was working with a number of ad hoc left-wing organisations. Robertson had even approached the United Congregational Church of Southern Africa (UCCSA), the Presbyterians and others for support. Much effort was thus being made by the SB to stop him dead in his tracks.

We looked at the legal prospects, and the Defence Act of 1957 offered a provision for those 'encouraging, influencing, aiding and assisting persons' who were not prepared to do their military service. Armed with this legislation, we prepared a memorandum suggesting that action be taken against Robertson and many others.

But Cronwright and the Investigation Branch ignored what we felt was a cut-and-dried case in terms of the Act, and simply insisted that we keep up the pressure on Robertson and his 'satanic' associates. 'Boys,' said Cronwright, 'julle moet hulle opvok', so from time to time we'd hurl a brick or six through someone's window, puncture a few tyres or make threatening phone calls – futile and amateurish actions that had no effect whatsoever and, at the end of the day, only increased our frustration.

I had already submitted numerous reports on RASP and Russell by the time the commune was raided, out of the blue, by Cronwright and the tenth floor, apparently following a directive from the Church Desk at the SB Head Office. They destroyed the place, finding nothing that could link Russell or RASP to any breaches of security legislation. So keen were they to get their clutches on Russell that they didn't even bother to consult anyone already monitoring RASP. The raid quickly sparked a witch-hunt, and soon I was battling to keep my agent motivated. We had to rethink our entire approach, and this really got my blood boiling.

As I saw it, our intelligence-gathering capability was paramount and our first duty was to protect the few decent sources we had. But this wasn't to be. In fact, the contest for power over the RASP and Russell files turned bloody in a way that disturbed even us, the usually rough-and-ready ones.

Late one night when Russell showed up at the RASP commune, he was struck off his motorbike by a giant of a man in a balaclava, who was then joined by a half-pint who proceeded to hold Russell down to be clubbed senseless. The story at John Vorster was that Cronwright and his staff were responsible, the giant being Captain Dries Struwig and the half-pint none other than Little Hitler himself.

When Russell came to, incapacitated and barely conscious, his mouth was stuffed with meds, later identified as sleeping tablets, heart tablets and other powerful pharmaceuticals. It was truly a miracle that he hadn't died. Another RASP member rushed him to hospital where his stomach was pumped and he was treated for concussion and massive bruising.

RASP closed down immediately afterwards, and Russell left for Canada. This solved our problem with them, but the whole incident had shown that there were many new directions being taken by our colleagues – an ominous sign for us. We obviously had to ramp up our response, but we were becoming desperately demotivated.

Sometimes I look back on our lectures from 1979, and consider the way in which we had been instructed to harass, intimidate and frighten by Captain André Beukes, who later became a general and commissioner of police for the Western Cape. In those lessons, Lieutenant Zirk Gous would complement Beukes, with his information on dealing with what he called 'Jesus renegades' – in other words, religious groups who were outside the 'true' faith. Gous would eventually retire as a brigadier and as head of Community Policing for Gauteng. When I think back on them now, I see how unsparing and severe they were.

Those two officers – Beukes and Gous – made sure that we understood that the SACC was part of an 'evil empire', and pivotal to that was the Dependants Conference, which provided a funding trampoline for those who fell foul of security legislation. The Dependants Conference was actively garnering the support of wealthy churches abroad and openly promoting the ANC's sanctions drive, which resulted in numerous corporations pulling out of South Africa. This was revealed to us as 'clear, active agitation against the state', and challenging its ever-widening field of support was thus a priority.

Because of their large following, the Catholic and Anglican churches were arch-enemies in our battle, but the real 'devil' was the Catholic Young Christian Workers (YCW) organisation, whose aims were to 'create a socialist state in South Africa'. The YCW was brazen in its efforts, spreading labour unrest, including a strike at the Eveready Battery Company in Port Elizabeth, and their anti-apartheid campaign was second only to that of the Southern African Catholic Bishops Conference. If the 'radical insanity' of the YCW was not countered, we were told, it would lead to our downfall. The Catholics, it seemed, posed one of the most significant threats to our values, even of 'gently leading the blacks in South Africa down the road to self-government in the homelands'.[9]

We were lectured on the dangers of not having church unity among whites. So much so that the SADF chaplains, to whom 18-year-old conscripts were exposed on an almost daily basis, were compelled to drive an agenda of fear, ensuring that teenage soldiers believed that 'terror movements' such as the ANC and the PAC were, in fact, anti-God.

Back at John Vorster Square, we were on a roll. A roll of failures, that is.

Many of these were linked to the Church Desk, and our attempts to stifle the appeals of the churches to overseas organisations and companies to divest from South Africa had failed. This failure, tied into the extreme demotivation that I and others felt, added to the frustration, the fury, the demoralisation and, in turn, led to even more brutality. Essentially, it meant that we were failing – at our jobs, and in our lives. It fed the sadism. It gave us the impetus to maim or torture. Of course, we knew we were pawns, cogs, cannon fodder, but the only way we thought we could out-muscle our own futility was to do worse and ever more terrible things – and try to get noticed.

So it was with some of my colleagues. Some of them killed people. Others shot themselves. Others taught civilians to shoot other civilians.

Chapter Eight

The De Klerk Whip

Johannesburg, 1990

A DECADE OF WORKING FOR the SB took me to the brink. By the dawn of the 1990s, it was speculated that the unit itself would have to be pushed over the edge, replaced by another form of itself. After all, apartheid was all but over; or rather, that's what the National Party wanted South Africa and the world to believe. But behind the scenes, we at Stratcom were only getting started. And it was Stratcom that would also determine my ultimate fate: to be drawn into the world of a most unlikely woman – unlikely, at least in my world.

If that sounds romantic in any way, it wasn't. In fact, my links with Winnie Mandela began under heinous circumstances, the roots of which were in work I did with a Stratcom source, Dr Harvey Ward, a former director of the Rhodesian Broadcasting Corporation (RBC) and media adviser to Ian Smith, the last prime minister of colonial Rhodesia.

After Zimbabwe finally won majority rule in 1980 – but before it fell under a ZANU-PF government – Ward fled his birthplace for South Africa, where his mother had been born, and then for England, his father's homeland. He entrenched himself as an international expert on counter-propaganda and disinformation, and it was vital to my job in 1990 to establish contact with him.

Ward looms much larger in my life than a simple work-related relationship, however. This was because he was my connection to Winnie Mandela, and the nature of that connection still haunts me to this day. It also enlivens me, however, because Winnie turned out to be one of the kindest and most compassionate people I have ever known. If that was Ward's purpose, I have a greater appreciation for everything else that was part of our working relationship – that 'everything else' being desperate, malevolent and, even in my already chaotic world, unprecedented.

Ward had gained journalistic experience in South Africa, working at the *Cape Argus* and Reuters in the 1950s and 1960s, before he joined the *Rhodesia Herald* and then the Rhodesian Broadcasting Corporation, a Smith propaganda vehicle. As a foremost 'anti-communist consultant', he was thus well placed to advise the apartheid government on how to combat the effects of sanctions.

His connections in the UK's Conservative Party-linked Monday Club – a support group for right-wing Tories at the time – were going to be useful, as I needed access to its network to bolster the National Party's contacts in that intelligence and political community. I also needed access via this network to American organisations that shared – but were even more strident about – this particular right-wing belief. Today, this ideology has regained impetus as a fight against the left, and is said to be the philosophy behind a number of supremacist massacres, including those in Christchurch, New Zealand, and the 2019 attack on the Chabad of Poway, an Orthodox synagogue in California.

In the early 1990s, American right-wing groups such as the Western Goals Foundation (in the UK, later known as the Western Goals Institute) posed less of an actual physical threat than supremacists do today, but they were just as dangerous in other ways. The Western Goals Foundation had been dormant for about five years when Stratcom started to grapple with the advantages of its original principles in the early 1990s. This foundation was part of a lucrative and wide private funding network that broke US government sanctions and assisted massive corruption through illegal arms trading in Contragate (also known as the Iran–Contra affair), the scandal that was exposed in the second term of the Reagan administration in 1987.

Publicly, Western Goals was a publisher and media distributor. Secretly it was a laundry. The US intelligence sector had been under the whip from the 1970s, when its sophisticated domestic vigilance operations were barred by law. Counter-intelligence forces still working for the state – some of whom were already retired but retained an active interest in 'neutralising' dissenters – needed financial and other kinds of support from those private funders. And we in Stratcom could, of course, only learn from this because we were heavily under the whip after F.W. de Klerk unbanned those organisations that apparently still posed a threat to national security and the existing social order.

We were inspired by the FBI's Counter Intelligence Program

(COINTELPRO), which ran from the mid-1950s to 1971 when the US government cracked down on it. Its psychological warfare consisted of all our favourite SB techniques: smears; surveillance infiltration; planting fake materials; demonising and using the media to serve our interests; and creating mayhem inside enemy organisations so that they collapsed.

Of course, COINTELPRO wasn't the only government project of its kind in the world. Almost every country – including a seemingly benign one like Canada – had a programme like it, and probably still does. When Stratcom was at its height in the 1970s, our main enemy was the same as that of most other Western countries: communists and communism.

Not much changed between the 1970s and the 1990s in terms of whom we considered to be the 'demons', bearing in mind that – especially in apartheid South Africa – a communist was not necessarily someone who admired Lenin and sought a socialist state. It was anyone who threatened the National Party's power, anyone, in other words, who opposed apartheid.

Back to Ward. He was a nasty piece of work and his adopted country, the United Kingdom, had read him correctly back in 1977, when immigration officials at Heathrow Airport refused him entry and put him on a plane to Munich instead. On that occasion, he was supposed to address the Africa Committee of the Monday Club at the House of Lords. That meeting had been organised by Tory MP Harold Soref, who appeared to get away with his white supremacist philosophies because he was just so 'British', an ardent admirer of all things Anglo. He and Ward must have got along famously because they both supported apartheid and Rhodesia's Ian Smith to the bitter end.

And because I myself remained unquestioning about these views at the time, the only aspect of him that disgusted me was the British kind of snobbery, that tendency of the wealthy, well-bred English prat to behave as if their very presence meant that they were doing everyone else a favour. Ward fitted that brief exactly.

By 1990, some 13 years after he had been turned away at Heathrow, Ward was back, safely and comfortably ensconced in Britain. A year after settling in England, he – who was on the Monday Club's Foreign Affairs Committee and a member of its Executive Council, aside from being president of the World Anti-Communist League and an 'honorary' Austrian baron – got involved with the Western Goals Foundation. Xenophobic to the core, he identified with its ethos.

Ward's interest in Western Goals had been piqued at a Tory conference in the late 1980s when the foundation had raised concerns about high-level links between the Irish Republican Army (IRA) and the ANC. That's how some of my own, much-needed contacts would be made, without my even being there. I used this information for Stratcom purposes by forging an invitation from Raymond Suttner to Sinn Féin, the political wing of the IRA, to attend the ANC's 75th Conference.

By then, the apartheid government had honed its machinery to the point that there was little more they could do. Its racist system was being dismantled – it could no longer resort to the gallows, for instance – but this didn't mean that the National Party or other, even more conservative, forces wanted things to go the way they were going. Ending apartheid was just a strategy to retain power behind the scenes.

The party needed to implement a more sophisticated operation, and those of us in the SB had to face the fact that we could all be out of a job within a few years unless we came up with a strategy to outmanoeuvre the prevailing glasnost. So De Klerk and his government decided that, since the apartheid laws that had propped up the Afrikaner elite for so long were no longer available, they needed to be reinvented as a front for their old faithfuls – their super-rich, white, right-wing funders. The engine for the strategy would be through the establishment and workings of a clever and effective Stratcom, and this was to be my function from 1990: I would make my move on behalf of Stratcom to rig the 'rainbow nation' project. For about four years, I'd associate with Ward, and many others, to that end. It would prove to be the worst decade of my life.

I saw with eyes wide open how the National Party not only tortured and murdered but also ruthlessly used and abused its own deployees throughout the early 1990s 'rainbow nation' period. If we wanted to stay employed, we had one job – and that was to ensure that the Afrikaner elite maintained power, by hook or by crook, by proxy or through patronage. We were to have their backs 24/7.

As with so many issues concerning the SB, though, we were never properly renumerated. Neither were most of our sources. In Ward's case, he neither demanded nor expected the R2 000 per month plus expenses that some were receiving. His commitment was more ideological than mercenary. However, I felt that we should at least cover his considerable operational expenses – telephone, postage and travelling costs – either by making a deposit into a local account for him or arranging for the money to be transferred via our embassy in London.

Lesser payments, such as compensating a source, were generated from the SB's SECFIN (secret finance) system, but Major Gerrit Bruwer – in charge of those and other key matters within Stratcom – found ways to make this difficult. My having to use my home phone to call Ward, for instance, caused problems with Linda because, more often than not, I wasn't fully reimbursed for those costs at the end of the month.

As far as I was concerned, Bruwer acted like a dyed-in-the-wool racist, an ignorant security officer who was more concerned about his body-building and tan than the task at hand. He was my immediate superior at Stratcom, and I couldn't stand him. He couldn't stand me either. What irked me most about him was that he was unable to grasp the significance of our actual work. He had absolutely no understanding of strategy and hamstrung all our efforts in his rude, entitled, apartheid-era Afrikaner way and, I imagine, contributed to the demise of the National Party, while the system's intransigence allowed him, and others like him, to eat away at it.

Bruwer, for instance, refused to take Ward on as a source until a formal recruitment had taken place, and in the argument that ensued between Bruwer and me, I told him I'd be happy to go to England and have Ward fill out the source registration papers there. With this in mind, I headed off to the Koedoe Arcade in Pretoria to visit Tanner Promotions – 'Tanner' being a front for the Stratcom HQ. I planned to go over Bruwer's head and sidestep the red tape of the John Vorster Square idiot factor. General Johann Coetzee and the big guns were ecstatic at the prospect of my recruiting Ward.

Within the first week of being on board, Ward was disseminating disruptive material on the ANC and the SACP through his network in the United Kingdom and the United States. Meanwhile, he also made arrangements for me to approach some of his contacts directly. This resulted in me having lengthy conversations with, among others, the legendary – in fascist circles – General Sir Walter Walker, KCB (Most Honourable Order of the Bath), CBE (Most Excellent Order of the British Empire), DSO (Distinguished Service Order), former NATO commander-in-chief of the forces in northern Europe. Walker informed me that he was committed to making the world aware that the end of the Cold War was a myth.

As patron of the Western Goals Institute (by then separated from the Western Goals Foundation), Walker – who died in 2001 – was deeply concerned about an imminent communist takeover in South Africa. During our very first conversation, he questioned the veracity of the dirt I had dug up on Winnie Mandela, to check up on me, and I gave him my SB bona fides.

I was given regular accounts of Winnie and her family's activities by the Soweto SB. Most had little Stratcom value. A report that Winnie, Zindzi Mandela and Dali Mpofu had gone to some or other function would also have had little Stratcom value. I then added that the three were drunk, and that

Zindzi and Mpofu had sex somewhere along the line. I also added that Winnie was regularly drunk and out of control. The interesting thing in all of this was the Stompie matter. The most valuable cherry on the top would have been if Soweto SB could supply proof indicating Winnie's direct involvement in child activist Stompie Seipei's death. But they couldn't. Why? The evidence simply did not exist. If I had any evidence whatsoever, I would have released it to the world and Winnie would have been roasted and toasted.

Ward pledged that he would do whatever he could to raise awareness about the 'true intentions' of the ANC. Once he had primed them, I was also in contact with Sir David Rodgers and Merlin Charles Sainthill Hanbury-Tracy, 7th Baron Sudeley, president of the Monday Club, to whom I forwarded Stratcom material. Right-wing British peers, distressed by the unfolding scenario in South Africa, with the prospect of the ANC becoming the ruling party, were exactly the kind of well-padded supporters the National Party needed to proceed with its secret campaign after 1990.

Tory MPs Andrew Hunter, later leader of the Monday Club, and Jonathan Aitken, later imprisoned for perjury, briefed then British prime minister John Major on what they considered was the 'true situation' concerning the ANC, in order to influence his government against the liberation movement and Nelson Mandela. Our aim was to shatter the image of Mandela, who had become something of a sainted figure in the United Kingdom, and to persuade those in power that he was not the answer to South Africa's issues. Nonetheless, we had to be careful not to come across as hysterical in pushing this agenda. What was required was that the British government would pressure the ANC into adopting a more moderate political and economic stance. This would facilitate continued economic power and class advantage for the National Party's elite.

Our activities were conducted according to Operation Wigwam, the most significant Stratcom operation of that time aimed at discrediting and neutralising the ANC, but I still had problems with the capacity of those back at John Vorster Square to grasp this. When I, for instance, briefed Bruwer that the channels to John Major's people were now open, and that our material was to be forwarded to them on an ongoing basis, Bruwer's response was almost unbelievable: 'Nou wie is hierdie man en wat kan hy vir ons doen?'

'He's the fucking British prime minister, for fuck's sake!' I spluttered.

I was so enraged that I grabbed the heap of fax transmissions to and from Ward and tossed them into the air before storming out of Bruwer's office. The head of Stratcom in the biggest operations area in the country did not know who John Major was – and they were about to promote him to colonel!

I immediately called the national Stratcom coordinator, Johan Putter, and told him what was happening. I demanded to see Brigadier 'The Guru' Alfred Oosthuizen of the Intelligence Branch.

The next day I was in Pretoria where I explained everything to the Stratcom hierarchy, having established that Bruwer was even translating my reports and memoranda into Afrikaans and sending them to the Head Office, presumably under his own name.

'You must be patient,' advised Oosthuizen, informing me that there were 'other big things in the air' in which I could play a key role. They advised me that they and the government had taken note of our British operations and were very excited at the prospects. They then also made me an offer of a position at Head Office, but I refused. It was enough for me in that moment to leave Pretoria feeling as if a weight had been lifted from my shoulders. Clearly 'The Guru' seemed to have the situation under control, and I believed that I could now bypass Bruwer if need be.

As our efforts among the right-wing British peers and their ilk gained momentum, I made inroads in other areas too. For instance, a senior lecturer in International Relations at Wits and a lecturer to SB recruits put me in contact with Professor Leo Raditsa of the University of Minneapolis, described as a 'great friend' to our cause. Raditsa's historical essay, *Prisoners of a Dream: The South African Mirage*, was published as a short book, which damned the ANC and SWAPO. His findings were apparently based on the US Senate Sub-committee on Security and Terrorism hearings of March 1982 into 'the role of the Soviet Union, Cuba and East Germany in fomenting terrorism in southern Africa', to decide whether those liberation movements were a threat or not. The contention centred on Cold War issues and, as the USSR supported the ANC, many senators saw the ANC as a potential enemy. It was all about anti-communism. In conclusion, the US position was that the ANC practised terrorist activities and was, therefore, a terrorist organisation and an obstacle to negotiations. Thus, Raditsa was just the sort of person Stratcom needed to foster a kind of last-minute hysteria around looming communist rule in South Africa by bloodthirsty terrorists.

I had lunch with Raditsa when he visited South Africa in the late 1980s. We wanted him to write a second book (with a pro-Inkatha Freedom Party, anti-ANC theme) and to act for Stratcom in Washington, so I set out to gauge what the man was capable of, and to prime him. I took him to Soweto where he was given a first-hand account of how the 'communist ANC' was, as I told him, 'wreaking havoc, murdering and intimidating its political opponents at will'. This was followed up with a similar visit to strife-torn Natal, where Raditsa travelled to places selected by our Natal representative, Major Louis

Botha, the Stratcom liaison officer to IFP leader Mangosuthu Buthelezi.

After meeting with Buthelezi and senior Inkatha members, Raditsa left South Africa armed with a mass of Stratcom material. I then put him in contact with other friends in the United States, including the Reverend Colonel Robert Slimp, a member of the Council of Concerned Citizens (CofCC), which, as recently as February 2012, was featured in the Free South Africa Project, a right-wing American campaign to throw a spotlight on the murders of white South African farmers.

Slimp had visited South Africa on several occasions, once as a guest of Andries Treurnicht, Vorster's Deputy Minister of Education, who gave the instruction that black children should be taught some of their subjects only in Afrikaans – the final spark for the uprisings of June 1976. In time, Treurnicht gravitated even further to the right, and left the National Party to found the Conservative Party, and was Leader of the Opposition until the first democratic elections in 1994.

Another American with whom Stratcom was in touch was Dr Edwin Feulner, one of Washington's most powerful conservatives and, among other things, an adviser on domestic policy to President Ronald Reagan. Feulner was founder and president of the reactionary Heritage Foundation, more recently known to supply advisers to the Trump government.

Men like Raditsa, Slimp and Feulner weren't workshopping ideas. They were already well positioned to serve Stratcom the kind of high-level advice that we needed to temper growing international affection for the ANC as the first ruling party of a democratic South Africa. But time was tight.

Raditsa was to work on an operation in the United States similar to the one we were fostering in Britain, by lobbying congressmen, senators and academics. Our anti-ANC message was designed to reach into the White House itself as pro-IFP propaganda, with the IFP promoted as anti-communist free-marketeers. In fact, Buthelezi visited the States fairly regularly – delivering a speech as a guest at a working dinner of the Heritage Foundation in 1991. On an earlier visit he met Reagan, Bush and then Secretary of State George Shultz. That visit was helpful to Stratcom, in that conservative Americans would now have a firm idea of which black leader was an alternative to Mandela (and communism), and which black-led organisation could rival the ANC (and communism). Or so they thought.

Meanwhile, Stratcom was still going strong in Britain and in the USA. Journalist Graham Boynton wrote 'How Bad Is Winnie Mandela', a lengthy critical essay for *Vanity Fair*. In the late 1980s, Stratcom had worked hard on having the future 'Mother of the Nation' portrayed as no better than a common degenerate and nymphomaniac, and possibly even a murderer.

At the same time, our work was slowly gaining on the ANC as tales of its internal corruption began to emerge just as the De Klerk government was hoisted as virtuous and noble, having unbanned the liberation movement and freed Nelson Mandela. Not only had it done away with apartheid, but it was also making what were considered to be courageous advances in dealing with the apparent communist threat.

It suited the SB to perpetuate the notion that one of Nelson Mandela's first acts, if the ANC took over, would be to bring in the Russians. Even more emotive was the story being propagated that he would officially embrace the Cubans and the Libyans. American interests in the subcontinent would be practically destroyed. Ward was thus tasked to also target one of the most vociferous supporters of Nelson Mandela in the United States, shadow Democrat senator and civil rights campaigner Jesse Jackson. But this was no small task. Jackson was a nationally revered figure and, in my opinion, a liberal rather than a leftist, and he occupied an ambiguous position in conservative American society. Nevertheless, Ward's report-backs from Britain were encouraging and he gave us much to work with.

Senior figures in the John Major government were apparently startled to read a Stratcom gem: an 'ANC' booklet entitled *Negotiation and the Way Forward*. Having helped compile it, I faxed a single copy to Ward in Glasgow, before mailing hundreds for him to channel to all and sundry. With artwork reminiscent of Chairman Mao's China and Kim Il-sung's North Korea – workers with bandanas and pitchforks heading out eagerly to the fields under gracious, benevolent communist leadership – the booklet openly played the sympathetic Marxist card. Ward reported that there was shock and disappointment at the ANC in British establishment circles.

Ward also spread our message of stepping back from the ANC to captains of industry in the United Kingdom, exhorting them to apply further pressure on John Major's government. The line was that if nationalisation took place in South Africa – as the ANC promised it would in the Freedom Charter – the effect on investment and imports would be devastating. Britain was South Africa's biggest trading partner.

Meanwhile, regular anti-ANC letters appeared in the British press and critical editorials began to surface. To substantiate this effort – in keeping with the Stratcom projects Operation Gordian, aimed at offsetting the growing influence of the South African Democratic Teachers' Union (SADTU), and Operation Wigwam (any action of whatever nature to damage the liberation movements and or the right wing) – I supplied Ward with masses of material on Winnie Mandela and other prominent ANC members, which didn't stick to the perfect Stratcom formula of 70 per cent truth and 30 per cent fabrication. It was more like 100% vicious fabrication.

I would utilise intelligence reports of, say, contact between Winnie, her daughter Zindzi and the former Wits Black Students Society (BSS) activist, the lawyer Dali Mpofu. Then I would twist or change the facts and send these on to Ward and other Stratcom sources as examples of Winnie's marital infidelity – a notion already vigorously promoted by our unit in the late 1980s.

Stratcom was eager to pin the 1989 murder of Stompie Seipei on Winnie, too, but it didn't quite succeed at that. Our bid, nonetheless, caused distress and fury in the ANC's funding circles, as did Winnie's 1986 public endorsement of the use of the necklacing method to liberate the country – which we, of course, hyped up big-time. All of this was spiced with stories we made up of Winnie's supposed excessive drinking and dagga smoking, giving Ward plenty to direct at the moneyed upper-crust – and he did.

Ward even supplied material to Chapman Pincher, author of the 1991 British espionage book, *The Truth about Dirty Tricks: From Harold Wilson to Margaret Thatcher*. Pincher – notorious for his conservatism – was very interested. An investigative journalist on the *Daily Express*, Ward hoped that he'd make use of his extensive contacts on Fleet Street – where he was known as the Spycatcher – and in the British intelligence community to help filter it upwards to where it mattered most.

To bolster Ward's effort, I sent out copies of the ANC booklet and material on Winnie to churchmen, city councils, mayors and politicians as 'a concerned and despairing South African'. I used *noms de plume* like Paul J. Roberts to plead with them to grow opposition to the ANC and refuse it donations.

A favoured source of mine, Old Man George (OMG), took to faxing and phoning 10 Downing Street and a number of British MPs directly to complain about the ANC's links to communism. He had also built up a friendship with a journalist for a Japanese news agency, Kyodo News, and agreed to share original material on South Africa and the ANC with him. I duly supplied OMG with SABC videos showing people being necklaced. The footage was screened there with appropriate Stratcom messages, interspersed with Winnie's statement from 1986 about 'together ...with our boxes of matches and our necklaces we shall liberate this country', the plan being to plant a notion in Asia that the ANC was plotting to kill white people. We timed the release of that horrific footage with Mandela's visit to Japan. Unsurprisingly, Winnie wasn't well received there, and promised grants to the ANC failed to materialise.

We regarded responses such as this as a triumph, even though our efforts were continually hampered by an ongoing battle with Bruwer over the authorisation of funds. He even turned down my claims for buying Pincher's and Raditsa's books. What Bruwer failed to understand was that it wasn't only I who needed books and other international publications to gauge Stratcom's impact and identify possible targets – so did our sources.

But then Bruwer amazed even me by offering to cut a deal over expenses still owing. He said he could find an AK47, which could then be handed in to redeem the SAP's going reward of R6 000. I was irate but, because I needed money, I agreed to this.

Obviously we wouldn't be able to simply hand in an AK47 ourselves, so I approached my old friend and ex-colleague, Nannie Beyers, who had left the force in 1989 an embittered man, and persuaded him to come in on the deal, which, I assured him, was to cover outstanding operational expenses. Nannie 'found' the weapon, handed it in, and a year later we split the reward three ways. In the end, not much of a deal.

Chapter Nine

The Gloves Come Off

March 1979 to October 1980

IN JANUARY 1978, DR RICHARD (Rick) Turner, an academic at the University of Natal, was gunned down as he opened the front door of his home in Durban. It was a straight-up murder. It had the SB's fingerprints all over it, and it shocked everyone at John Vorster Square because Turner was white.

We might play what we called 'dirty tricks' on white activists and the white left. We might mess them up a bit. We might even shove multiple tablets down their throats while they were unconscious. But assassination! This was extreme – entirely in another dimension, and department.

This wasn't going to go well for us as a unit. Someone would have to go down, but knowing how things worked among us, there would have to be a fall guy and a scapegoat. We knew that the ones who gave the orders and supplied the weapon would never be named or known.

Fast-forward 18 years.

In 1996, the feared Durban SB member Andy Taylor – who would later become a colonel – was subpoenaed to appear before the TRC. It had long been suspected, both inside the force and out, that he knew who had killed Turner. Some thought that he had done it himself. Many were executioners themselves, but no one wanted to own up to the Turner hit. And no one has, even now – more than 40 years later.

The TRC didn't subpoena Taylor to talk about Turner, though, and he didn't apply for amnesty for that murder, but he was, indeed, connected to a range of horrible deeds, one of which was the 1981 assassination of human rights lawyer Griffiths Mxenge.

At John Vorster Square, we knew some of our colleagues in Natal could be even more murderous than we were. They were very violent, at least as violent as us, but with a more lethal bent. There were no angels among us – we were made of evil stuff. But a few members of the Durban SB were enmeshed in the actual politics of what they believed to be 'saving' the country from the ANC and 'the communists'. This was a clear response to the increasing violence in Natal, where the state-supported Inkatha Freedom Party was slugging it out with the ANC.

They were part of the Third Force into which Inkatha was integrated as a militia. They were well armed, well covered and bloodthirsty. Yet, when the TRC granted Taylor and his colleagues (Frank McCarter, Adrian Rosslee, Izak Bosch, Laurence Wasserman, Johannes Steyn, Hendrik Botha, Solomon du Preez, Casper van der Westhuizen, Roelf Visagie and Jacobus Vorster) amnesty in 2001, we felt that they got a free pass. And yet, they had only applied for amnesty for the abduction, assault and murder of six ANC activists from Swaziland in the late 1980s, whose bodies they had disposed of by blowing them up. Attached to their amnesty applications for those six slayings were bids to be forgiven for housebreaking, theft and the illegal possession of firearms and explosives. Small change. To their extreme good fortune, however, the applicants were told by the TRC that it found that their acts were 'associated with a political objective and that they had all made full disclosure of all the relevant facts'.

Taylor and Coetzee were named on the same charge sheet for the murder of Griffiths Mxenge as former Vlakplaas informer and askari Butana Almond Nofomela – who was already serving a prison term for another murder – and fellow askari David Tshikalanga. The other former cop arrested for the Mxenge slaying was Taylor's Durban colleague Johannes van der Hoven, who ran the SB in that city.

Taylor and Van der Hoven had by this time left the service. In fact, most apartheid-era SB members had scattered by 2001. The SB we had known was long since gone, but its history and a number of its recruits from that time were very much alive – and active.

I wasn't. I no longer wanted to be a part of any intelligence or spying unit. But my curiosity was such that I couldn't stay away completely either. If people called me with stories about someone with whom we had worked, or I caught sight of an article, or some information reached me, I was interested. I wanted to hear more, and to talk about it.

Then I came across an article by Rick Turner's daughter Jann – who was a child when she held her dying father in her arms in the passage of their house in Durban. It had been published in the *Mail & Guardian*,[10] and I read it voraciously.

Jann Turner wrote her piece when it became clear that no one would apply for amnesty for her father's murder. She asked her readers: 'What do you think went through his mind in those 20 long minutes after the bullet ripped through him? Those 20 minutes before he died? How much fear? How much regret? How much love? How much forgetting? How much forgiveness?'

I took a really deep breath when I read that.

If I could have, I would have assured Jann Turner that not too many of us in the SB at the time cared too much about forgiveness. We had none of the regret or love she said her father must have felt.

To try to get to the truth, she'd approached a gallery of rogues: Dirk Coetzee (whom she described as a 'chaotic, half-crazed human being, not a cold, calculating monster'); BOSS agent Martin Dolinschek ('In 1993, I found him in Zambia – in ANC "custody"'); in 1978, former investigating officer at Durban Murder and Robbery, Chris Earle (whose 'hands shook' when he told her he remained convinced that 'the murder was not a political one'); and Vic McPherson ('I've met him twice and each time the smell of alcohol hit me from several metres away'), who had kept the Turner house under surveillance and used their neighbour as an agent (later he became the national coordinator of Stratcom). She'd also spoken to Taylor, who refused to meet her but finally admitted to her on the phone that 'it might have been one of our guys, but we kept our noses out of each other's business'.

An SB member, whom Turner doesn't name, met her in his rental car in 1997 with documents he claimed were lifted from NIA files by another colleague 'as insurance'. These were top-secret papers and included a transcript of her dad being interviewed by Dolinschek after Rick Turner had applied for a fellowship in Germany, having become severely depressed under five years of banning orders. As was always the case, the SB was required to vet applications, and Dolinschek was given that task in Turner's matter in 1977.

It haunted me to read Jann Turner's words published more than two decades ago:

> The TRC offered the first and last hope that my father's assassination would be officially investigated. It was a real chance to break through the wall of silence surrounding BOSS and the Security Police.

This week sources within the Commission told me that their investigations have uncovered a high-level cover-up. But that is all. It seems the TRC have been thorough in checking out the police, but have they requested BOSS and Security Police files? Have they subpoenaed everyone I listed in my submission with something to tell us about my father's murder? If not, why not? (*Mail & Guardian*, 29 August 1997)

I don't know who killed Rick Turner, but the silence around the identity of that person may yet be broken. The turning point may be the trial of ex-SB member João Rodrigues, who tried to lie his way out of his involvement during the inquest into the death in detention of Ahmed Timol in 1971. I didn't hesitate when I was asked by the Timol family's lawyers, Webber Wentzel, to join them in gathering information for a new inquest in 2018 and 2019. What transpired at the end of the inquest was that murder accused Rodrigues was finally declared fit to stand trial on charges of premeditated murder and defeating the ends of justice. Rodrigues tried to get a permanent stay of prosecution, claiming that his age (80) and memory loss would preclude justice. In June 2019, Judge Seun Moshidi of the South Gauteng High Court denied him his way out.

I believe that the TRC didn't do its job as well as it could have done – and should have done – and that the process has left too many people without answers or justice. Of course, I'm really glad that I testified. I was such a wreck at the time that my ex-colleagues probably thought the likelihood of me giving coherent evidence was nil. I was found to have been 100 per cent honest in my submissions, with Judge Sisi Khampepe stating that 'Erasmus has taken the meaning of the word truth to a new level'. I'm able to leave this legacy to my children.

We knew that some of our SB colleagues, who had made a big show of going to the families of people they'd killed and begging to be absolved, were more terrified of death than they were about seeking forgiveness. The sometimes spoken, sometimes not, directive not to speak was all too real. For most of them in the end, it was all about self-preservation. Sure, many of us only admitted to what we believed we could get away with, but Andy Taylor and others had far, far more hibernating in their dark souls.

The Mxenge case, like the Turner one, was a source of appalling bitterness within the force. The whistleblowers – Coetzee, Nofomela and Tshikalanga – were found guilty, while Taylor and his boss, Van der Hoven, were acquitted. It seemed that some in the SB were untouchable. And I wasn't one of them.

The instruction that came down was that no one was to work on their own

or without the full knowledge of their bosses, and preferably the Head Office
– at least this was the official line.

This was plain stupid because the state was merciless and ruthless. If we
found you, chances are we would treat you like any other victim. In reality,
it was often tricky to spot the red herring from the real threat. We had to try
to stay one step ahead, but not everyone in the SB had this kind of initiative.
Some simply followed orders from Head Office. Many were merely incapable
of thinking outside the box.

There was also competition from other quarters, including private
gangsters, right-wingers, and those who saw an opportunity to seize the
moment and make money protecting our targets from us.

Of course, there were also organisations outside the SAP that we could use
to reinforce our reign of terror. One of the most effective was Scorpio, a right-
wing group in Cape Town that was carrying out successful attacks on the left,
using everything from petrol bombs to death threats against anti-government
factions.

We liked their name, so we set up a fake organisation by the name of
Omega as a front for our actions. I took the name from the biblical verse 'I am
the Alpha and the Omega, the beginning and the end, the first and the last'
(Revelation 22: 13). It was particularly useful when we called newspapers and
blamed our attacks on Omega. Initially used only by SB agents targeting white
activists, Omega was later also adopted by those targeting black activists on
the East Rand and Soweto, and even further afield.

But then, as we intensified our campaigns, the left started to hit back. One
of its responses to our fresh wave of violence and intimidation was to carry
out armed patrols of one another's homes – a development that we actually
welcomed. We looked forward to confrontations with our enemies, who we
believed didn't have the guts – and certainly not the weaponry – to mount any
significant counter-vigilante-type actions.

Another reaction – refusing to publicise our attacks in the media – was
considerably more powerful. The left believed, and rightly so, that perpetrators
like us were adrenalised, spurred on when what we had done made the
headlines. So, if the media didn't know that something had happened, the
left simply didn't tell them. And activists now refused to cooperate when the
media wanted comment, an interview or pictures, after an attack.

In those days, being unable to confirm an incident by means of a source
made a story tough, if not impossible, to publish. Journalists always needed to
corroborate their stories, so we were under pressure to refine our techniques
and find alternative ways to conduct our crusade, our own war. We had to

be creative. And because much of the disillusionment within the SB and the SAP in general was linked to pathetic salaries and appalling treatment by our bosses, we had to try to make the work we were undertaking enjoyable for ourselves. SB members were, after all, expected to be the embodiment of an ongoing nightmare that used fear to overwhelm the enemy. We were the gatekeepers of state institutionalised terror.

Real corruption began escalating in our ranks by the beginning of the 1980s, when violence by the security forces intensified. When the apartheid government decided to square up to international push-back by weaponising its policies, this gave some in the SB further opportunity to abuse their positions.

My partner, Sergeant C.C. 'Kallie' Prinsloo, once received watertight information about gun-shop owner Frikkie Botha selling automatic weapons and ammunition under the counter to anyone with the necessary bona fides, who could pay cash. Busting Botha was an opportunity for us to earn some old-style cop kudos, but of course we couldn't simply waltz in and slap the money down on the counter. After all, Botha could be an agent for another organisation. We had to have a strong story to back us up.

Kallie's source introduced us to a sub-source directly linked to Botha, the sub-source having been told that Kallie and I needed weapons to improve the lax security at a mine we were buying into on the Lowveld. We arranged to meet the individual over drinks, and in keeping with our businessmen cover, the venue was the five-star Carlton Hotel in the Johannesburg CBD.

As usual, there was no money available in the SB expense account. I was earning about R300 a month, and Kallie had a wife and two children to support so he wasn't much better off. It was a mess. The sub-source bought our story, but it took copious amounts of expensive whisky to persuade him, and when we submitted the claim, we were told that we'd been wasting state money. Kallie and I lost something like R100 on our very tight personal budgets when the bill was deducted from our salaries instead.

Nonetheless, we readied to do the deal, Botha having offered us an AK47 and an R1 rifle with spare magazines and abundant ammunition for R700. He indicated through the sub-source that if we were interested, he had plenty more stock in this category. And this was exactly what we wanted so as to pull off our manoeuvre to garner praise. The weapons were clearly of communist origin – the USSR providing the ANC with AK47s and other rifles – and anyone in possession of these was in violation of security legislation. We assumed that we had this in the bag.

It didn't come without hitches, however. On the day we were due to spring the trap, the SB allegedly didn't have the R700 trap money in its Secret Fund. Several frantic phone calls later, the money was secured from one of the detective branches at John Vorster Square, counted and a record made of the serial numbers on the notes.

Kallie and I met Botha in a secluded area near the dam adjacent to the SAPS rugby club. Botha opened the boot of his car to reveal the weapons. We concluded the deal, which we taped on a Nagra recording machine concealed under my shirt, with Kallie handing over the cash. This process covered all possible legal requirements for a conviction.

Once the money was in Botha's grip, Kallie shouted: 'We are members of the South African Police and you are under arrest, Mr Botha.'

Botha's hand instantly shot behind his back, where he was carrying a concealed pistol, but Kallie and I quickly disarmed him.

We returned to John Vorster Square, flushed with success and with Botha in handcuffs, but rode right into a storm between the Investigation Branch and the SB staff. Cronwright refused to have anything to do with the case, stating that it wasn't SB work and, therefore, it had to be handed over to Strafsake, which handled serious criminal cases for the Criminal Investigation Department (CID). We maintained, as did all our colleagues at the SB, that the offence fell within the parameters of legislation as it concerned 'supplying military weapons of communist origin'.

Nonetheless, Cronwright got his way. Kallie and I had to take Botha down to Strafsake, its suave commanding officer, Colonel Karel 'Blondie' de Beer, having been informed that we were on our way. But the moment we walked into his office, I immediately caught a flash of familiarity between him and Botha. We were instructed to leave the suspect there.

Heading towards our floor, Kallie confided that he'd picked up something odd in the exchange, which came as a relief for me – I thought I was becoming ultra-paranoid. But as we had to get cracking with the tedious business of transcribing many hours of recordings necessary for a trial, we didn't talk much about it.

I had nearly finished the transcription a couple of days later – that's how long it took to write out by hand – when Kallie walked into our office, his face pale with anger. He sat down and, holding his head in his hands, told me that Botha had appeared in court the previous day, charged with possession of unlicensed firearms. He had pleaded guilty and was given a light fine.

The matter of being in possession of stolen property (the R1 rifle) and an AK47, which clearly fell under security legislation, hadn't been mentioned. It was immediately clear that this was a set-up, involving either Blondie alone, or together with Cronwright, who we thought might have engineered it. We knew that many of the SB and Investigation Branch officers conspired in the background for personal gain.

As it turned out, however, Cronwright had had nothing to do with this one. Some months later, Kallie and I were subpoenaed to give evidence in a case against the original owner of the R1 rifle, to whom it had been issued by the SADF. The man had subsequently swapped the rifle for a bottle of brandy and a few rand. He was jailed for six months.

The matter with Botha didn't end there, though, because Botha called Kallie and invited us to lunch. Our curiosity piqued, Kallie and I accepted the offer and met him wearing a concealed wiretap. Many drinks into the afternoon, Botha started spilling the beans. He wanted to make amends, he said, because 'some of my best pals are in the force'. He had no hard feelings. He admitted that he and Blondie were old friends and that if the SB hadn't been involved, Blondie would have quashed it entirely.

But as the liquor flowed, Botha became more arrogant and self-confident, and revealed that his house hadn't even been searched. The weapons were never produced as evidence – we knew that the AK47 had remained in pristine condition in the 'care' of the SB hierarchy, licensed eventually to Colonel Jack Olivier – and arrangements had hastily been made with the prosecutor.

After we'd transcribed that wiretap, we discussed whom we might take it to. At this point, Kallie – who was senior in rank to me – wanted to drop the whole thing. He knew it would create problems for us. I was raging. This was corruption! How could they be allowed to get away with this? As a result, Kallie and I had a serious falling out, and I wondered whether we would ever be able to work together again; then he invited me over for a braai. He told me that he had taken the transcription to a number of big shots, but that nobody wanted friction between the SB and the other specialised units like Strafsake. He reminded me, too, that Blondie was very popular at the Head Office.

A few months later, there was an article in the *Rand Daily Mail* about the disappearance of a crate of 9 mm pistols from a Johannesburg gun dealer. I made a few discreet enquiries and established that Botha was a suspect and that Strafsake was investigating. This case, too, quietly disappeared.

It wasn't only gun-running, though. Corruption in the force was mounting, especially when it came to settling personal scores or, among our seniors, needing to show a higher tally of successes. It was subdued at first, but became more brazen when they chose to use us, the rank and file, to do their dirty deeds for them – without the necessary paperwork.

In 1983, I received a rare instruction to go and see Cronwright on the tenth floor – and to go alone. Little Hitler was crouched behind his enormous desk. He told me that he had heard I'd been 'doing some good work lately'. I stared at him, trying to figure out what was coming next. My suspicions proved right.

'In what way, sir?'

'Fucking up the lefties. I'm glad to hear that you're starting to wake up. That's why I called you here. There are two names I want to add to your list. The first is that fucking Tom Lodge. He's giving us a hard time. I want to hear what you plan to do to him.'

Lodge, a Wits University academic who'd authored *Black Politics in South Africa since 1945*,[11] was a significant enemy of the apartheid establishment, and I'd wondered when he was going to be handed over to us.

'The second is that k-----r minister at Rosebank Union Church,' Cronwright spluttered between mouthfuls of his huge jam sandwich.

If I wasn't surprised by the mention of Lodge, I was by this name, because I'd already submitted reports to Head Office about the Reverend Nathaniel 'Nat' Nkosi. A source had outed him to me for his anti-state work sometime before.

'What do you people on white staff do the whole day?' Cronwright spluttered, crumbs and flecks of jam flying. 'There's shit going on under your noses and all you do is submit endless fucking reports. You need to get out there and do something. Go out and fuck these people up. Do you understand? I want progress reports. I want to know what you're doing!'

Having decided to ignore the orders from Little Hitler, I confided in Kallie – I was a little worried about the consequences of not doing what Cronwright had instructed. Kallie was on my side.

'It's one thing to put pressure on, but I'm not going to kill or injure people just to make the tenth floor's numbers look good,' he said. 'Those guys are insane.'

That camaraderie between us didn't matter, though. Kallie was gradually succumbing to depression, and he confessed to me, while under the influence of booze, that he wasn't coping with the stress of the job. He told me that he had joined the police to uphold the law and was completely against the Third Force that seemed to be taking root in the police. Kallie, who had an increasingly evident problem with alcohol, was eventually transferred to the police canteen – the pub at Hillbrow Police Station – as punishment. This is where he committed suicide with his service pistol. Right there in front of everyone.

A week after Kallie's death, I was back to being fed into the cannon.

I was contacted by a woman whose husband had been in jail when I was dating their daughter on and off. I'd never asked them why he was behind bars, but now Dawn, the mother of my ex, called me out of the blue. She needed help.

Her husband, Patrick (Paddy) Fahey, had been released from prison after serving some 15 years. She revealed that he had been convicted on charges of placing dynamite in the speaker boxes at a Johannesburg drive-in and attempting to extort money from the management by threatening to set off the explosives.

Fahey was, by all accounts, very dangerous – with or without dynamite. Arrested by the infamous Andries Struwig, Fahey had escaped from the cells at John Vorster Square after using a smuggled steel file as a cutting tool hidden in a birthday cake. He was eventually hunted down again by Struwig and had now been paroled.

Dawn said that she was terrified because, on his release, Fahey had immediately started experimenting with gas lighters and had told her that he was going to make a bomb to kill Struwig. I called Struwig the next day.

After a few hours, he called me back to chat a little more, beginning with the words: 'Paul, do me a favour ...'

I knew that something was coming. Something serious.

'You know where Fahey lives now, right?'

'Yes, sir. In a flat in Alberton.' I knew the area well.

'Go there tonight and wait for him,' Struwig instructed, 'and when you see the bastard, blow him away.'

'You mean *kill* him, sir?' I'd kind of anticipated something like this, but I was still shocked.

Struwig was adamant. He said he would 'take care of everything' from the side of the SB and the SAPS. 'Just get rid of this piece of shit. Do society a favour. But you do it on your own, okay?'

'But, sir, I only have my service pistol,' I protested. It was obvious that I would quickly be identified as the shooter and that would be the end of me.

He insisted he would 'organise everything' with the East Rand Murder and Robbery squad and instructed me to call him as soon as I'd done the job so that he could 'sort things out'.

I felt sick. I knew I wasn't going to be gunning a man down in cold blood just on the instruction of Struwig – certainly not when it had nothing to do with national security or saving a life. This was all about Struwig's cowboy attitude and I wasn't prepared to follow through. But what the hell was I going to do?

Struwig and Cronwright were close, and I was under no illusion as to what they were capable of doing. After all, Andries 'Oom Dries', a massively built man, had smashed a young man named Mondy Johannes Motloung – who had been arrested with Solomon Mahlangu – through the glass partitioning on the tenth floor at John Vorster Square on the day of the Goch Street shootout on 13 June 1977.[12] That punch damaged the MK cadre's brain so severely that the state declared him unfit to stand trial.

Mahlangu, who was tried from 7 November 1977 to 1 March 1978 on two counts of murder and other charges under the Terrorism Act, was hanged on 6 April 1979. My colleagues in the SB were intimately involved in every moment of Mahlangu's last 22 months.

That SB policemen were torturing and murdering people in my ambit, at my workplace, did not elude me. That peers were seemingly in concert with arms smugglers did not confound me. But this was also my world, my bread and butter. I was cooked.

That night I changed the number plates of my car, drove to Fahey's flat, parked a block away and waited, my idea being that I could at least tell Struwig that I had made the effort. That, yes, I'd been there.

After an hour or two, I climbed out of my car and walked slowly down the road past the flat. On the opposite side of the road was another parked car. There were two men sitting inside, smoking. I read their front number plate and then crossed the intersection to the next corner, before turning around and heading back to my car.

When I crossed the road, I read the rear number plate and wasn't at all surprised that it was different from that of the front – swapping plates was a very common ploy used in the force. This was, in fact, often a hallmark of specialised police units such as the SB and Murder and Robbery.

Was this a set-up or were they simply there to ensure nothing went wrong? Or was it just coincidence? I wasn't taking any chances. I made my way back to my car and drove past them with my headlights on bright to get a better look. Animals always smell each other out, and these were definitely cops. The driver turned away as I went by, his hand – with a burning cigarette between his fingers – obscuring most of his face.

An hour or so later, I returned. The lights in Fahey's flat were off. I circled the block, and the same car with its occupants was parked around the corner. I was tempted to stop and confront them, but instead drove slowly past again and then headed home.

I didn't sleep well that night, resolving to be very careful of Cronwright, Struwig and the other heavies at John Vorster Square. I didn't hear from

Struwig for a couple of weeks and gradually started to relax – until his call came. I was ready.

'What happened with Fahey?' he bellowed. 'Why haven't you let me know?'

'Sir, somebody had the flat under observation.'

Long silence.

'Who?'

'I don't know, sir … possibly Murder and Robbery. Whoever they are, they're not very bright.'

'Why?'

'Well, they sat outside the flat advertising their presence. Any fool could see they were cops because they had different plates on the back and front of their car.'

'Oh.'

Another long silence.

'Okay, Paul,' he grunted. 'But let me know if Fahey moves.'

I got the message. He wasn't going to push me any further.

But that wasn't to be the case with one of Cronwright's henchmen, Lieutenant Robbie Bouwer. He once accused me of pocketing source money – a staggering amount of between R100 and R200 per month. Not only did he insist that I was a thief, but he also spat at me and accused me of being a 'shit investigator'. Bouwer, like his idol Cronwright, was an avowed racist and, I suspected, hated English speakers as much as he hated black people.

Enough was enough. I started scouring the 'situations vacant' columns in the newspapers. My only other alternative was to volunteer to serve with the SAP in South West Africa. And that was how I arrived in Ovamboland in 1981.

I've seen how Dylan reacts when something triggers my memory of that place. It can be anything – a song, some disturbing news about someone who was with me on the border who had gone *bossies*, the sight of an SANDF tank, a police Casspir – and I'm immediately apprehensive. As a father, you have to watch yourself in moments like this. Is there a time limit on how long you allow it?

There is no denying, though, that my time in Ovamboland, where I witnessed and participated in atrocities, provided me with insights I would otherwise not have had when we embarked on Stratcom. Much of our SB propaganda work was adopted by the SADF, starting with how we handled conscientious objectors.

A good example of how the SAP and the SADF spread the Stratcom word as a unified force was the case of Russel Crystal and his Students Moderate

Alliance (SMA) – a body set up at Wits University that worked with an American right-wing organisation, the International Freedom Front (IFF).

Crystal led the National Student Federation (NSF), a front organisation in South Africa created and funded by the apartheid regime in the early 1980s. The International Freedom Front's leadership had initially bonded with the NSF through the College Republican National Committee, which started out as a campus-based structure active at Harvard and other universities in the Massachusetts area.

While it was originally set up to assist student supporters of the Republican Party (under the auspices of its National Committee), it became a tool of right-wing activist Jack Abramoff and others, who expanded it into Washington in the 1980s to push their political agenda. The mainstream Republicans weren't keen on this association, however, and so Abramoff got involved with another organisation called Citizens for America. More important for South Africans and the cause of Stratcom, though, were his links with Jonas Savimbi, whose UNITA movement had representatives in the United States at the time – even though Angola had a legitimate government (the MPLA) and a freely elected president in Eduardo dos Santos.

Savimbi, who was finally killed by Angolan government troops in 2002, is believed to be mostly responsible for how long Angola's civil war lasted – 27 years of bloodshed with the loss of a million lives – and South African security forces, working in cahoots with him and supported by the Americans, contributed significantly to this.

Savimbi was Africa's most virulent anti-communist guerrilla leader, so all those Americans associated with Savimbi, supplying arms and support to UNITA, were thus apartheid's allies too.

An individual like Russel Crystal may, on the face of it, have seemed like not too much of a threat, but his SMA at Wits, and even the NSF, were extremely helpful to Stratcom and the apartheid government. This was because of the links Crystal and his cohort here had with Americans who, in turn, bolstered Savimbi in what came down to a brutal war against communist forces in southern Africa.

Abramoff – who was heir to a fortune and had very wealthy friends serving the right wing in the United States – was as vehemently anti-communist as the apartheid government and us, its puppet foot soldiers. He went on to produce two mainstream anti-communist movies, *Red Scorpion* (1988) and *Red Scorpion 2* (1994), both starring Dolph Lundgren and filmed in South West Africa. On a far more serious note, however, Abramoff gathered right-wing militias from Asia and South America in a bush camp in Angola to share ideas.

Although Abramoff was said to have parted ways somewhat acrimoniously with some of his partners in the United States over time, we were more interested in the well-paid work he did for the apartheid government, so much so that his name even came up at the TRC.

Yet, this was a complicated business and Stratcom was created to bring together the different strands of our operations: sanctions-busting to secretly refinance the existing government, which believed it could, with sufficient resources, mount a successful election campaign and even win; and smearing the ANC by means of a calculated dirty-tricks campaign, while image-washing the National Party to make it seem as though it really believed in negotiations, thus reassuring its 'moderate' and right-wing supporters in the United States, Britain and Europe.

What was at the heart of all this? Money? Power?

The only way to achieve our goals, we were told, was to operate under a Stratcom 'umbrella' that would embrace all the fronts operating out there to create a 'new' political party (which would, of course, be the National Party in disguise). Everyone who handled sources and agents or – as in my case – was a control officer in a national operation was directed to actively promote this effort, using all available avenues.

We decided to draw up a draft constitution for what such a 'new' political party would look like in order for the SB members involved to properly understand this shift in tactics. We could no longer use racial language or descriptions; our propaganda and tactics had to be scrubbed clean, at least in public. The apartheid laws would soon be gone, done and dusted, so Stratcom decided that the ideological underpinning of this new organisation would be liberal, putting forward values of freedom of speech, free association, free enterprise and, most importantly, one person, one vote.

This was a big moment for me, a warrant officer in the SAP with limited knowledge of political science or any kind of academic background, helping to conceptualise a constitution for a political party. This was where our own academics' experience came into good use, helping us turn our ideas into a working document.

Bruwer and I were part of the logistics planning. Funding for the exercise would have to come from the Head Office in Pretoria, where we would be based as the plot intensified.

General André Pruis, supposedly an expert on constitutional affairs and the ANC, suggested the addition of a clause 'promoting Christian ideals'. I strongly resisted on the grounds that such a clause would be alienating to many and immediately carried the taint of state involvement. Put like that, 'Christian ideals' simply reeked of the apartheid National Party. 'Why alienate everyone in the country who isn't Christian?' I asked. Naturally, the clause was added. Nobody – especially a nobody like me – told Pruis and the SB Head Office what to do.

Finally, the go-ahead came from Cabinet and Bruwer immediately rented premises and office equipment at Portland Place in Braamfontein, Johannesburg. The building was the home of several anti-apartheid organisations, including the Release Mandela campaign and my old friends, the Alliance of Black Reformed Christians in Southern Africa (ABRECSA).

Because these organisations were based in the building, I already had a full set of keys to the premises, so Bruwer and I were able to check it out. Later, in a haze of cigarette smoke and booze at the police pub, we decided that De Kock and the Vlakplaas crowd would have to be brought in to assist with stealing the computers, fax machines, telephones, typewriters, and whatever else we could lay our hands on, from these organisations. But this ended up being just another lunatic plot that finished with a massive hangover.

Harvey Ward was to be brought out to South Africa to act as the principal agent on the project, the belief being that with his extensive anti-communist contacts, start-up funds would pour in and the new party could become self-financing. This self-financing was a primary aim of all SB fronts because this was a really dangerous phase of these operations – there should be no chance that someone would be able to prove that the state was picking up the bill for the new party. In the political climate at the time, such a revelation would have been catastrophic for the National Party.

I was given directives that the University Freedom of Speech Association was to align with anti-apartheid organisations that were considered to be reasonably moderate, such as the South African Institute of Race Relations (SAIRR).

Ward was initially reluctant to accept the offer. This was understandable because, as he said, he would have to give up everything in Britain, so I was authorised to offer him a salary of R6 000 per month, a vehicle, a housing subsidy and an expense account. He jumped at the offer, but wanted to discuss the details, including who would pay for his move.

His partner at Ossian Books, James Gibb Stuart, would meanwhile take over Ward's position as our principal agent in Britain and would receive directives from Ward in South Africa. I, of course, wanted to fly to London and then on to Glasgow to meet Gibb Stuart, to whom I had only spoken on the phone, but the Head Office thought Stratcom national coordinator Johan Putter was a better option for that assignment. I was left to sort out printing facilities for the party – a problem, as the project was so sensitive that the SAP printing unit could not be used. Bruwer and I thus went to see a Military Intelligence-funded business federation, with a view to using their machines. We also wanted to secure this federation's support for another Stratcom initiative called Businessmen for Growth and Stability (BGS). A staggering amount of R140 000 was set aside by Head Office for this purpose.

BGS was a big project, one that was already up and running countrywide, aiming to get business to persuade or force the ANC to review its stance on nationalisation. It boasted a membership of 100 000, and it was envisaged that it could ultimately operate in tandem with the new party we were setting up.

Because of his British background, Ward could not be the party leader, but would act as principal agent – he would coordinate and steer the whole project. Credibility was critical, and much thought was put into solving the vexing problem of who would head the party. Suggestions included Judge M.T. Steyn for reasons of impartiality, and even a disenchanted member of the Democratic Party, who was not favourably disposed towards the ANC. Other suggestions were traditional liberals such as Ken Owen, editor of the *Sunday Times*, or even John Kane-Berman of the SAIRR.

While all this was going on, the ANC was holding its key 48th national conference in Durban, and it was attracting plenty of attention. This took place in 1991, about 18 months after the organisation was unbanned, and the first time it had held its conference in South Africa since 1959.

This was the conference at which Nelson Mandela was elected president of the ANC, succeeding the ailing Oliver Tambo, who became national chair. There were other big names in attendance too. Walter Sisulu was chosen as ANC deputy president and Cyril Ramaphosa as the secretary-general, with Jacob Zuma as his deputy.

Back then we didn't grasp the historic importance of that moment because we operated strictly under directives from the Head Office. Our instructions were clear: Stratcom was to spare no effort in hammering the ANC. Arrangements had been made, for instance, to intercept all telephonic communications to and from the conference. Since there were about 3 000 delegates and hundreds of international guests, we had one hell of a job on our hands. This, of course, made a joke of De Klerk's 'levelling of the playing fields' or his earlier announcement on 30 July 1991 that 'every secret project is being looked at again … the government has nothing to hide …we do not have a hidden agenda'.

In the background, a major incident was under way.

Using the signature of former ANC political prisoner Raymond Suttner, I'd forged an invitation from the ANC to Sinn Féin leader Gerry Adams to attend the ANC conference. It was hoped that a copy would be given to John Major and other politicians and further raise their indignation against Mandela and his party. When I set about making the necessary calls to England and Ireland, Bruwer nearly had a seizure about the cost, but eventually the invitation was sent off, with copies to Ward, who later confirmed that senior Tories were distressed to hear that the ANC was climbing into bed with the political wing of the Irish Republican Party.

Copies were duly forwarded to the Americans too.

We vigorously promoted the notion that the ANC was practising anti-capitalist terrorism, and our next plan was to invite Libya's Colonel Muammar Gaddafi and the Palestine Liberation Organisation's Yasser Arafat to the ANC's conference – on their behalf, of course. The intention was to rile the Americans as much as possible, especially influential Jewish people who were keen to support the ANC. However, as the hours ticked into the party's conference, with fascinated international media attention focused there, we began to worry that we might be over-playing our hand. We were walking a tightrope, and our form of Stratcom was hardly nuanced. We were still learning those more sophisticated ropes on the job.

We supplied the conference fax number to all our sources, and manufactured tons of material, ranging from complaints about the ANC's economic policies to exhortations – supposedly from within the Congress movement itself – to get rid of 'radicals' such as Winnie Mandela and Peter Mokaba. We also planted what appeared to be inside information about Mokaba being an SB informer, and that the white communists were undermining black moderates like Thabo Mbeki.

This was not a complete waste of time. It certainly intensified existing power struggles within the ANC at the conference. Fortunately for me, my efforts did not go unnoticed by the government, which conveyed its appreciation for the work to the SB Head Office.

I later received two commendations for 'exceptional work' and 'ad hoc action initiated to achieve the aims of Operation Romulus', which was set up to focus exclusively on damaging the ANC. This was in addition to my 'great initiative and enthusiasm to launch actions that created great interest in Britain, and that have had positive results for the [South African] Government'.

The commendations were signed by General P.J. Viljoen and Brigadier M.D. Ras, who had regularly turned down or halved my personal expenses claims. Perhaps that was why they felt obliged to add that Head Office was 'aware' of my 'massive contribution ... dedication, enthusiasm ... and initiative [which] does not only reflect on himself the honour of the SA Police and this office, but serves as a motivation for younger and other members of the SA Police'.

Bruwer, however, was enraged that commendations were not forthcoming for him, insisting that he and the whole section should have been mentioned. He went to the Head Office to complain.

I can't help but link that time – the ANC's national conference and the power the party started to cultivate in its aftermath – with two other major life shifts. One was what was rapidly unfolding at the SB (a sense of doom as our agents' myriad fears and bitterness exploded into view); the other a call from the psychologist at Dylan's school.

Linda and I were informed that our son was developing major behavioural aberrations, which were ascribed to the imbalance he was experiencing in our home life – *when* I was home, that is, since I worked non-stop and was spending virtually no time with Candice or Dylan.

The commendations from Head Office thus came at the same time as I had to face up to the consequences of being an absentee father. The commendations came years too late. When the school told us it was now or never, that Dylan was going to plummet further – and irretrievably – if something was not done immediately to change the way we interacted as a family, I had to force myself to accept I'd had enough. The workload and frustration were excavating what was left of my soul.

Exhausted, depressed and all but on the verge of collapse, I disconnected the odometer of my official car, and Linda and I escaped for a few days away to the southern Cape. We drove from beach to beach until we found Herolds Bay, a haven near George. Within two weeks, Linda had started negotiating for what was to be our dream home – a double-storey with a sweeping view over the ocean. Southern right whales come to calve in the little bay between the two headlands. Dolphins could be spotted playing in the surf, and on a clear day you can see Mossel Bay on the other side of the water. What I didn't see, as is usual with me, was the storm heading right for us.

I decided – to hell with Stratcom, the stinking National Party and the accumulated filth of 17 years in the SB. I'd work for the good old SAP, plodding the beat if necessary, with the sound of the sea in my head rather than my pounding and tired brain trying to conjure up yet another sleazy little Stratcom escapade. I wanted – *needed* – a life and, more importantly, I needed the admiration of my family rather than the slick handshakes of a slimy police general.

It was July 1991, and while I was waiting for my transfer from the SB to the SAP to be processed, the Inkatha scandal exploded. It was publicly revealed that the National Party government had been funding the IFP, and that its trade union, the United Workers Union of South Africa (UWUSA), was a body set up by Stratcom to counter the Congress of South African Trade Unions (COSATU). De Klerk, an accomplished liar, had been caught out. After all, had he not told the world just a year earlier that 'all secret projects' had been terminated?

On the morning that the news broke about the IFP, I was at what we called the casino, the main Stratcom safe house in Midrand, at a seminar organised by the Head Office. The casino was packed with Stratcom reps from all over the country. As the reports came in about the extent to which the National Party had been compromised, the shock on senior Stratcom members' faces was apparent. Colonel Louis Botha, the SB liaison officer to Mangosuthu Buthelezi and the IFP, was particularly upset. We'd been trained to believe that we'd never get caught or, if we did, it was unlikely that there would be any serious repercussions – at least not out there in the real world. But Botha's game was up and he was, indeed, soon arrested for alleged involvement in Third Force activities, on charges relating to the investigation of the murder of 11 people in Natal.

Revelations affecting our bosses changed everything quite radically for some of us too.

Ward had packed up his life in Britain, and his arrival in South Africa to manage the establishment of the new political party was imminent. We were good to go, despite 'Uwusagate' – and then we were summoned to the Head Office. Foreign Affairs Minister Pik Botha had decreed via the State Security Council (SSC) that all overseas SB operations were to be terminated with immediate effect. He said that the government could not afford to be compromised any further. But by then it was too late to call a halt to our plans for Ward, so on his arrival I had the unenviable task of telling him that it was all over. I had to do much the same to all my sources. Ward walked away with nothing, while other sources, their services also terminated, were allowed to keep technical equipment in their possession, such as fax machines, or were paid off.

This was the second time we had been told that our secret operations were over and that Stratcom was being terminated. And because it had all happened amid such drama, we almost fell for it.

It wasn't long before there was a directive from the SSC that all records of Stratcom operations – every tape, every document, every scrap of paper, every trace – had to be destroyed. Even our desk blotters were checked to ensure there were no indentations that could be lifted by rubbing pencil lead over the pages. So, too, the bulk of the SB main filing system was to be obliterated on orders from the Commissioner of Police, General Johan van der Merwe.

At the SB offices at John Vorster Square, the process took just a week. Industrial shredders seized up under the strain as some 185 000 files and millions of person-hours were destroyed. Just like that.

State funding for Stratcom was officially withdrawn – but there was to be no fullstop here. No operation was shut down. As it transpired, many of the Stratcom fronts were simply required to become (allegedly) self-financing, and thus most remained in a position to carry on as before once the hurdle of the state having funded the IFP (and many other such operations) had been cleared.

When my transfer to Mossel Bay came through, I monitored a conversation between Bruwer and my new commanding officer at the SB. Bruwer blamed my '*fokken vrou*' for my having requested the move, but I didn't react. I knew that I would be set up from the start, but there was no way I was going to stay within Stratcom and be a throwing knife for De Klerk.

The Head Office had in the interim decided that people with stress problems should no longer be part of the SB, and my natural response was to take it personally. What an insult! I managed to keep my mouth shut, and persuaded myself that it didn't matter. My family and I were on our way to a fresh start in a quiet area where nothing could go wrong, and where I could fade into obscurity.

Chapter Ten

I Wish I Knew What the Fuck Was Going On

Training in 1979, Operation Marconi in 1988/89, and more training in 1990

WHEN MAJOR R.F. MARITZ presented us with Stratcom operation Project Marconi – directed at the electronic media, the most persuasive vehicle for conveying our propaganda to South Africans – in late 1990, we knew our enemy.

The problem was not the state-controlled SABC but the independents, especially private radio stations such as Radio 702. The host we hated most was John Robbie. He was effectively running a one-man anti-Stratcom show and directives flew thick and fast to stop him at all costs. As was often the case, Bruwer passed the problem over to me.

After investigations, I had no choice but to report that Robbie came up clear. I had found no avenues to smear him in the usual SB fashion: no drug abuse, no homosexuality, and no criminal activity with which he could possibly be persuaded to change his tune. Not only that, but investigations into the 702 programme director also proved fruitless. If everyone has some skeletons in the proverbial closet, with rattling bones our favoured leverage, theirs were empty.

So, masquerading as listeners, we loaded the Radio 702 talk shows with calls. My favourite moment was when I tackled its guest of the day, Chris

Hani, on a morning programme about the ANC's lack of control over its self-defence units, which I claimed were running amok, robbing and beating up political opponents and intimidating non-ANC elements. Other flunkies concentrated on Robbie's evening chat shows. They didn't stand a chance of shutting him down, though. He seemed to become more radical with every dissenting caller, and so we decided we had to take more direct measures to shut up the 'bloody Irishman'.

Since Robbie was continually attacking the SAP, we planned to arrange for him to be challenged on air into accompanying a police patrol in Soweto during which a firefight would be staged and Robbie would be shot. The attack was not to be too serious, but enough to make the police – who would, in effect, have 'saved' his life – look really good. The plot was discussed with General Erasmus and Police Minister Vlok, the latter a close friend of one of my principal agents, who revealed that Vlok thought this was an excellent idea and had given the green light to proceed.

Bruwer, however, was disgruntled by what he saw as my having a channel to the minister via my agent. My boss was fed up that he hadn't been included in the plotting, so it was decided that, because Bruwer was a personal friend of Eugene de Kock, Bruwer would meet De Kock and the Vlakplaas unit and work out the details. Vlakplaas would carry out the operation, with us assisting if and where necessary.

At the last minute, the SB decided that harming Robbie was too much of a risk for Stratcom.

As the propaganda unit of the SB, we were in our darkest place in the early 1990s. While operations such as Project Marconi became more honed and considered, we became more debased, not even able to hang on to the Christian values that had been pounded into us when we were rookie cops and junior SB police. We were told, over and over again, that we were working for God and country – a white country. But now, as everything was spinning to its most destructive close, it was every man for himself. Nobody knew who would make it out alive, anyway. Every one of us had our own enemies; every one of us had our own fears.

To fulfil the desperate mandate of a dying National Party – to ruin the ANC's chances at an inevitable election – we were being more persistently trained than we had ever been before. Now the pressure was really on. We – and those of us within the SB, particularly – had to adapt, and one of the ways in which we did this was to mould the old rules of interrogation into our strategies.

Interrogation only succeeds when the interrogator is able to exert his will on another person, and to be a good interrogator one has to have a well-developed memory to identify and exploit the slightest weaknesses or chinks in the armour of the detainee.

The brain functions like an electrical unit and, as interrogators, we would alternately intensify and de-intensify our input. This inevitably created confusion in a detainee; and if we also messed up their body clock by feeding them at odd times, or suddenly shifted the pattern of interrogation – say, with light in the person's face – we could fairly quickly disorientate them enough to crush their rebellion.

A major objective was to emasculate male detainees, and when it came to women, we would 'spiritually rape them', as we savagely dubbed it – diminish them and reduce their sense of self-worth. Add sleep deprivation, an excellent technique in itself, and you were halfway home. Of course, we were also specifically trained to leave no physical marks, or as few and as minor as possible.

In the early years after the unbanning of the liberation movements, we in Stratcom weren't interrogating many people. After all, the left was now largely free to do as it pleased. Apartheid was crashing and burning around us. However, although we may have been doing less interrogation, we were busy adapting our sophisticated persuasion techniques for the new era.

We took ten infallible interrogation techniques forward in Stratcom for the purposes of developing new sources and agents. These were old, familiar tricks of the mind, only this time they wouldn't be used to make detainees talk, but to 'assist' the empowered left, newly radicalised whites, black people who'd returned from exile to an uncertain future, having abandoned their families years before, former political prisoners and others to support the National Party government's leadership in the 'reconciliation' process.

These techniques were:

1. Question the person's self-identity.
2. Create a feeling of guilt for what they (may) have done.
3. When the sense of guilt is in place, question their ability and create a sense of fear about whether they can actually make change happen.
4. Create anxiety that they are still being watched (and may yet be killed or hurt) by unknown enemies.
5. Reinforce the position that if they humble themselves to the unifying and moderate forces – that is, a Stratcom political party – going into negotiations, they will be vindicated and benefit from it.
6. Having achieved the above, allow the person to feel elevated.
7. Then switch this all around again and rechannel the old feelings of self-condemnation.

8. This triggers the essential 're-orientation' as the person feels confused about themselves and their past.
9. Concentrate on harmonising their sense of self, both past and present, carefully drumming in the importance of 'making progress'.
10. Bingo! The person's complacency and co-operation should be forthcoming.

Work towards just one goal – with the conviction that you are right and everyone else is wrong. Brigadier Du Plooy had lectured on all of this to us at that Polkol course in 1979 and, in his customary trembling voice, had reminded us of the ideals for which we all strived. He said that it was not easy to carry out these very difficult tasks; we were to be encouraged by knowing that we were doing this out of our love for and loyalty to our country. In performing these duties, he insisted, we were defending our Christian faith against godless communism.

Our mottos had always been '*Godsdiens, Vaderland en Vlag*' (Faith, Fatherland and Flag) and '*Vlag en Familie*' (Flag and Family). Du Plooy would repeat these mottos with tears in his eyes, leaving us spellbound. But at the heart of all this theatre was the truth, rooted in a regular joke: the SB had received a confession from a lizard that it was in fact a crocodile, but they neglected to tell us.

Back in 1979, of course, we did not need the ten points, as we could quickly and readily get a result by using Radio Moscow. By 1990, however, Radio Moscow was a memory, but one that made us shiver on occasion at the thought that it could be turned on us.

I was grateful for the history component of those Polkol SB lectures, which came into good use after 1990. We were taught at length, for instance, about the Anti-Apartheid Movement (AAM), founded in London in 1959 as the Boycott Movement before changing its name after the Sharpeville massacre in 1960. This meant we knew the names and identities of founding and predominant members or supporters, among them Mary Benson, Lionel and Hilda Bernstein, Brian Bunting, Phyllis Altman, Julius and Tamara Baker, Myrtle Berman, Ronnie Kasrils, Sonia Bunting, Mervyn E. Bennun, Dr Percy Cohen, Ethel de Keyser, Ruth First, Joe Slovo, Arthur Goldreich, Harold Wolpe, Michael Harmel and James Kantor.

Others also on our list were Adrian Leftwich of the African Resistance Movement (ARM) and another 'traitor', Stephanie Kemp. Du Plooy made no secret of his hatred for Kemp. She was born into an Afrikaner family in the Karoo and, he bitterly remarked, she had turned her back on that history when she joined the underground movement.

By 1990, many exiles had returned home after threats of their arrest and imprisonment were lifted by De Klerk, and many of these 'satanists' and 'communists' were working in the Johannesburg CBD. They were addressing open rallies. They were being quoted in newspapers, on the radio and on TV. We saw their pictures. And Operation Marconi and other similar initiatives struggled to counter this power.

In our heads these returnees remained powerful examples of the white brains behind an incipient black revolution. It was emphasised in our courses in 1979 that these were 'mostly Jews', and much of our discussion during our lectures was about those individuals in particular, especially Joe Slovo and Ruth First.

Ruth First was assassinated by a parcel bomb in her office at Edoardo Mandlane University in Maputo in 1982 in an operation approved by the SB Head Office, which meant that any of us would have been elated then to capture Slovo, whom we considered to be South Africa's Public Enemy No. 1. That would have been multiple medal territory, yet in 1990 he was free. Unbelievably, Joe Slovo, like Chris Hani, was walking among us. This blew our minds.

There were many such twists of the truth that we in the SB seriously battled to understand and internalise. Our instincts were to capture and turn these people, by whatever means necessary. Now we had to rethink every act, because 'turning' in this transitionary post-apartheid period was not necessarily about ideology, and we simply could not risk violence or old-school threats. 'Turning' in the Stratcom era was more often about who got to be included in the post-elections money game, and who was offered a position in the future dispensation.

During our training, we had learned about the history of the South African Non-Racial Olympic Committee (SANROC), which was behind the international sports boycott of the country, led by 'yet another fucking communist', Dennis Brutus. That committee had been among our most loathed enemies. Like the AAM, it had helped bring about the weapons and oil boycotts and other restrictions on South Africa, which, we deduced, had bankrupted the country and forced the National Party's hand.

I had put myself in my bosses' crosshairs once by suggesting that we were giving our enemies ammunition by banning black sportsmen from coming to South Africa or censoring them inside the country. Sports venues in South Africa were almost entirely 'Whites Only' establishments at the time, and I thought that if we switched it around a bit, and allowed 'them' in, we could gain on the propaganda front. But my bright-spark counter-argument wasn't well received.

And by 1995 we in the SB had to come to terms with a (slightly) multiracial Springbok rugby team winning the World Cup, and the President walking onto the pitch to congratulate them wasn't a white man defying the Soviet intention to isolate us, but a black man loved by all.

And to think that the Watson brothers, who played rugby in the Eastern Cape, had been ostracised by the sports establishment just a few years earlier for participating in mixed-race games. They had played 'our' sport with black men, as if this were normal, and the rugby-loving public detested them. Yet by the early 1990s, there was talk of racial quotas in sport, meaning that the Watsons had been right. We hated this.

The Watsons, through their open alliances with black activists, had once been fair game for the SB, and we were all looking to make the showcase arrests. Anyone who arrested one of the big names would be considered a legend. We had, after all, a legend in our midst, South Africa's Sherlock Holmes, J.C. 'Kalfie' Broodryk, who took great delight in relating how he had caught the communist and human rights lawyer Bram Fischer in the 1960s after a massive manhunt. This appeared to be the highlight of his life.

At least there had been a logical sequence of events that had led to Fischer's capture, unlike the tracing and arrest of ARM member John Harris for the bombing of Johannesburg Railway Station in 1964.

The head of Intelligence at the time, General 'Lang Hendrik' van den Bergh, dramatically claimed that, on hearing the blast, he had suddenly received a name, John Harris, in a flash of 'divine revelation'. The actual source was Gerard Ludi, also known as Security Police agent Q018. But the establishment never missed an opportunity to claim that God was on their side – so much so that he even handed out tip-offs from God to the police.

About five years or so before I was trained in the SB, the National Union of South African Students (Nusas) became quarry for the unit. After 1990, I recognised name after name, person after person, who had been involved in Nusas, now free to be what they wanted to be, many of them jockeying for positions as much as any of us.

The war between Nusas and the apartheid government had intensified between 1973 and 1975, when students were in open conflict with the authorities. By 1974, however, many members of the Wits Student Representative Council (SRC) were SB informers or agents, including Craig Williamson, Arthur McGiven of BOSS (who later defected to Britain) and Derek Brune (who went on to hold a senior rank in the post-colonial Namibian Police Force).

The apartheid government's Schlebusch Commission would, later that year, declare Nusas an 'affected organisation', which meant that it could not be funded directly from abroad. The commission also stated that not one dime of the many thousands channelled through Nusas from the International University Exchange Fund (IUEF) to BC student organisations could now be used for that purpose. The IUEF, based in Geneva, had been 'another communist front' until Williamson started working there full-time. He would help to break the back of its affiliation to Nusas.

'I wish I knew what the fuck was going on,' I remember a voice mumbling from behind me in the lecture hall at Polkol in 1979. Most of the others had drifted off to sleep.

'Communism is a godless collective system in which everyone belongs to the state', Du Plooy taught us. He quivered as he quoted Marx: 'My highest ambition is to dethrone God and destroy capitalism.' 'En ons moet baklei teen die euwel!' Du Plooy had eventually shouted, jolting some of the guys awake.

We got the message: the ANC's ideology was satanic and it aimed to destroy whites by giving voting rights to all people aged 21 years and over, compulsory and free education for all, with food for the children, freedom of speech, the freedom to seek employment, and by revising the laws on land ownership and tax. The ANC were Bolsheviks, we were told. They were waging guerrilla warfare. They were committing acts of sabotage. We were thus a nation at war! We were, therefore, duty-bound to go out and make every effort to obtain new informers. We adhered to the National Party morality. This meant that there were no constraints, no laws, no morality when it came to our pursuit of information.

As Williamson summed it up at the TRC: 'The SA Police were the armed wing of the National Party, and the Security Branch were the cutting edge of the sword.'

I'd achieved the highest marks in the class in the 1979 Polkol exams, but my seniors could not be humiliated or embarrassed in any way, so it wasn't mentioned; a lowly sergeant couldn't be seen to be outperforming the officers. Du Plooy told me how proud he was of me and shook my hand until it nearly broke. I'd resolved then to improve myself.

All student constables were obliged to study further if they held out any hope of being promoted, and required subjects included Criminal Law, Law of Criminal Procedure and Evidence, Investigation of Crime and Criminology, and Ethnology.

The SAP crime manual was our Bible. Crimes were codified from Class A to Class F. Class A involved crimes against the security of the state, such as high treason and sabotage, while Class F involved crimes such as traffic offences. Our first function, however, was the 'preservation of the internal security of the Republic', followed by 'the maintenance of law and order', and police officers were mandated to 'take action against persons whose aims were to promote subversive activities against the state'.

'The reason for this difference is that murder, just like assault, is a crime occurring mainly among people of the lower strata of society,' according to the manual. It was simple: 'South African blacks' were 'more liable' to commit crimes such as murder, manslaughter, assault, theft, burglary and robbery.

'The primary reason for this phenomenon [is] that the "levels of civilisation" of [black and coloured people] are much lower than that of the Whites. Criminality among the Bantu exceeds that among Whites by far, although Coloureds scored the highest percentages. The more primitive a people are, the more they resort to violence and cannot distinguish between serious and less serious matters,' vented the training manual. 'When, in addition, they grow more and more conscious of the extreme differences in prosperity existing in the city, for instance, or on the farms of White farmers in the boundary zones, where the prime condition of the White farmers' cattle stands in sharp contrast to that of the Bantu's own little K-----r herd, the desire is aroused to possess these things without working, or paying, for them. This results in theft, burglary, robbery and plundering.'

All ethnic groups were discussed according to their own 'crime characteristics'. Jewish people were pretty much despised, although it was acknowledged that 'since they form a closed unit (due to being despised), this is the reason for the low incidence of juvenile delinquency among them'.

In terms of ethnology, there was an introduction titled 'The Angle of Government Policy', which told us that 'culturally backward people have to be led to the level of civilisation'. Knowledge of ethnology was apparently 'indispensable to the person who has to act as the guide'. We whites had to 'possess profound knowledge of the life and outlook of primitive peoples, particularly of the Bantu'.

Indeed, 'the racial problem' in South Africa was acknowledged, with our textbooks stating that the 'relations between White man and Bantu in particular [are] the most urgent and momentous of all our national problems today'.

Of course, this didn't mean that we were being asked to *improve* these relations. Rather, it was the rationale to separate us.

The hateful manual went on: 'We dare not shrug our shoulders at the tremendous responsibility. It is a challenge to all of us, both Whites and Bantu; a challenge demanding supreme statesmanship, sober-mindedness, tolerance and financial sacrifices … The South African Government's policy of separate development is … a matter of profound conviction and unshakeable faith … The idea of renouncing it is not given a thought. There is no alternative …'

Our manuals were thin on detail and drenched in Nazi-style ideology. Apparently, all we were required to know was that black people should have their own homelands and that they needed to be among us whites only when they came to work.

I remember a chapter in one of these manuals being devoted to 'the Bantu's belief in and worship of ancestral spirits and witchcraft'. To us students, the question was: Would we ever be able to civilise and control these people? And it wasn't only 'the Bantu', of course. The textbooks also described the 'free Indians in Natal', who were 'a poor and backward group [with an] unhygienic way of living', but having 'strong political capital resources'.

So, in 1979, it was clear that if I wanted to 'improve myself' – after getting the highest marks in the class – I'd have to fight against blackness with all my white might. It seemed, after that course, that the only way I'd be able to avoid being relegated to insignificance when I went to John Vorster Square as a junior SB operative was to seek out the love of 'my people, my God and my flag' in a self-created war zone. The training had worked. I received it as gospel and set out to rein in the bastards.

Chapter Eleven

The Satanists

Johannesburg and Grahamstown, 1982

THE FLOSSIE (A HERCULES C-130) touched down at Waterkloof Air Force Base in Pretoria and an hour later I was home with my father and stepmother in Bedfordview. Home for seven days' compulsory leave during which one was expected to 'normalise' and readjust to society after border duty.

Jesus, but a lot had changed!

Everything just seemed so insignificant. It took all my patience to listen to my folks chatter on about what I considered inanities, unimportant things that had happened in my absence. To make it worse, I wasn't home for very long when my father presented me with a record of my phone calls from Ovamboland (I had phoned regularly, reversing the charges), for which I was expected to reimburse him. Secretly, I was seething. Why the fuck had I bothered to phone them, anyway?

I had a light delivery van parked at home and discovered that its gearbox had been broken in my absence, so I had to fork out another R91 for repairs. This was insane! I climbed onto my motorbike and went off to see friends. But they, too, had changed somehow and my visit was short, the crushing banality of their lives was just too much to bear.

To clear my head, I headed down the highway, red-lining my motorcycle through its gears, faster and faster, until my fear was replaced solely by the effort and concentration required to keep the machine on the road at 20 kph. That made me feel better – until I was clocked by the traffic police.

I felt the rage building. I told them that I'd just come back from the border. I thought they might give me a break since this was our national duty. Instead, they insisted that they'd have to arrest me. So I climbed off the bike, which was so hot that the engine was clicking and ticking.

'Go ahead!' I taunted. 'What you are waiting for?'

The cop turned and walked over to his senior while I waited impatiently. After a while he returned and asked: 'When did you get back from the border?'

'Today,' I said. 'Can't you see that I'm a policeman?' I was still wearing my camouflage uniform.

'Okay,' he said, taking in my uniform and badges with a nod. 'Seeing you've just come back, we'll give you a chance this time.'

I thanked him and started the bike so I could roar off. Fuck them as well! I had no choice but to go back to the stifling atmosphere of my father's house. Within just a few hours, it had stopped feeling like home. It was just a house – a place to which I felt no connection. And then suddenly, everything I thought mattered was starting to come undone. I had rapidly become alienated from what I thought was a family structure. Now even those people, my blood, felt somehow less than me. I can't say what I thought I was at that time. Did I feel more than them? Probably.

I was even irritated by my earlier self, the person I had been before Ovamboland, and that rapidly ballooned into anger. Even my music collection meant nothing to me. All I wanted now was Paul Simon, Pink Floyd or Jethro Tull. I wanted to wallow but also to get really loud.

After three days, I could not stand the humdrum of civilian life a second longer, so I headed to a rundown hotel nearby, had too much to drink and picked a fight with some locals. Outnumbered, I retreated to my vehicle to retrieve that great argument-settler, my trusty 9 mm. I produced it with a flourish.

'Now we'll see something,' I howled at them. I saw them only as aggressors.

They took off, but I was too quick for one of them. I lunged for him, grabbed him and swung him around, cocking the weapon and placing the end of the barrel between his eyes.

'Now you're going to die!' I growled.

'Jesus, you're mad!' he shouted back at me. 'Please! You don't know what you're doing.'

I pressed the barrel harder against his forehead, staring into his eyes. 'I know what I'm doing and don't tell me I'm fucking mad.' For a long time we were locked in this position, but I eventually returned the weapon to 'safe', shoved him away and stumbled off in the direction of my car.

'You're fucking mad,' he screamed after me. 'You need help, you fucking mad bastard!'

On the way home I stopped at some other obscure drinking hole and tossed back several more drinks, somewhat mollified by the anti-climax of that little scene. More than anything else, I wanted to get back to Ovamboland. That was all that was playing in my head.

The following day I tried to talk to my father, who had himself been through a war, and not just a regional (albeit ideological) fight for power, like ours, but a world war. He was having none of this, though. He simply couldn't open up and so I was shut down. Only when I was much older did I realise how trapped he must have been by that inability to talk, to release his emotions about it. It wasn't just that the Second World War had messed him up, but also that there was no way he could share how it had done that.

We had church, of course. Prior to my spell in Ovamboland, I had been attending a Baptist youth group meeting on Friday nights, having broken away from the Methodist Church after the security course in 1979, when I decided that I couldn't be part of a denomination that supported the SACC. Anyone who advocated the 'Red gospel' wouldn't get a cent of my money in the collection plate. I decided Baptists were apolitical and I had made some friends there.

On the first Friday after I got back from the border in that severely depressed state, I swallowed a couple of Obex, a 'slimming' tablet popular in the SAP, not for its weight-loss properties, but its ability to keep you wide awake, especially when taken in large doses. I then poured several stiff pegs of whisky down my throat.

I had already come to terms with my decision – that I would leave as soon as possible for Ovamboland. So, in that drugged and drunken stupor, I ended up at the youth group meeting in uniform with my rifle and just sat there, not speaking to anyone. I wanted somebody to talk to me. I felt completely alone.

The irate youth leader called me the next day and demanded an explanation. He insisted I pray about it and never drink again. That had been, after all, the 'Lord's House', he reminded me. I promised I would go to church on Sunday and agreed it would be better if I didn't go back to the youth group meetings. Instead, I took out my brushes and painted a picture of a man sitting with his head in his hands in a room with black windows. My nightmares were vivid, one rolling endlessly into another. A very angry Jesus would appear, but I was never able to reach far enough to grab the outstretched hand.

Ashamed at my behaviour at the meeting, I wrote out the lyrics from Jethro Tull's 'Aqualung', and pinned them to the door of the church.

I went back to work a day earlier than I was supposed to, but no one even noticed. All I did on that first day back at John Vorster Square was swap experiences about Ovamboland with everyone else who had been there.

That was the start of many months wandering around like a zombie, battling the insomnia and tiredness that wore me down. When I did sleep, I'd wake up startled, afraid and sometimes in tears. I had an unending series of nightmares and vivid recollections, distortions, of buildings bursting into flames or of me trying to shoot someone but the cursed gun would just not fire.

Because many of my old sources had fallen off the radar when I went to the border, I had to recruit new ones. I became more and more devoted to nailing the white left, particularly those I knew or assumed to be conscientious objectors. After being in Ovamboland and witnessing first-hand the 'sacrifice' other whites were making, my hatred for white lefties increased a thousandfold.

By this time, the SB was developing its relationship with Military Intelligence (MI), and more specifically with Colonel Roy Allen, whose name often comes up in connection with the assassination of Dr Robert Smit and his wife, Jeanne-Cora, in November 1977. He denies this. Allen headed up the MI's probes into conscientious objectors, and I met him for the first time after interviewing deserter Clifton Westraad, who had fled South Africa when faced with two years of national service. Westraad had ended up in New York in the hands of the South African Military Refugee Aid Fund (SAMRAF), which assisted 'runaways' – we called them 'traitors' – like him. SAMRAF was the US counterpart of the Committee on South African War Resisters (COSAWR) operating in Britain and Holland. We were taught that these were both ANC fronts.

Westraad had been employed by Don Morton, a 'Red gospelist' at the SAMRAF office in New York, but he'd started getting homesick and had ultimately come into contact with MI operatives, who offered him a deal: he would help with their investigations into SAMRAF and, in return, he would not be prosecuted for draft-dodging. He would also be excused from any other commitment to the SADF.

In a major intelligence coup, MI operatives, led by Allen, apparently met Westraad in New York over a weekend. He unlocked the SAMRAF offices and the team relieved the organisation of its entire filing system and administration, which was packed into steel *trommels* and placed on a Johannesburg-bound South African Airways flight.

By the time Morton opened the offices the following day, Westraad and SAMRAF's entire stash of secrets were already in the hands of the MI in the Poynton's Buildings in Pretoria. Included in this haul was a mass of correspondence from young men who had contacted SAMRAF for advice on leaving the country to avoid being called up, including many who were already doing national service but had had enough and wanted out. The SADF quickly transferred these undesirables to 'safe working environments' where they could be watched.

As a result of my contact with Allen and the MI, I was appointed as a sort of SB liaison officer on conscientious objection and general matters. It was at about this time that the SB intensified its contact with the MI by supplying it with the names of troublemakers. Once those men were identified and placed in 'suitable environments', they were given an especially hard time.

Some of the treatment was what we considered to be fairly mild on the face of it, but the intention behind all of it was to drive people what we called '*slapgats*', slightly crazy. One suspect, who had had a long academic career at Wits before he finally had no choice but to accept his call-up to national service, did his basic training and was then appointed a 'director of vehicles', spending 15 months showing drivers where to park in the huge military lot at Voortrekkerhoogte army base in Pretoria. Eventually, he became so desperate to do something that tested his brain and made use of his academic ability that he wrote daily requests for transfers during his two-year stint. These were slowly and sadistically torn up by his commander, who told him that because he was a 'communist', the army was going to keep him at Voortrekkerhoogte 'doing a k-----r's job'.

One of my top sources at Wits University was a different kind of person entirely. Patriotic and true to the apartheid cause, he had prepared himself physically and mentally for his national service. He strongly resisted my offer of a cushy job, insisting that conscription was his duty, and as he was so fit and *paraat*, the army held no fear for him. He was undoubtedly officer material, but while on the officers' course, he made the mistake of embarrassing the instructors by outperforming them physically. One of them, said to have an IQ lower than room temperature in an Arctic blizzard, then insulted him because of his Jewish heritage. He was taken before the commanding officer and, after a brief exchange, was branded a troublemaker and kicked off the course. I tried to rectify the situation via the MI, but to no avail.

Some three years later, when he was in private legal practice, a field in which we desperately needed sources, I approached him with a view to renewing the working relationship. It was a 'no'. He told me that the army had done to him in two years what the lefties at Wits hadn't been able to do in four.

A major blunder was our attempt to arrest a suspect and former detainee, Auret van Heerden. We discovered that he had been posted to MI in Poynton's

Buildings after basic training, and that the MI knew about his past as an activist. So we in the SB simply turned the situation around and put out word in his political circles that he had been an agent of the state all along.

Another of our prime targets in 1982/83, Jeanette Curtis – wife of Marius Schoon, sentenced to ten years in prison for attempting to blow up Hospital Hill Police Station in Johannesburg in 1964 – had fled to Botswana with her husband. I called Jack Curtis, Jeanette's father, and left a message, ostensibly from the Botswana police, that Marius was gravely ill with yellow fever and that he, Jack, should go to Botswana immediately. Jack, having been caught before by SB machinations, phoned the right sources in Botswana to verify the information. The lines were down, and so, in a state of anguish, Jack left immediately, taking a hellish drive through the night, only to arrive in Botswana the following morning to find Marius fit and working in the garden.

This is how we thugs entertained ourselves. We interspersed petrol bombings, arson and other acts of vandalism with plain cruelty. We dreamt up new acts of spitefulness all the time. At a non-violence symposium held at Wilgespruit Fellowship Centre on the West Rand, we ruined vehicles, but I remember that our favourite trick that day was hacking tyres to pieces.

Throughout all of this, I had an overwhelming longing to return to Ovamboland. It was clear to me even then that we had all come back with our ghosts. Eugene de Kock, South Africa's most highly decorated policeman, went on to head up Vlakplaas and would face 108 charges, ranging from murder to fraud. SB members Willie Nortjé, Eugene Fourie and Rolf Gevers testified against their former commander at the TRC.

John Adams was later implicated in the bombing of the ANC offices in London, and I heard that a former colleague, Buks, had gone back to Koevoet where he was renowned for his fearlessness, before succumbing to PTSD – as did Nortjé, Fourie, Gevers and many others, including me.

John Deegan served in Ovamboland for four more years than we did, and then resigned. Out of the police and with no medical aid and no treatment for his PTSD, he was found crawling around in his father's flower beds, reliving a hell from so long ago. He was riddled with guilt after carrying out an instruction to execute a Swapo unit commander, 'Tokyo', in Ovamboland. He threw it all away and lived an itinerant life for many years, before passing on.

In the meantime, I was battling my own demons in my own way. I would more and more often try to satiate my desire for excitement by playing chicken on my motorcycle, racing through red traffic lights at full speed. From time to time, I'd get involved in fights. Anything to get the adrenalin pumping. The few friends I hadn't managed to alienate remarked that I had changed, and secretly I was concerned that I was heading for some sort of breakdown. I had become detached from what was going on around me, and the slightest trigger could bring on a blind rage.

I once got into a fight, provoked by a stranger after a friend's bachelor party, and beat him up so violently that he was hospitalised for three months. As usual, in my private time following these public outbreaks of fury, I'd be tormented by the incident and, in this instance, was horrified when I heard that my victim might have sustained a brain injury.

In 1983, the year I got married, a light at the end of the tunnel, as I saw it, was that I had enrolled at Unisa. It was an opportunity to study, to distract me from my life with the SB and the SAP. I chose a Bachelor of Arts, one of my subjects being Philosophy, but I found it really difficult to balance the complexities of my job with tranquil after-hours intellectualising. Likewise, it was tough to philosophise when I couldn't even figure out my own psyche. I couldn't concentrate. Nothing registered. I thought of asking for a transfer to another branch but didn't want to be seen as anti-SB, worried that I'd end up forgotten in some lonely hell like other SB members who had been perceived to be anti the establishment.

I once plucked up courage and spoke to Colonel Daniel Mahoney, the head of white affairs – the unit that targeted the white left – about the insomnia and nightmares. I explained that I wasn't handling things too well at work. Colonel 'Mac', as we called him, fished out his snuff box and, after a few lengthy pulls into both nostrils, considered my predicament. With retirement looming, he wasn't going to get involved in other people's problems.

'*Here, buurman. Wat kan ons doen?*' he shrugged. 'It's that border that's buggering you up. Everybody changes when they come back from that place.'

More snuff.

'You must go out more and relax,' he suggested. 'You know … get stuck into the girls!'

I laughed. We laughed.

'Take Dalene here.' He pointed to where his secretary usually sat. 'I'm sure she's never had it with a guy. If you get it right, I'll give you a week's leave.'

More laughter.

'You must drink less beer, Paul. You must learn to relax. When you get home, pour yourself a lekker brandy and Coke.' That was the SAP panacea for all ills: *brandewyn* by the bakkie load.

Then he promised he would give me more interesting and stimulating work, and every opportunity to recruit sources. In this way, he assured me, I would forget all about Ovamboland.

The SB was receiving numerous offers of assistance at the time, especially from Rhodesians, and, true to his word, Mac passed some on to me. Many recruits were, however, inveterate liars. Most claimed to have been Selous Scouts or said that they had had specialised military or intelligence training, and a lot of my time was spent listening to how they'd won all the battles but, nevertheless, lost the war, with many contending that this was because they were sold down the river by South African prime minister B.J. Vorster.

Yet, there were a few spin–offs and the occasional positive result from these quarters for me. For instance, I was able to lay my hands on the Zimbabwe Defence Force's 'shopping list' of arms and ammunition, which came via telex to a South African importer and was of great interest to MI. The list included 2 million 7.62 rounds, AK rounds, 69 mm patrol mortars and Semtex. There were also masses of names, addresses and personality profiles of persons of interest who had remained in Zimbabwe.

Other information received concerned the KGB, SWAPO and the newly restructured Central Intelligence Organisation (CIO) in Zimbabwe, which also operated in neighbouring southern African countries. It was this kind of information that was used to set up anti-ANC operations in Zimbabwe. But with some of the expats from Rhodesia, it was often difficult to separate fact from fiction, so a lot of the information was completely disregarded. My biggest failure in this, I believe, was not taking seriously enough information on what would be an attempted coup in the Seychelles led by mercenary Mike Hoare. Thinking that it was no more than yet another bullshit-baffles-brains pub story, I didn't report the intelligence. Indeed, the South African government denied knowing anything about it. This one was complicated, however, by the fact that members of MI were in on the coup and had supplied the weapons. Even today, though, I doubt if the SB could have interfered with or put a halt to the coup attempt had the Head Office been forewarned.

It was through the ex-Rhodesians that I came into contact with anti-communist groupings and with individuals such as Ivor Benson, who published the right-wing *Behind the News* newsletter, the Reverend Ed Cain and his *Encounter* newsletter, and the Christian League of South Africa. With Rhodesia having supposedly 'fallen', leaving only South Africa and South West Africa to counter the inexorable march of communism across Africa, people like Cain were picking up on the South African scene where they had left off in Rhodesia.

In the early 1980s, the SB was not as geared up to fight on the propaganda front as was MI. Psych operations were largely the domain of the military and BOSS, which were supposed to operate only beyond the borders of South Africa.

Paul Erasmus (left) with Sgts 'Tubby' Campbell and Nel in Ovamboland Central. (Undated)

A young, stupid and somewhat 'paraat' (committed and ready) Paul Erasmus on passing out of Police College on 3 December, 1975, showing off a copybook salute.

Paul Erasmus and Security Branch friends on 9th Floor of John Vorster Square, 1981. From left Warrant Officer Piet van Greunen, Paul Erasmus, Warrant Officer Roy Baker, Constable Jorrie Jordaan, Constable John Deegan and Sergeant Leon 'Rabbitpants' Haasbroek. John Deegan worked in Koevoet commanded by Eugene de Kock. Deegan suffered from PTSD, returned to South Africa, and committed suicide in 2015.

Ovamboland 1981. From left: Sergeant 'Giepie' Nel, Const Rolf Gevers (later posted to Vlakplaas), Sergeant 'Tubby' Campbell, Constable Buks Delport and unknown. Paul Erasmus, front, kneeling.

Paul Erasmus and Sergeant 'Das' Coetzee dressed up for a fancy dress 'sokkiejol' during the Oktoberfest, Ovamboland, 1981.

From left: Paul Erasmus shares a joke with 'White Affairs' Section Head, Colonel D Mahoney, Captain Neville Els, Constable 'Boet' Van Wyk, Sgt Gert Horak and Warrant Officer Roy Baker, official Security Branch photographer on the occasion of the Colonel's retirement.

A Security Branch clippings book.

*The Security Branch hierarchy having a drink at John Vorster Square, 1983.
From left: Colonel Daniel Mahoney, Section Head, White Affairs, Brigadier Hennie
Muller (Commanding Officer), Colonel Arthur 'Little Hitler' Cronwright and Colonel
Jack Olivier (Deputy Commanding Officer)*

*Paul Erasmus at his desk at John Vorster Square. Note the posters on the wall: a Black
Sash meeting poster, a Save the Children poster, World Day of Prayer for Peace poster.
Erasmus created many posters which mimicked the anti-apartheid posters of the day to
create mischief, especially in Alexandra Township in the mid-1980s.*

Linda and Paul at a Security Branch supper event, mid–1980s.

An example of a business card from a Stratcom front company.

ธ7-9ร

RECEIPT

SOURCE NO. .... CLAIM NO. SQQ870................... ....

I ....cknowledge

receipt of the amount of R *eighty nine thousand and ninety*

(in words) *five cents only (R89·95)*.........................for

services rendered.

Division: ....

....
SIGNATURE

Place: ....

Date and
Time: ....

Witnesses: (1) ....

(2) ....

An example of a receipt for fees paid to a Stratcom agent. The SB were penny pinchers.

WH10, the SB department which intercepted mail, would destroy letters each morning in a furnace. Paul and many other SB members asked the officer responsible to save the stamps for their collections.

Dylan! my grand-Son- All my Love and Best wishes in whatever you do! Winnie Mandela 11. 7. 2000

A note on a photograph of Dylan from Winnie Madikizela-Mandela, 2000.

Dylan and Paul Erasmus, 2019.

Paul Erasmus and Roger Lucey at the SABC Moshito Conference, 2016.

Zamaswazi Dlamini-Mandela (left), Winnie Madikizela-Mandela, Paul Erasmus & Dylan Erasmus, 2016. © The Trials of Winnie Mandela Documentary Series, *African Oral History Archive*

Paul, Dylan and Gretchen at Dylan and Gretchen's wedding, December 2020.

Candice and Paul, 2020.

From our first contact with Cain and others, we were left with little doubt that MI was in the process of filling the vacuum that had been left after Eschel Rhoodie and the Information Scandal in the late 1970s. Rhoodie and his cohort had used, abused and stolen state funds on a staggering scale to fund secret propaganda campaigns. They even tried to buy the *Washington Star* newspaper along the way. The government-appointed Erasmus Commission – set up by Vorster's successor P.W. Botha and led by Judge Rudolph Erasmus, with two other judges on a panel – was later dismissed as a whitewash, but it certainly revealed some of the corruption that emanated from this secret, MI-initiated five-year propaganda campaign between 1974 and 1979.

The Information Department – under Minister Connie Mulder and Information Secretary Eschel Rhoodie – moved more than R64 million around on Vorster's watch. Other ministers knew about aspects of the campaign, including the funding of *The Citizen* newspaper.

For us in the nascent SB of the 1980s, this scandal was immense and it was fresh. For the apartheid government, though, it was a calamitous comedown internationally, especially since pressure was already growing for it to reform. It was also something of a blow for the country's national image because voters (whites) had been raised to believe that Afrikaners were upright, moral people who wouldn't dream of stealing money or doing anything against the '*Volk, Vaderland en Vlag*'.

Even Hendrik van den Bergh, the founder of BOSS, who was like a hero to us SB rookies because he was such an intelligence legend, was fingered. We got the impression at the time that our SAP seniors felt that individuals like him had been thrown under the bus by Vorster's administration, and this only made them all the more obedient to the new Botha government.

By now the screws were really tightening on the security establishment, but it took another four or five years for the SAP to properly get going in the covert psych ops and propaganda field. We were on a roll in 1984 when Stratcom was officially established at a full Cabinet and State Security Council meeting. Prior to this, any actions instituted in terms of propaganda by the SAP had been purely ad hoc. The elimination of the country's enemies by Section C, which was run by the SB Head Office via the internal hit squad at Vlakplaas under Dirk Coetzee, was a slightly different affair. We didn't blow up, set alight or murder people – at least not directly. Instead, we were trained to manipulate people's minds – and, yes, often with physical intervention.

I see clearly now that the Info Scandal – or Muldergate, or whatever people preferred to call it at that time – was a precursor of the kind of corruption that was to become endemic in South African government. This was straight-up corruption, complementing the race laws that defied human rights. For decades, it was all interwoven so as to give selected individuals employment, farms and other properties, and unimaginably fine perks. That scandal, which saw the disappearance or 'reallocation' – theft, in other words – of many millions of taxpayers' money, was the most public example of apartheid government officials not being held accountable and of being protected in their greed and misuse of resources. And it was far from over.

In the early 1980s, the SB detention cells at John Vorster Square were full of suspects. We were wall-to-wall with lefties. Then, on 5 February 1982, Dr Neil Aggett was the first white detainee to die in detention; there had been 52 other deaths in detention before his –– all black people.

The first we heard of this was when Cronwright announced that one of Aggett's interrogators, Lieutenant Stephen Whitehead, had reported it. Whitehead had apparently told Cronwright that the suspect's 62-hour interrogation over the weekend of 28–31 January had yielded dozens of pages of information, as well as a confession. But this was not all.

I had just returned from a meeting with an informer and was standing in our office on the ninth floor when, to my surprise, Whitehead walked in. Chubby and freckle-faced, he was a member of Little Hitler's staff, but was rarely seen on the ninth floor. It was clear that something was afoot.

I drew up one of our battered green chairs and Whitehead sat down. He offered me a Camel and we both lit up. I made no attempt to conceal my animosity. I always found him rude and condescending, but on this day he was in an entirely different mood.

'We', he said, suggesting us in the SAP, 'have a problem, a very serious problem, and we feel that you may be able to help, considering the experience you've had over the past couple of years in covert operations.'

I already knew that much of Whitehead's energy was being spent on preparation for the Aggett inquest. When he asked me if I was available to leave immediately on an investigation to another part of the country, I wasn't keen to travel with a character from the tenth floor. The idea of travelling with one of Cronwright's henchmen sickened me.

'It's only me and you, Paul, top secret', Whitehead said matter-of-factly. 'We have authority to go where we like and for however long, so long as we get the job done. We have access to the expense account and we'll get full subs.'

There was even an afterthought: 'And we'll have a lot of fun.'

My mind raced. Subs! These were for accommodation and food at prescribed government rates, but we, the SB juniors, invariably slept in our cars and ate as little as we could just to skim off some extra income. Officers got higher subs than other members, however, and Whitehead was an officer.

'So … you interested?' he asked.

Interested? Hell, yeah. I was broke and needed the cash.

Whitehead took me to the commanding officer, Brigadier Hennie Muller, who confirmed that he had authorised the trip with Head Office's blessing. It was essential, he said, that we 'work as a team'.

'Contact me daily, Stephen,' he told Whitehead. 'And I would like to tell both of you boys that the success of your mission will be of cardinal importance to the future of the Special Branch, and in fact the country itself.'

The intention was clear. If the state fared poorly in the Aggett inquest, there would be serious problems to come. Muller's position was that the SAP had no choice but to win this one. He compared it to the Biko case.

'If we lose, it will sink the whole ship.'

Five hours later, Whitehead and I were on the road to Grahamstown, about 900 kilometres from Johannesburg. He filled me in en route. Our mission, he said, was to gather evidence to the effect that Aggett had been a 'walking suicide'. His life had to be put under the microscope. As Whitehead put it: 'We must be able to show that Aggett dropped from his mother's womb holding a loaded and cocked pistol against his own temple.'

Government had instructed the Head Office that the Aggett inquest had to be won; it was imperative that the world believe we had arrested a man who would have committed suicide even if he had not been captured.

The reason we were heading to Grahamstown was that Aggett had attended school at Kingswood College, which is where we'd start our research. Whitehead kept referring to the brown SB file on Aggett, which he had brought with him.

The spire of St George's Cathedral, which dominated the skyline, made an impression on me, and I said so, but Whitehead was quick to point out that the church was also the city's primary venue for anti-government meetings. I decided not to take a picture of it in front of him.

Our first stop was the local SB office, which was located in an arcade off the main street. I was immediately uncomfortable in the presence of the branch commander, Captain Alfred Oosthuizen. He immediately asked Whitehead what cover we intended to use during our enquiries, and Whitehead, naturally, was at a loss for words. Unbelievably, he had not even considered this aspect of the operation. There was clearly no workable plan of action.

Oosthuizen knew what we were up against and his probing questions to Whitehead left me under no illusion as to his ability. I wondered what a man of his intellect was doing in the SB, later recalling the words of one of Roger

Lucey's songs: 'Down in Grahamstown Prison sat Peter Jones alone. For 17 months he sat there and nothing was done.'

Peter Jones had been Steve Biko's friend, and was arrested with him at a roadblock near Grahamstown in August 1977. Biko was banned at the time and restricted to his village outside King Williams Town, but had travelled illegally to Cape Town with Jones to meet with members of the BC movement. After their meeting, Biko and Jones had headed back to Biko's home, but were caught just outside the university town. They were taken into custody and separated. Biko was so seriously beaten by members of the SB who interrogated him that he died from his injuries a few weeks after.

The comparisons between Biko and Aggett might have played on Oosthuizen's mind because, just for a moment, he seemed to empathise with us.

'You guys have a difficult task ahead of you,' he said. 'Trying to prove that someone was suicidal even as a child. If there's anything I can do for you while you are here, just let me know.'

Oosthuizen then stood up, indicating that our meeting was over. I couldn't help but notice a strange smile on his face as we left. It might have been sarcasm, but it unsettled me. I didn't mention it to Whitehead, but then I didn't think I needed to.

'What a fucking pig!' said Whitehead as we climbed into the car. 'Who the hell does he think he is? You notice how sarcastic he was?'

I agreed. But there was something else that bothered me. My impression was that Oosthuizen was not someone you dared underestimate. I would find this to be true in very personal ways some years later.

Whitehead told me that Oosthuizen had achieved remarkable success in intelligence operations in the Eastern Cape, and especially at Rhodes University in Grahamstown, where he had infiltrated informers into various organisations to the point that he was effectively controlling those entities. He was thus highly regarded at the SB Head Office.

Our next stop was at the local National Intelligence Service (NIS), the agency that replaced BOSS. All that drama had played out in 1978, the year before I had been inducted into the SB. In the wake of the Info Scandal, in which BOSS had become mired, its head, Hendrik van den Bergh resigned, and BOSS was renamed the Department of National Security (DONS) in 1980. When Vorster resigned in 1979 and P.W. Botha was appointed as the new prime minister, intelligence was brought under Cabinet control. This was good for MI because Botha loved the SADF, and would allow the military to dominate the security establishment.

Botha then split the intelligence function up into four agencies: MI,

BOSS/DONS, the SB and Foreign Affairs – the four arms of state that would ultimately be central to Stratcom and its operations. At the same time the Erasmus Commission was investigating the Info Scandal, so BOSS officials decided it was time to shred any documents that could be used against them.

In 1980, Botha finally put all the intelligence agencies under the control of the State Security Council (SSC), and in January 1981 we were told that it would work like this: the NIS would be responsible for analysis, political intelligence and counter-intelligence; MI would, as its name implied, develop 'contra-mobilisation'; and the SB would concentrate on 'counter-subversion'.

So it was that the NIS representative in Grahamstown organised accommodation for Whitehead and me. The relationship between the SAP and the intelligence sector was fragile after a year of this revised set-up under the SSC. However, we seemed to get along better with the NIS – a far more subdued version of BOSS – than we did with our own SB colleagues on that trip.

But a pivotal event – with which I have grappled for nearly 40 years – was about to take place. It all started when Whitehead and I travelled to his in-laws' holiday home in Port Alfred, just under an hour's drive from Grahamstown. It was here, over numerous whiskies, that Whitehead told me about his father-in-law, Dennis Rothman, who was the deputy director of the NIS and the only senior official in the agency, who was 'fully trusted' by Botha.

Rothman had been all over the world on NIS missions, including to Ethiopia, where the KGB had apparently engineered his arrest. Whitehead's story was that having been detained for six months – during which he was beaten and starved – the apartheid government managed to secure his release through the CIA.

Regular drinks and Whitehead's discloures meant that he and I were becoming something akin to friends over the next few months, and it was in that time that he showed me a photograph of Botha pinning a medal on Rothman's chest at a discreet little garden party in Pretoria – the badge being for his 'services and sacrifices' in Ethiopia.

The Port Alfred evening was not only my introduction to Rothman as a figure to be feared, but it was also a warning to me. It should also have set off alarm bells that we'd gone to the holiday home to solve the immediate problem of our cover story, yet Whitehead remained indecisive about our cover the following day. We spent the morning on Port Alfred beach before heading back to Grahamstown – at Whitehead's insistence – 'just to look' at Kingswood College. This was a futile exercise in my opinion, but I was trained never to argue with an officer.

Later he asked what plans I had made to approach the school headmaster. When he called me 'the undercover expert', it became obvious to me that I was being buttered up, flattered. Naturally, I was reluctant to make any call on this, but that just gave Whitehead a gap to lecture me on how privileged I should feel to have been chosen for the trip. In fact, he turned quite brotherly when he said I wasn't to 'let him down'.

I was furious! I had a feeling that I was going to be the fall guy here.

Whitehead really turned on the charm that second evening when, once again, we had plenty to drink and he switched to his casual self, plying me with compliments and insisting that, since we were now friends, I should forget about formalities and address him by his first name.

There were pitifully few reasons for us to go to Kingswood, but I told Whitehead on our third day that our cover would be private investigators hired by a well-known author based abroad, who wanted to write a biography of Aggett. The author, we would say, had requested us to gather as much information as possible and present a framework of facts that could minimise the time he would have to spend doing his own research on a visit to South Africa.

My name would be Paul Edwards and our 'employer', the Industrial Security Agency (ISA), an established firm in Johannesburg run by an ex-colleague, Adrian Hamman. Hamman would confirm our story should the headmaster ever check up, and provided us with a letter of appointment and ISA identity cards.

Two days later, we were ready.

The headmaster showed us around the school and discussed Aggett's time at the school at length. Nevertheless, this entire series of events was freaking me out, because our attempt to find any evidence of suicidal tendencies in Aggett was completely futile. Two hours later, when we left Kingswood with Whitehead seemingly elated at our success, I asked him why he had overlooked that we still had absolutely nothing to contribute to the suicide theory.

Aggett had been an exemplary student and stable youngster, popular with his teachers and other children. He had excelled in extramurals, been elected class captain and was an exceptional young scholar, an all-round achiever with no hint of mental instability or psychological problems. From what we had managed to piece together during our tour of the school and the headmaster's tribute, there was simply no way Aggett could have been classed a 'walking suicide' at school. We'd fallen at the first hurdle, failed on step one, which was to find any inkling of a troubled childhood.

We'd have to look at his student years at the University of Cape Town

(UCT) as well, but that was going to be another kind of assignment entirely. As it was, none of this had made much sense to me as a professional operation, and I had reservations about Whitehead. As for us going to UCT, the moment we walked in there, the alarms were bound to go off. Whitehead spoke with a clipped Afrikaans accent and I'd witnessed how he clammed up in front of the Kingswood headmaster. He would never be able to do the undercover act. He was a torturer, not an agent. He was a man paid to destroy people and he enjoyed doing it. Nothing else to it. Now Aggett – a dead white detainee – was threatening his peace and livelihood, and Whitehead was terrified.

He didn't mention that, while we were on this assignment, he was in regular contact with a state psychiatrist, who I later established had been in on the planning of our trip, and who was already primed to be an expert witness at the inquest. The psychiatrist had apparently told Whitehead to forget about tapping Aggett's peer group at UCT for proof and proceed directly to Somerset West to interview Aggett's parents. Whitehead was adamant: everything depended on this, he said.

We left immediately for the Aggett family home in the Cape. Whitehead remained secretive throughout, and it was patently clear that he was now telling me only what he thought I needed to know. The trip was a nightmare 700 kilometres, our only stops being for petrol at Swellendam and Plettenburg Bay, where Whitehead took pleasure in entering the police station late at night, when the members on duty were at their most relaxed.

The senior member, a constable, was lying back with his feet on the desk. After appraising the two unshaven strangers for a minute or two, he greeted us with the usual, 'Yes? Can I help you?'

Whitehead flashed his ID card, and the constable nearly toppled the table in his haste to remove his feet. It was a light moment, carefully orchestrated by Whitehead, before we set off for Cape Town and got there as the sun came up.

Dishevelled and travel-weary, we presented ourselves to Brigadier Kotze, commanding officer for the Western Province SB division. Arrogant and bombastic, Kotze stared at us grudgingly from behind the refuge of his desk, and then told us in no uncertain terms that he thought our enquiry was 'a lot of nonsense'. It was clear that he thought we were intruding on his territory and resentful that he had not been consulted. He would, however, accept us into 'his' division for the time being, and would render us whatever assistance he could.

We spent most of the day reading the divisional files on Aggett, but a lot of the content comprised security reports (SAP 67s) that had originated in

Johannesburg and was thus old news to Whitehead and me. Only marginally more useful was the SB agent who specialised in UCT, who stated that Aggett had been a communist who 'hung around with k——rs and gave us *kak*'. Whitehead confirmed that Aggett's confession had included the line 'I am a Communist and subscribe to a Marxist philosophy.' Finally, at the end of the day, etiquette demanding, we were ushered back into Kotze's office where Whitehead thanked him profusely for his assistance and hospitality, which had consisted of two cups of government-issue coffee with three heaped teaspoons of sugar.

We then made our way to Bellville, where Whitehead had organised accommodation for us with relatives. We spent four nights in unsavoury and unhygienic conditions boarding with his elderly aunt.

This was supposed to be our 'planning' time for Somerset West. It was all but that.

Aggett's parents lived at 20 Bo Oranje Street. That was all I knew when I began to psych myself up for what would be the most challenging interview of my career. Whitehead and I rehearsed the answers to questions we were likely to face, and I convinced him that the battle would be won if we could just get past the front door, turn on the charm and get them talking instead.

On 15 March 1982, we arrived in our best three-piece suits. I had planned for us to turn up on their doorstep at 7 pm – a respectable hour at which most South African families would have had supper and would be settling down for an evening of TV. But it took us longer than we thought to find their house, and after driving around aimlessly for about ten minutes, Whitehead stopped at a restaurant and suggested we get up some Dutch courage with a whisky or two. I ordered a Coke.

By the time he was on his fourth double whisky, I realised I was on my own on that evening's mission. When I said as much, the relief on Whitehead's face was like a light going on. I even told him that I would feel more comfortable being on my own – and he didn't argue.

Ten minutes later, I knocked on the front door. The house was already in darkness and I was about to leave when the door was opened by the Aggetts' domestic worker, Sarah Isaacs. I enquired as to the whereabouts of the Aggetts', and she said they had gone to Johannesburg.

I edged my way inside.

Here was a golden opportunity to search the house and find evidence relevant to the inquest. I contemplated my options. First, I would have to neutralise Isaacs, either through physical strength or by bluffing her, which was by far the better option. I was determined not to compromise the operation. I turned on the recording device in my pocket.

Without specifying where I came from, I explained that I was a private detective, and offered her money if she would allow me to have a quick look through the house. She hesitated and I moved forward, reassuring her as I went. My aim was to dominate her and, ignoring her protests, I began my search. All the while she was behind me, until finally my confident steam-rollering started to take effect and she followed me from room to room.

Finding a bound pack of letters written by Neil to his parents, I asked her to check whether anyone had arrived, and while she was gone I slipped the envelopes into my briefcase. I found more letters from Neil to his parents in a desk drawer and slipped those into my pocket.

Having completed the search in record time, I was on the point of leaving when a neighbour, an elderly man, burst into the room.

'What are you doing here?' he shouted at me. 'Who are you?'

The secrecy of the mission being uppermost, I could have taken him out right there, but that would have entailed doing the same to Sarah Isaacs as well. So I opted to repeat the same story, that I was a PI contracted to research the family background of the late Dr Aggett.

He said the Aggetts had asked him to keep an eye on the house, and he'd seen the lights on and a strange car in the driveway. I was able to leave then, and he was none the wiser about the search I had just wrapped up.

I arrived back at the restaurant where a very drunk Whitehead was waiting for me. I reported back on what had happened and produced the bundle of letters I'd pinched. I assured him that we were in the clear but he wasn't budging, even in his inebriated state. We'd have to ensure that we hadn't been compromised, he insisted, and instructed me to go with him to Somerset West Police Station to find out whether an incident had been reported. He told me that, if necessary, we'd have to convince the local constabulary to keep quiet.

I felt that we should just get out of sight, but the inebriated Whitehead wasn't happy with this and so we ended up speaking to the relief commander and even visited the 'crime scene' before heading to a nightclub in Sea Point where Whitehead treated me to a lavish meal.

There was nothing remotely suicidal in Aggett's communications with his parents. He was a normal son. They were normal people who had raised him well. But that didn't convince Whitehead, who insisted that the letters be checked by psychiatrists – they'd be the ones who'd 'tell us what's what', he said.

He was genuinely elated by my find and launched into a discussion of my prospects in the force. He assured me his contacts would speed up my promotion. After all, his father was a brigadier and a personal friend of General Johann Coetzee, head of the SB.

Whitehead told me how the first step on the promotions ladder – from constable to sergeant – had come easy to him, and he 'sometimes felt guilty' because his father had arranged for him to write the exams a year before he was entitled to. More than that, he had taken exam papers home with him to study beforehand.

I shouldn't have been shocked. It was no secret in the force that the promotion system stank from top to bottom.

Whitehead woke me early the following morning, his eyes wide with fright. 'There's big shit!' he shook. 'The whole operation's blown and we have to be in Kotze's office immediately. The cops at Somerset West have betrayed us.'

An hour later, we were summoned into Kotze's office at Caledon Square, where police station staff had conveniently placed themselves in positions all the way down the long corridor so that they could see John Vorster Square's two 'criminals'.

Kotze stared at us in icy silence for a full minute. Then he shouted: 'Do you know what you've done? The Aggetts' neighbour reported you to the Somerset West police and they gave him your true identities. You have disgraced the whole SB and the force! How the hell did the Somerset West police know it was an SB operation?'

Kotze was raging like a bull. 'Now I've got to face all the shit!' He glared at us. 'I'm going to give you an hour to get out of my division. One hour!' He looked as though he was about to have a stroke. 'You get in your bloody car and drive straight back to Johannesburg! Now get out!'

We retreated down the passage. Here and there we noticed smirks on some of the faces of Kotze's staff. Fifteen hours later we were standing in front of Muller at John Vorster Square. Cronwright, Whitehead's section head, was present, as was Major Jan Visser, who was mine.

Cronwright was almost frothing at the mouth. Muller asked me to wait outside, not wanting a junior to witness what was sure to be an unpleasant scene between officers. However, I could hear the raised voices, and listened with interest. After a very long half-hour, Visser summoned me back into Muller's office.

'Paul, Stephen has told me the whole story. I appreciate that you both tried your best and it is very unfortunate that things have turned out this way. The General [Johann Coetzee] has been on the phone and we're in for a hard time.'

'Who told you to break into the bloody house?' hissed Cronwright as he stepped forward. But before I could reply, he told me that I was stupid and had buggered up the whole Aggett inquest. He would refuse to accept responsibility for the stuff-up.

I was astounded. For a moment, I believed he was going to throw a punch.

'I was against Erasmus going in the first place,' he thundered at everyone in the room.

Muller assumed some control. 'That will be all, thank you, Major Cronwright. This conversation is now closed.' We all left, but I returned to my office, my face burning in anger and humiliation. Moments later, Whitehead walked in.

'What the hell is going on, Steve? I'm not taking this type of insult from that little jerk. I thought he was going to take a swing at me. I didn't break into that house.'

Whitehead told me that the knives were out for both of us, and the best way to protect ourselves was to avoid any argument. We should let things cool down. Everybody was panicking, he said, and the general feeling was that the inquest was as good as lost.

How would Whitehead be able to testify at the inquest when the world knew that he had been charged along with me for breaking and entering Aggett's parents' home? That was what everyone believed.

Nonetheless, Whitehead pacified me, saying, 'We will sort it out.'

After Whitehead left, I went back to Muller's office, passing Visser in the passage.

'Listen here, Paul,' he said. 'I will be thrown out of here if you repeat what I'm telling you. Whitehead is a snake in the grass and is trying to pass all the blame on to you. He claims he specifically ordered you not to enter the house if the Aggetts weren't there.'

Whitehead did, indeed, make this statement later at the inquest.

'He says that his orders to you were just to establish whether the Aggetts were at home – not to break into the place and search it.'

When I arrived at Brigadier Muller's office, he was on the telephone. I caught snatches of the conversation and it was clear that Muller was talking to Coetzee, who would be the next National Commissioner of Police. The call ended and he told me that I could not expect him to take my side against an officer; that there were ethics involved. I, in turn, told him that I had a tape recording to prove that I didn't break in and that I felt I had had Whitehead's approval regarding how I would proceed.

'Well, Paul,' he said, 'I suggest that you hang on to it for your own sake. And one other thing – this incident is not to be discussed with anyone. Do I make myself clear?'

A week later I was informed that I would have to appear in front of Coetzee at 7 am at the SB Head Office in Pretoria. Whitehead and I spent the previous evening going over the facts and then I made a transcript of the tape I'd recorded in the Aggett home.

On the drive to the Head Office, Brigadier Muller never once referred to the inquest, chatting amicably instead about the weather, traffic and rugby. It was very different, though, when we got to the boardroom on the seventh floor. Coffee was served. I couldn't help but notice that the brigadier's hands were shaking.

Present were General Coetzee, Colonel Pieter Viljoen and Brigadier Broodryk, whose presence lifted my spirits. At least I had a friend of sorts; I had become quite popular with the garrulous Broodryk, who endlessly bragged about himself.

The general gave a brief overview of the situation. Aggett's death, he reminded us, had been the 53rd in detention. The country was under severe diplomatic pressure. South Africa could not afford another Biko affair. We had created a situation almost as bad as that, and, whatever it took, the Aggett inquest had to be conclusively won by the state.

The problem was that Whitehead, Aggett's chief interrogator, would be the key state witness and now he had been severely compromised by our blundering. What credibility would a man have when he had literally held the power of life and death over a detainee, who had died, and had then, as his interrogator, conceded to having broken into that man's aged parents' home to try to substantiate that the man in detention had suicidal tendencies?

The media would certainly go to town with this.

Whitehead had to somehow be recused from accountability for the Aggett home search, the general said. But how to do this? The ideal situation would be to have no charges brought against Whitehead and me, but this was impossible. Too many people knew about the incident: the domestic worker, the neighbour, the local police and everyone they had respectively told.

I then heard a full account of what had taken place.

The neighbour had gone to the Somerset West Police Station early the following morning and routinely reported that he had found a strange man in the Aggett home. As luck would have it, the warrant officer on duty was the same one we had encountered the previous night when Whitehead insisted we head to the station. The warrant officer told the neighbour that we were SB, and the neighbour then reported that I had threatened him with a gun. Out of fear, the domestic worker substantiated his story, adding that I had 'broken into' the house and had threatened her with a firearm too.

At this point Muller informed Coetzee that I had a tape recording that would absolve me from the allegations of breaking in, threatening people and whatever other crimes the policeman at Somerset West had decided to charge me with. Head Office had already been in contact with the Western Province, he said, and the Cape Attorney-General, Neil Rossouw, would 'make the necessary arrangements from his side'. Coetzee's attitude was that we had made a silly mistake, but the situation was not entirely lost.

For the next two or three hours the discussion centred on the major issue, which was to somehow separate the incident in Somerset West from the Aggett inquest.

I was taken into Colonel Viljoen's office where I made – or, rather, Viljoen made – a full statement as to what had happened. A story was concocted that trade unionist Gavin Andersson – whom I knew from having harassed him during my early days on the SB – was supposedly hiding out at the Aggetts' home. We, of course, all knew only too well that Andersson had left the country, but this tied up rather well with the fact (a neat coincidence) that the neighbour's surname was also Anderson – a gem that would help to muddy the waters.

By midday, we all gathered again in the boardroom.

The charges of attempted murder, house-breaking and so on were dropped by arrangement with the Cape Attorney-General, who would in turn 'prime the staff' and the presiding magistrate. Instead, a case of Illegal Search of Premises, under Section 28 (1)(b) of the Criminal Procedure Act, would be brought against me. It was to be made clear that Whitehead had not been present during the search and, although in charge, he would state that he had instructed me not to search the house, but only to establish whether Gavin Andersson was, indeed, hiding there.

The illegal search case would only come up after the inquest and no mention would be made of the fact that we had travelled across the country to find a needle when we knew there was no haystack. There was also to be no probe into how it could have been that, coincidentally, an SB policeman and a torturer, while on investigation together – which almost never happened – had randomly received information on Andersson.

That day, after all our negotiations were done, General Coetzee looked at me with his two-tone eyes (one black, one grey) across the table and asked how I felt about pleading guilty to the charge, how I felt about 'the arrangements as they stand now'.

Before I could answer, with his most charming smile he proceeded: 'You're probably worried about the trial, but I give you the reassurance that you definitely won't go to jail. We don't expect that from you. That R200 fine will, of course, be paid out of the Secret Fund. This has been arranged with the magistrate. I will further arrange that you don't receive a criminal record and neither will this incident appear on your personal record or affect your future in the force. You know, it's the chaps who are the workers who always get into a bit of trouble. In fact, this sacrifice will even help you in your career.'

We returned to John Vorster Square. I was more than relieved at the turn of events. I might even benefit from it all, I thought, but in the back of my mind lingered nagging doubts. What if I hadn't made the recording? Had Whitehead really reported that he had instructed me not to search the house? Would they still throw me to the wolves?

In preparation for the inquest, mock trials were held on the tenth floor in which Whitehead was put through the mill by his colleagues, with every possible and conceivable avenue of questioning explored and analysed. As Coetzee had said, the eyes of the world would be on South Africa with this one.

During this time, Whitehead's mood fluctuated from elation to sombre depression. I regularly went for lunch with him when he was feeling down – to cheer him up and get his mind off the forthcoming case. Discussion would, however, invariably turn to Aggett's death. He spoke about the interrogation and specifically Aggett's last hours. I felt at the time that Whitehead needed to get it off his chest. It was as if he really needed somebody to confide in.

'I never lifted a hand to him, Paul. I swear to God, I didn't. You know, the night he committed suicide, we even played music in the office while we were going over his statement.'

Whitehead told me about the Mike Oldfield song they had apparently listened to, one that Whitehead had played over and over while we were in Port Alfred.

'You know, Paul, when Neil and I parted that night I sensed that there was something wrong. I know, and could feel, that he had given up. We had really pushed him over the edge, but I swear I didn't know he was that bad – that he would kill himself. But I knew that he was broken. He confessed immediately before his death, as you know. It was like he had just fallen apart.'

I was more than aware of the effects of sleep deprivation and 62 hours of interrogation. Aggett must have been devastated, let alone depressed, after making that supposed confession. Keeping someone awake wasn't considered as assault in terms of the law then, and the SB interrogators' methods relied heavily on this. Such was our training.

But the Aggett case was not going to simply disappear like so many others. Despite General Coetzee's charm, I did become linked to the case, and not only in terms of the illegal search of the Aggett house. I heard rumours that the Aggett family and their counsel had connected me with his death too.

The story went that I was with Whitehead and Aggett on that fateful night, and that I was the bully who had tortured him while Whitehead asked the questions. I even heard that I had strangled Aggett with a wet towel.

But then, again, Whitehead soothed my concerns, suggesting that this was typical of the SB, where members sought to settle personal grudges at every turn. He said nothing had been picked up about me playing a role in the torture during the discussions between the Aggetts and their esteemed SC, George Bizos. It was important that we were aware that the SB was sparing no expense or effort.

We were in for a hard time.

The inquest started in September 1982.

Bizos was not fooled by the bullshit concocted about looking for Gavin Andersson, and even suggested that the SB had been asked by the state lawyers to gather information for a psychological report on Aggett. He claimed – correctly, of course – that this was why we had searched the house. Of course, Cronwright denied any knowledge of the incident and Peter Schabort, SC for the Minister of Law and Order, distanced himself from it too, stating that it had nothing to do with the SAP's legal representation.

As planned, the Cape Attorney-General, Neil Rossouw, waited to see what the outcome of the inquest would be. It was finalised late in December that year, absolving Whitehead (and the state) of any direct blame for Aggett's death.

After the inquest, the Aggett family apparently tried to institute a private prosecution of Whitehead, and in May 1983 Rossouw decided to prosecute Whitehead and me for an illegal search. We eventually appeared in a Somerset West court in July of that year, where the state immediately withdrew the charge against Whitehead, as arranged, and I pleaded guilty, as arranged, and was fined R200 or three months after I repeated the story about Andersson. I paid the fine, which I had drawn from the Secret Fund the previous week.

The Aggetts declared that they were disappointed that Whitehead had not been charged, Aggett's father stating that, as far as he was concerned, I had been 'merely fulfilling orders'.

Of note, there were other considerations too. Whitehead was studying law and would never have been able to practise if he had been convicted. He was an officer and his father a senior officer, close to the future commissioner. His father-in-law was deputy director of the NIS and someone Whitehead considered to be President Botha's friend.

I was irrevocably on the losing end.

General Coetzee, who did indeed become the next Police Commissioner in 1983, and who had persuaded me to take the rap, reneged on his promise. The offence appeared on my service record and, unsurprisingly, I was not promoted. All subsequent attempts at promotion also failed. It was only in 1987 that I found out what had actually transpired when I managed to lay my hands on my personnel file. Detailed there was precisely how the bastards had lied to me.

Whitehead left the force after Divisional Commissioner General L.P. 'Louwtjie' Malan, who was not afraid of anyone, told him to cut his hair or be transferred. He then went to the NIS, where his wife worked, and where he'd spend his time working on the Australia Desk. I heard later that Whitehead's 'misuse' of a junior in rank – me – was offered up on the SAP officers' course as an example of disgraceful conduct. He had left me in the lurch.

I was the patsy, and even when I could see that, I soldiered on because every moment that I felt I had actual power was a great moment for me. It was a rush – a rush that, most of the time, led to a desperate anti-climax, of me feeling that I had been let down, of being treated as less, of being made to feel as if I were inferior.

Take the case of the Afrikaner activist Berend Schuitema.

I had been in contact with Johannesburg-based business tycoon Tony Factor for about two years because he had been receiving letters addressed to him for 'forwarding to the Prime Minister of Israel'. There were about 20 in total, all unsigned, and we were unable to identify the author, who signed off simply as 'Boerseun', and 'Jou lekker ou vriend', 'Bliksem' or 'Jou eie rooi hoenderhaan'.

The content was endless verse, much of which rhymed, most of it in a mix of Afrikaans and English. It was made up of lines such as: 'Ek is 'n boer en jy is 'n moffie / Ons sit op die stoep en ons drink koffie.'

We decided that this was the work of a crank, but because some of the phraseology had an anti-South African, anti-establishment flavour, we kept an eye on it. Tony Factor – who maintained a high public profile – was also worried that the letter writer might injure him or his family. We tried unsuccessfully to lift fingerprints off the pages and sent copies to the Head Office on the off-chance that they'd picked up something similar from another area and were able to match the scripts.

One of the suspects, whose activities I had been monitoring, was Berend Schuitema, who had been involved with Afrikaner poet Breyten Breytenbach[13] and a number of Dutch anti-apartheid activists. Schuitema was part of a group of white international revolutionaries known as Okhela, which was run by the ANC, mostly from Paris.

Our information was a mixed bag of hunches, disinformation and reports, which indicated that Schuitema had been in contact with the Japanese Red Army. In May 1982, Broodryk – who had arrested Breytenbach when he had visited South Africa illegally in 1975 – asked me for a memorandum containing all our intelligence on Schuitema, as well as the letters to Factor. He arranged a meeting the following day, convinced that Schuitema was not only the author, but also the prime suspect in a bombing incident in Cape Town because he fitted a description given by a witness. That, or Broodryk needed a scapegoat for the bombing. It could well have been perpetrated by the SB -- my colleague Nannie Beyers later told me that the SB was responsible for bombings in which the blame was laid at the door of the ANC. He had participated in some of them.

With considerable difficulty, I arranged access to Schuitema's flat, which I searched illegally, removing a mass of photographs and stealing dozens of pages of Schuitema's writing. SB forensics would later show there was no link between the letters sent to Factor and the writing, but Broodryk remained convinced that Schuitema was 'dangerous'.

Schuitema had already been a victim of Stratcom disinformation, which was leaked by Broodryk and the Head Office internationally, claiming that he had sold out Breytenbach and Okhela to the SB. He had thus been discredited in Europe, where he had been part of the Dutch Anti-Apartheid Movement, and amongst the left in South Africa. It was felt that he could possibly have resorted to placing a bomb in an attempt to regain some credibility. After forensics turned up negative, Broodryk decided on a direct confrontation with Schuitema at his flat.

Smiling and confident, Broodryk told Schuitema that it was no secret in the intelligence world that he was the main suspect in the bombing, and that they knew he had done it because he wanted to win back some ground in the activist community.

After a heated argument, an enraged Schuitema kicked Broodryk's partner, Colonel Hans Gloy, in the groin. Thereafter, my instructions were to 'neutralise' Schuitema, who, Broodryk maintained, was 'on the brink of insanity'. It wouldn't take much to push him over the edge, and we could put him away for good – in an asylum or in a morgue. 'Maak 'n plan,' I was thus told – essentially, a licence to kill.

Broodryk was an egotist. He carried around with him an album with photos and press reports of his exploits with Fischer, Breytenbach and others, which, to my embarrassment, he produced and discussed at length with an unregistered source I had recruited at Schuitema's flat to help with observing his movements.

It seemed to me that Schuitema seemed somewhat unstable and so, since he was living with and being supported by his girlfriend, Louise Stack, we decided that the best way to get at him was to bring about a split between them. I visited Stack several times at work to humiliate her, openly announcing to her employers that I was from the SB. Her boss was told that she was dangerous, living with a communist suspected of terrorism.

Schuitema, who worked from the flat during the day, was also given what we called 'the basic treatment': I would knock on the door and run away, arrive at odd hours and regularly threaten him with arrest. When he went out, we'd follow him at a discreet distance and – still out of sight – call his name, or we'd enter the flat and interfere with the contents. On one occasion, I even typed the words 'Ek is mal, ek is mal, ek is mal' over and over on a sheet of paper left in his typewriter.

Broodryk was entertained by these details and phoned me every day to get updates, but Schuitema was stronger than we gave him credit for and survived the onslaught. It appeared that the SB had been dealt a losing hand on this one. I certainly wasn't going to give in to Broodryk's wildest notions and, whenever he even hinted at the possibility, I would have an excuse as to why an attempt to physically harm Schuitema hadn't been made.

It didn't help either that Louise was devoted to Schuitema. I once engaged her in conversation, and she told me, 'He's absolutely harmless, Paul. Why don't you people let him be?'

I kept quiet.

'I know what you're trying to do to him. Why? He's lost everything that he has lived for. Why don't you people just leave him alone? I won't let him do anything silly, and if he tries I'll let you know.'

There was something in her that touched a raw nerve in me, and I scaled down the onslaught, which was, in any event, becoming tedious. There was no outcome, but still Broodryk wouldn't let me stop, insisting that Schuitema would crack as long as we kept up the pressure. Broodryk said that when he finally exploded, we would be ready to finish him off.

So we kept Schuitema under 24-hour surveillance, much of which I did on my own, living and sleeping in a car while continuing with other duties in between. It was exhausting, and eventually I walked away from the assignment, although I did phone Louise from time to time.

Broodryk eventually realised that his plans weren't materialising and the calls from him stopped, but because I had followed his orders for so long, I became something of a 'glory boy' to him. He liked to summon me to the Head Office where he and Gloy were the resident trouble-shooters, specialising in driving suspects, such as ANC activist Carl Niehaus, over the edge. Niehaus was being tracked by an SB plant, Lieutenant Robert Whitecross, and as soon as Whitecross reported to the Head Office that Niehaus was sufficiently rattled, the surveillance unit pulled the same tactics we had used on Schuitema. Suspects were always distressed when we chipped away at what mattered most to them – what gave them a sense of security or protection.

Encouraging, or egging on, suicide was a tactic we favoured. I once made numerous copies of a book by assisted suicide advocate Doctor Jack Kevorkian, and sent them out to selected suspects. My appalling act nearly ended tragically when I handed a copy to a media informer who read the book and subsequently tried to kill himself.

Satanism was always a lure for us. I was tasked to watch a Romanian couple, 'Mr and Mrs Vaharshagian', who had immigrated to South Africa and set up a perfume and cosmetics business in central Johannesburg, somewhat appropriately named Cult. Our intel was that they were the high priest and priestess of satanism in South Africa and were setting up and running covens across the country.

One night I set off with two colleagues, Jorrie Jordaan and Barry Groenewald, to search their home in Northcliff, as we had heard that they were out of town. Inside the house, we found huge paintings of figures tearing limbs from a baby and grotesque monsters with snarling teeth. One empty room had a pentagram outlined on the floor and two black robes with hoods hanging in a built-in cupboard. Jordaan and Groenewald took fright and fled. I stayed, but the only other item of interest in the otherwise unadorned room was a small framed pen-and-ink sketch of a young girl, whose eyes stared straight back into mine. That's when I left.

When a WH10 piece of evidence was handed to me for investigation, I was both spooked and intrigued at the same time. Two youngsters living in Hillbrow had written to Anton LaVey, the self-proclaimed head of the Church of Satan in California, requesting membership and asking to be put in contact with LaVey's followers in South Africa.

My colleague Nannie Beyers and I put our heads together and came up with a plan. I called the applicants and, disguising my voice, told them that I was LaVey's chief representative here. I explained that 'getting involved' was not just a matter of attending a meeting or joining a coven. One had to prepare spiritually, a lengthy process through which they would be guided, step by step, by me.

The two were thrilled, and Beyers and I sensed that we had an opportunity for some sick fun ahead of us.

Our first instruction was that they had to save like mad and have finances available as 'one's commitment to the brotherhood of Satan' was also a commitment of one's material possessions, which would have to be shared with us. Applicant One had a job as an usher at a cinema and immediately started working double shifts, while Applicant Two was at college, supported by his parents.

Their first task was to write the Lord's Prayer backwards and learn it off by heart, to be tested within a week, telephonically. Applicant One passed with flying colours and had also accumulated several hundred rand, so we declared him ready for Step 2: Initiation Night, which, as any good satanist was supposed to know, involved sex. A lot of sex.

That night, at a late-night meeting in a dark alleyway, Applicant One handed over every cent he had and the following day was given instructions in respect of the sexual aspect of the initiation. We told him he'd be judged on his performance with several women, so he would have to start training. We instructed him to masturbate 50 times a day before we could prepare him for the next step. We also told him to give us silver jewellery to be 'blessed' for the initiation. And when he confessed that he had no money to buy jewellery, we instructed him to get it on account.

Applicant Two went on to pass the Lord's Prayer test with a lot of stuttering and so he too, after being relieved of a few hundred rand, was promoted to Step 2. This guy's enthusiasm was beginning to wane, though, especially after two days when he reported that he had managed to masturbate successfully only a few times.

'Keep at it!' I roared, and slammed down the receiver.

Applicant One then reported that he was experiencing problems. He said that he was exhausted, and his mother wanted to take him to the doctor because he was spending so much time in the toilet.

'We will not tolerate this weakness!' I insisted, and once again ended the call. After a week, Applicant Two gave up, crying and begging me to 'forget' about him. He no longer wanted to be involved with Satan and was going back to church.

That night, Beyers and I met Applicant One to discuss his situation. Heavily disguised and with false plates on Beyers's car, we drove around Hillbrow with the young man in the back of the vehicle, talking softly to each other and dropping phrases like 'Where are we going to dump him?', while the youngster's terror levels were rising.

He handed over several silver chains, a ring and another few rand. All of a sudden, Beyers accelerated and headed out of town, driving like a maniac with a demented look on his face.

I turned around and glared at the victim, eyes blazing.

'You've let us down, and now you're going to die!'

I produced my pistol, cocked it, and pointed it at the initiate, who started screaming.

Beyers and I laughed like maniacs, as I yelled, 'We're all going to die!'

At the Braamfontein Cemetery, just outside the city, Beyers slammed on the brakes. With my pistol in the young man's mouth, I told him that we would be watching him; that he was useless to our cause; and that we would kill him if he ever came near us again.

We dropped him off at the graveyard, terrified and shaking, and Beyers and I went to celebrate with a roast chicken at Highpoint, Hillbrow, convinced that the youngster would never go near the occult again.

Soon I sported a flashy new silver chain and Beyers's and my personal debts were paid off.

And we thought we should look elsewhere for satanists.

Chapter Twelve

The Waiter's Hell and
Other Crimes

Ovamboland, 1970s, and Johannesburg, 1983–1989

IN MAY 1983 A MASSIVE car bomb exploded at the South African Air Force headquarters in Pretoria, killing 19 people and injuring scores of others. In retaliation, an SADF strike was ordered on Maputo, Mozambique, and we were told that the attack took place some ten minutes after the prime target, Joe Slovo, had left one of the target buildings.

The sheer horror of the bomb blast in Pretoria gave rise to seething anger and demands for retribution. Physical attacks on activists increased and there was a new impetus to Omega activities in Johannesburg. But while all of this was going on, I met Linda and it was love at first sight for me. I was immediately struck by her humour, her uncomplicated, apolitical and happy-go-lucky existence, compared to my intense and fanatical approach to life. Linda and I would debate, sometimes for hours on end, issues like the word 'peace', which to me, in a political sense, was a word that concealed some diabolical communist plot.

Opposites attract and we were engaged in June and married in October 1983. I didn't know how I would ever be able to tell Linda what much of my job entailed. By that point, I was already struggling with insomnia and had developed an ulcer. I went through long periods of depression.

When I felt the time was right, I approached Colonel Olivier. I had just completed an assignment that had met with his approval, so I felt he might be more receptive to a request for a transfer, or at least a position in the SB where I could work normal office hours.

He listened to my story with obvious impatience.

'Are you unhappy here?'

'No, sir, not really. It's just that I seem to be developing something of a nervous problem.'

'Nervous problem from what?'

'Well, I think it's Ovamboland, sir.'

He reflected on this for a minute.

'I don't want people on my staff who are unhappy. I don't believe that you are overworked here. If you insist, however, I will have to consider your request. Think about things and I will talk to you about it at a later stage.'

He reached forward for a file from his in-tray, which was his manner of dismissal.

The following day he walked into our office, just as somebody had cracked a joke. Our laughter stopped instantly as he entered.

'You don't look too unhappy with life here, Erasmus,' he said, 'but when you have decided, I will arrange to send you to some small place where you won't be nervous again.'

Shortly before my wedding, I broached the subject of a promotion. Olivier was silent for a long time. I didn't know then that things were going to become very dark indeed as Cronwright was set to take over command of our section. Olivier was being promoted himself, and transferred to South West Africa, where he was to take command of the territory as the divisional commander of the SB.

Not long after he assumed office, Cronwright informed me that he knew it wasn't me who had reported him to the Head Office about the National Front meeting. He explained that there had been an NI agent on the committee. He wanted bygones to be bygones between us, and he hoped to see Omega vigorously rejuvenated.

It was clear, however, that Cronwright was an unchanged man. He harboured an obsessive hatred for particular suspects with whom he had previously dealt; among these was Dr Liz Floyd, who had been Neil Aggett's girlfriend.

When information was received that a commemoration was to be held at Aggett's grave at West Park Cemetery, and a tombstone unveiled, Cronwright instructed us to 'fuck it up'. So we headed off to the cemetery where I promptly started the day by spraying a hammer and sickle on the tombstone. We had also arranged a 'laughing bag' to be placed under the stones at the graveside.

Cronwright was ecstatic, especially when he was told that the clergyman who was conducting the service nearly collapsed when the device was activated mid-prayer.

At this point, we were at the height of our powers at the SB. Cronwright was authorising finances left, right and centre for even more dirty tricks, including the release of a mix of sneezing powder and tear gas in the Catholic cathedral on Saratoga Avenue, Johannesburg. But it didn't stop there. We also made use of catapults, from which half-inch steel ball bearings were fired, reaching the target with hardly a sound. I once used this on a crowd with raised fists on a main road, hitting a priest in the chest. Sometimes we would shoot cast lead bullets from the catapults into big groups of protestors, to create the perception that the SAP – or someone – was opening fire on them. This, naturally, caused panic, which was our desired outcome. All of this kept Cronwright happy and off our backs.

There had to be a breaking point, though, and it came after a night of drinking mampoer, when Cronwright and I argued again about the right wing and the National Front. He eventually grabbed my lapel, just like the previous time, and I was on the point of lashing out when a colleague pulled us apart.

A few days later, Cronwright phoned me at home and asked me to visit him at his house in Florida, a suburb west of Johannesburg. There, he became more and more agitated, launching into a diatribe about his dedication, how he had wrecked his family life, how the 'communist Jews' at Wits had thrown him down the stairs and broken his back, and his fears about the way things were going politically, certain that the ANC 'would one day hang him' for what he had done.

I carried a concealed recorder, and I played the tape to Linda when I got home. We carefully considered the situation. I was no longer in any doubt that I had to make a move for my own sanity.

Linda had been encouraging me for some time to make the break and resign. She was concerned about my health. I was drinking a lot; the nightmares and fear of sleep were crippling; and she was worried that I was going to end up like Cronwright – a pitiful, disturbed, lonely wreck of a human being who had wasted his life serving the SAP.

Nevertheless, Cronwright did keep his promise to me and drew up a memorandum for my promotion, but it never got any further because the Aggett search and conviction was always there – on my file, as my shadow.

Something turned in me one night when Beyers and I were called again to Cronwright's house, and found him in a blind rage, pacing up and down like a caged animal.

'The fucking station commander at Florida Police Station has been giving me a hard time. I want him killed. I don't care how you do it. Just get rid of him. Tell me what you need. He's an enemy. Kill the bastard!' Apparently the said station commander had been giving Cronwright's son, who had just become a policeman, a very hard time.

The next day, Linda and I resolved to start our own business, which she would run until we were in a better financial position for me to leave the force. I couldn't tell anyone and I didn't want to leave under a cloud, but I was in a fog, easily provoked into saying too much.

I continued with my usual investigations and received two commendations from the Head Office for reports I submitted on the End Conscription Campaign and the Conscientious Objector Support Group. These included photographs of suspects, their IDs and transcripts.

Yet, there was no challenge left. I'd had enough, as I'd had before, and more than once before that.

The watershed moment finally came in 1984, when one of my seniors called me to the Head Office to discuss some artwork that was needed to counter community action in the townships. I agreed to do some designs and submitted a portfolio of about 15 images a few days later. I was asked to do some colour separations quickly and was given R50 for the necessary materials. Roughly 250 000 pamphlets were printed and distributed by the SB and the SADF throughout the country, and this campaign was so successful that Head Office asked whether I was prepared to be transferred to Pretoria, where I would become the in-house artist for Stratcom.

They weren't pleased when I refused, but I was determined not to become embroiled in another dirty tricks campaign again, especially now that Linda and I were planning for me to leave the service.

Destiny being what it is, a golden Stratcom situation then unfolded. Out of the blue, the SB at John Vorster Square picked up that Dr Allan Boesak, a Dutch Reformed Mission Church cleric and anti-apartheid activist – someone we considered an enemy – was regularly visiting Johannesburg and conducting a relationship with an SACC staff member. A team under Captain E.P. van Wyngaardt began monitoring them.

Here was an opportunity like no other to neutralise a particular threat, either by exposing him as an adulterer – Boesak was married – or blackmailing him into stopping his anti-apartheid activities or, the ultimate prize, persuading him to work for the SB as an informer.

Put on the alert, we secured adjoining rooms to Boesak's on his next visit and bugged his room. Our first few attempts at obtaining a recording failed because of unexpected technical problems with the equipment. We then drilled a hole through the wall and inserted a mini-camera lens with fish-eye capability into it. Finally, we had the evidence we needed.

Of course we leaked the information to the media. But Boesak was ahead of the game, as he announced his separation from his wife. The SB's opportunity to blackmail or influence him was thus lost.

This was February 1985, and MP Frank le Roux of the Conservative Party couldn't resist asking the Minister of Law and Order, Louis le Grange, and Minister of Justice, Kobie Coetsee, whether Boesak would be charged under the Immorality Act – the legislation that made sex between black and white people a criminal offence. This, after Le Grange had told Parliament that the SB had 'discovered' the relationship between Boesak and his girlfriend 'during the normal course of its duties'.

No instructions to prosecute were, however, given.

This all proved a welcome distraction for me because by now Linda was pregnant, I was building on at our house and there was talk that Cronwright was soon to retire. I was the only member of the SB invited to his wedding – I think it was his third marriage – where he treated Linda and me like royalty. This was the first time that Linda met Cronwright, and she found it tough to accept that he was the monster who had cast such darkness over much of my career. She even had tears in her eyes during the intimate ceremony.

Cronwright did indeed retire soon after this, and his replacement was an accomplished young captain, Alfred Oosthuizen, formerly SB branch commander in Grahamstown, whom I had met with Whitehead during the Aggett search debacle. Oosthuizen's reputation preceded him. We heard again of how he had virtually run the student political infrastructure at Rhodes University.

There was double trouble on the way for us, though, as the Eastern Cape divisional commander, Colonel (later General) G.N. 'Sterk Gert' Erasmus, a strict disciplinarian with a fearsome reputation, was to become our commanding officer.

The 'terrible twins', Erasmus and Oosthuizen, had been deliberately moved to Johannesburg, where our intelligence-gathering capability was regarded by Head Office as all but non-existent at that stage. Their job was to steer our show back on the road.

None of this was of much concern to me, however, because Linda's business was showing outstanding potential and we believed that, if our expectations materialised, I would be able to resign within the following six months.

However, Oosthuizen – Oosie or the Guru, as we called him – was not fooling around. He instantly demanded all source files, and SB members were called in one by one to discuss their informers, their handling of these agents and their management skills. Those sources that didn't meet with Oosie's approval were summarily scrapped from our lists, and a stream of instructions was issued on those that remained.

'Ag, Johannesburg will soon break this *plaaspolisieman* in,' quipped one of our disgruntled section officers, unfortunately within earshot of Oosie. Within a week, the man had been transferred from John Vorster Square to Soweto.

Then came the organisation's files. For days, there were mountains of the ubiquitous brown government-issue folders on the Guru's desk. Every morning, there would be a meeting of the entire staff and Oosie would turn up the heat, exhorting us to intensify a recruitment drive of agents in the primary target organisations. He also asked each of us about our vision for our own career prospects.

As he got rid of staff members, they were replaced with mostly younger policemen and women, interviewed and selected by Oosie himself. He intended to train and oversee their jobs himself, determined to work only with people who had not been 'tainted' by the rot that had set in at John Vorster Square over the years under Cronwright, Olivier and Mahoney.

Oosie laid down the rules concerning Omega too. Its activities, and even the use of its name, were to cease with immediate effect. His argument was, 'no name, no blame'. Give it a name, he said, and our enemies would be able to investigate it. In future, all Omega activities were to be conducted with Oosie's knowledge and were to be carefully planned and executed.

Among the few survivors of the purge were Beyers and I, so we continued with our prime task, which at that time was the investigation of church matters. Oosie initially showed disdain for our efforts, especially when we shifted our attention to the United Democratic Front (UDF) and its many affiliates, but he nevertheless pumped us up and allowed us some resources.

Things got busy when Anton Lubowski of SWAPO visited Johannesburg and we put a 24-hour surveillance team on his tail. Lubowski would be gunned down in front of his home in Windhoek in 1989, probably by agents from MI's Civil Cooperation Bureau (CCB). In the ensuing political debacle following his death, Defence Minister General Magnus Malan stated in Parliament that Lubowski was a 'paid agent of MI'. But if Lubowski was ever employed by MI, the SB certainly didn't know about it. He was given 'the works' by us, with full monitoring of his activities: we searched his luggage, I followed him intensely and photographed him. We sent reports immediately to the Head

Office and other SB divisions. We would not have done this if he was an agent.

Even as the Lubowski episode and other events under Oosie were creating excitement among operatives at John Vorster Square, Linda's business as a polystyrene display provider was going from strength to strength. In May, heavily pregnant, she hired premises to start operating full-time. We even entered into negotiations with the Johannesburg City Council – which was planning celebrations for the city's centenary in 1986 – for the franchise for all polystyrene products on which the centenary emblem appeared.

Then the government declared the first State of Emergency on 20 July 1985, initially covering the Eastern Cape and the Pretoria-Witwatersrand-Vaal area, but expanded to the Western Cape a few months later. SADF troops were poured into the townships, where demonstrations and violent resistance were escalating. Most were conscripts hardly trained to counter anything offered by the ANC and its surrogate organisation, the United Democratic Front (UDF). The UDF's strategy was to make the country ungovernable. Revolutionary elements succeeded in establishing so-called liberated zones.

Suddenly there was much more to contend with in the SB sphere.

Our daughter Candice was born in July, and I worried about spending more time at home while other members of the SB were working longer hours with regular patrols and extra duties. Oosie started giving me pep talks that were little more than veiled threats about being transferred, as I was not shaping up to his high standards.

He then divided the staff, which had expanded considerably, into several new sections, with Beyers and me falling under the command of Lieutenant Michael Bellinghan, a suave, calculating, ruthlessly ambitious cop, studying for his degree in psychology. He later introduced psychometric testing into the SB.

Bellinghan's professional rival at John Vorster Square was Gordon Brookbanks. Although they were friends, they were skilfully steered by Oosie into competition, their individual sections being played off against each other. This eventually became a hard race where one had to outperform the other.

The success of this manipulation became obvious when we began to register new sources and agents on an unprecedented scale. Oosie, however, was adamant that our intel be qualitative rather than quantitative. He manipulated ordinary members too, placing individuals like Beyers and me in competition with each other on who was more dedicated, and who had more sources.

That Nannie Beyers was a better policeman was not an issue for me. He simply was. He had been transferred to John Vorster Square after being stationed at a one-person police post in Opuwo, South West Africa, where he and his wife Annatjie had lived a quiet life, miles from anywhere, sharing a love of wildlife and the desert.

When the SADF moved into the area in numbers in the mid-to-late 1970s, Beyers, being the one and only security policeman in the area, came under pressure. From day one of its encampment, the SADF invited Beyers, being the only policeman covering this huge area, to join senior military officers at braais, where the liquor flowed like water. Beyers, though, was never a drinker and, at some point on one of these social occasions, he was approached by one of the waiters, a national serviceman.

Curious, the young soldier asked why Beyers was wearing a different uniform. Beyers could tell that the youngster was anxious, and asked if there was a problem. Beyers explained that he was a policeman and so didn't fall under the SADF or its rules.

The conscript then told Nannie that he was gay and, in an emotional state, confided that he had been raped and brutalised by senior officers and civilians linked to the military. He said this had happened to many other gay conscripts and those deemed effeminate. The attacks had apparently been an ongoing nightmare from the start of his national service.

Fearless as always, Beyers went back to his SAP post that night and opened a docket for the assault, following this up the next day by going to the military base where he took statements under oath from several servicemen. Some revealed sexual assaults so shocking that Beyers told me he felt ill when he took down their words.

According to Beyers, some of the young men claimed to have been tied up and hung upside down and then, helpless, raped. Some believed they could identify their attackers. They said others who assaulted them were only on the base for short periods and were clearly civilians.

Later, when Dylan was an adult, I shared this with him. He had come to know Beyers as my loyal friend and fellow traveller, and it helped to explain to Dylan what we were doing when we were the same age as he was. I was grateful, then, that my son was a free man.

Earlier in my life, I didn't believe people were born violent; we were not animals whose predatorial instincts were there from the start. But, as time went on and the longer I was in the force, I realised what I myself might be capable of doing if pushed, and I changed my mind. We were, indeed, capable of the most horrific violence.

There were other events on the border to which Beyers was privy, including servicemen having to pack trunks of ivory ripped from elephants that had been killed by machine guns fired out of South African Air Force helicopter gunships.

Perhaps it shouldn't have been so, but the story that made the headlines in the 1970s was not the one of the sexual abuse and violence towards conscripts. It was the elephants. The media at the time alleged that senior politicians, MI and police were involved in the wholesale killing of elephants. Horrified by these deaths, Beyers had faithfully committed that to paper too.

One day, a vehicle pulled up outside the SAP post and a very drunk General Lothar Neethling, Chief Deputy Commissioner of the SAP, stormed into Beyers's house and demanded fresh meat, biltong, alcohol – and the dockets relating to both the rapes and the elephants. Beyers did not cooperate. Neethling, who was later to head the SAP forensic science department and earn notoriety as the go-to man for poisons to be used against activists and enemies of the state, stood up to Beyers's defiance. A furious exchange took place, during which Beyers told Neethling to get out of his house or he would open fire.

Beyers's next visitor, a few days later, was Colonel Ogies Viljoen, who had been sent from the SB Head Office to sort out this upstart sergeant. Once again, Beyers refused to comply with the order to close the cases, even when Viljoen told Beyers he was 'destroying SAP–SADF relations' and could, in fact, pose a serious threat to the good name of the SADF. He said Beyers had no right to 'interfere' in what were internal matters – matters that should be dealt with by the Military Police.

Beyers stayed on for a while, determined to stick to his guns, contending that he had taken an oath that superseded any other considerations. He refused to be bullied by anyone to close the dockets, to get rid of evidence or 'forget about what happened'. The threats, however, became impossible, relentless and more ruthless. Eventually, Beyers was compelled to accept a transfer to John Vorster Square, where he was overlooked time and again for promotion.

Nannie disobeyed direct orders from an SAP general to throw hand grenades at Uniformed SAP Radio Branch members – another example of the many false flag orders we were given. In another incident, Nannie and I were ordered to kill an SAP station commander. It was Nannie who took the initiative and refused this order, as the officer issuing the instruction was drunk and we ignored the obvious lunacy of the command.

Beyers is dead now, lost to the PTSD and depression that took him to his early grave. Like me and many others in the SB, he had reached saturation point, unable to contain in himself the numerous crimes and cruelties that we perpetrated on behalf of apartheid.

Beyers told me about the attacks on the gay soldiers years later when it was revealed that the SADF was running what it termed the Aversion Project, headed by Dr Aubrey Levin. The project identified gay conscripts and, in order to have their homosexuality 'cured', submitted them to 'treatment', including electric shocks. The project was also linked to some 900 gender reassignments in the 1970s and 1980s, which were performed under top-secret conditions at 1 Military Hospital in Voortrekkerhoogte. Levin was finally convicted of sexual assault in Canada, to which he had emigrated when apartheid ended. He was a professor of clinical psychiatry at the University of Calgary until 2010 when his licence to practise was suspended by the authorities there.

Even the slightest suggestion of a man being gay was an effective denunciation. When Arthur McGiven, a BOSS operative, defected to Britain in 1978, one of the damage-control measures that the SB used to discredit him was to point out that he was gay. The Little Hitlerites on the tenth floor spread the same story about me – a classic case of smearing a person in a strongly homophobic South Africa.

The McGiven case was an example of the SB's own machinery being used against a member of its own system. As McGiven had worked among us, we were instructed to use every available contact and the media to spread the story, not only of his 'perverted' sexuality, but also that he was 'never trusted by BOSS' and they were 'going to kick him out anyway'. To the best of my knowledge, however, the only intelligence McGiven revealed was Helen Suzman's 'S' number – her SB Head Office file number. The indomitable Suzman then, in Parliament, asked the Minister of Police not only about the existence of the file, but also whether he would let her have a look at it herself.

The SB had, however, been using WH10 to intercept correspondence from McGiven to his parents in Johannesburg's northern suburbs, and I was responsible for evaluating the material collected, looking specifically for anything that could be used to further discredit him. Although I never did uncover anything incriminating, part of the plan was to pass information to the *Rand Daily Mail* subeditor and SB source, John Horak (later a colonel based at the Head Office), whose handler was my subsection head, Lieutenant Koos Venter.

I expected to be able to resign early in 1986 as Linda's projected earnings for the first quarter of 1986 were realistically estimated at R300 000. My resolve to leave the force was further strengthened by rumours circulating that open violence was surging in the country.

In June 1985, activists Matthew Goniwe, Sparrow Mkhonto, Fort Calata and Sicelo Mhlauli had been killed by SB members in a joint SB–MI operation in the Eastern Cape. Then Victoria Mxenge, wife of human rights lawyer Griffiths Mxenge, was murdered on 1 August 1985, around the same time that activists Brian Mazibuko and Toto Dweba were killed, Mazibuko on the East Rand and Dweba in Natal. Many others mentioned in intelligence reports were also murdered.

This increasingly bloody atmosphere was affecting us foot soldiers at John Vorster Square, no longer sure that we wouldn't one day be drawn into the killing squads, particularly now that the government was more and more determined to crush the unrest by whatever means possible. We were told that we were involved in a life-and-death struggle, and that the country was teetering on the brink of disaster. All I could think about at that time was getting out of there. But this wasn't to be.

In September 1985, Linda and I had a major setback when our house was burgled for a second time and we were left with only the clothes we were wearing. We were not insured and now had huge commitments to settle around her business, with no money to cover these.

It was ironic that I was then privy to an intelligence report that the Community Support Committee (COSCO) – which fell under the auspices of COSATU – planned to boycott the Johannesburg centenary celebrations, stating that the city 'having been built on the blood, sweat and tears' of black people was not to be celebrated. As a result, in fear of labour action, big capital immediately pulled out of the big event, and Linda and I, having so much invested in the occasion, decided to quickly put the business and the franchise on the market. We sold at a financial loss shortly before the Johannesburg centenary celebrations collapsed completely.

Nonetheless, I had already made the error of smugly telling Oosie that I intended to resign, so with all our financial troubles descending on us, I had to do a hasty turnabout. Were it not for Stratcom becoming more important and powerful, and my artistic skills, I might well have lost my job.

Stratcom concepts and activities were already being put into practice at divisional and branch level 'to provide an effective utilisation of intelligence gathered in terms of and accordance with our line function', the direction of which was contained in the Preservation of the Internal Security of the Republic (Section 5 of the Police Act). So it was that I settled down to make my contribution to this, finding that Head Office was rather fond of my forgery skills.

Easy pickings were individuals such as a senior bishop within the SACC, who was sent a letter by his lover in South West Africa, the envelope also containing a photograph of their child. I was given the original by Oosie and Bellinghan in order to blackmail him.

Pretending to be a PI who had stumbled on his situation, I threatened to expose him and sell the information to the government or make it available to his colleagues in the SACC. After protracted negotiations, the bishop coughed up R1 000, which he wrapped in newspaper and, according to my instructions, left in a telephone booth in Plein Street, Johannesburg.

Bellinghan and I shared the spoils with Oosthuizen and a junior SB member, but subsequent attempts to squeeze more money or information from the bishop were shelved when he slyly demanded to see the evidence we had, which we obviously couldn't produce. The top-secret WH10 activities would have been compromised.

We followed up the success of this venture with other simple, even ridiculous, ploys to syphon cash from the unsuspecting. A popular tactic was to arrange a meeting with a member of a monitored organisation and, if the target agreed, hand them a large sum of money while they were photographed from a distance. Meanwhile, they would be surreptitiously encouraged to laugh at jokes told intentionally for the camera. At best the photos could be used for extortion and, if this didn't work, could be sent to an organisation to try to generate suspicion – or so we hoped.

In one instance, after handing cash to a junior SACC staff member, whom we believed we had lured into our trap, we were astonished to find that he had no understanding of the concept of blackmail. He was just delighted to see such good photos of himself. At least, that's what we thought. He had, in fact, seen straight through the set-up.

And so, because we had failed so dismally, we headed off to Khotso House, the SACC head office, and displayed the photos for all and sundry. But even that had little effect. The SACC staffers knew exactly who we were and where we were from, and our egos were further deflated when they simply laughed at the pictures. It was humiliating.

Stratcom tactics were key in the far more serious Chris Ball affair, which erupted in 1986.

Ball, the managing director of Barclays Bank, had already had the security cluster and the President foaming at the mouth after he'd organised the first visit by major white South African businessmen to the ANC in exile the previous year. But we were to take that one step further.

Ball had apparently advanced money for a UDF advert marking the seventieth anniversary of the ANC that appeared in a number of newspapers. He immediately garnered the ire of P.W. Botha, who accused Ball directly of paying for the advertisement and thereby furthering the aims of a banned organisation. It quickly emerged that Ball had established contact with Winnie Mandela – a golden opportunity for us in Stratcom to exploit.

For days, we made hundreds of calls to senior Barclays personnel and the media, pretending to be irate investors threatening to withdraw support from 'the communist bank' and demanding that Ball be replaced. This, naturally, fanned the fire of a major confrontation between Ball, the government and the Barclays hierarchy – one that was further exacerbated by the suggestion of a link between Ball and Winnie Mandela. We couldn't resist hammering on Ball's association with Winnie, spreading the word through the establishment that the two were having an affair and that Ball was handing her money on a regular basis.

Our efforts included spray-painting slogans like 'Winnie digs Chris's Ball' at strategic spots in Johannesburg, and rumours of Ball and Winnie Mandela having an illicit affair began to surface in the press. There was a bonus in this for the SB, as this cost Winnie some credibility within the UDF, and thus within the ANC.

Ball eventually resigned under tremendous pressure, and we regarded the entire episode as a significant victory. We felt that other businesses would now be more reluctant to venture support for the ANC.

By this time, WH10 was tampering with thousands of documents, feeding them into the ever-hungry jaws of the many industrial-sized paper shredders. This wasn't new; for example, letters to Botha calling for the release of Mandela or displaying any other anti-South African sentiment had always been summarily destroyed. I once saw a consignment of thousands of Christmas cards, written by Norwegian children to Nelson Mandela, being destroyed. It was one of the rare times when I was saddened – each one had a hand-drawn picture and a Christian message from a child who sincerely believed that Mandela would receive and get to read their message.

We did whatever we liked. We could get away with anything as long as it could be justified as serving our line function: the destruction of the ANC–SACP threat to our country.

WH11 – phone and wire tapping – housed on the tenth floor at John Vorster Square, didn't find its task as straightforward, particularly as it was dealing with its own internal problems. One of its staffers, an elderly warrant officer, faithfully reported for duty every Saturday morning and was admired for his dedication until it was revealed that he was overseeing a little scam: he collected illegal inside information by phone tapping, which he then forwarded to the country's top racehorse trainers, who would otherwise have betted on their own horses. Once again, the matter was 'handled internally' and the cop involved was immediately discharged, with the threat of death.

These, though, were no more than sideshows.

The big news was the infiltration of the ANC's Special Operations units into South Africa. These were not ill-prepared 'terrorists' issued with limpet mines, some of whom had been known to blow themselves up after a brief training period. These were well-trained and highly motivated individuals.

Things got going quite quickly on this front after a white woman placed a bomb at the Cambridge Police Station in East London in February 1986. The SBs throughout South Africa were supplied with intel after the name Marion Monica Sparg surfaced from the files. Sparg was an ANC supporter who, we believed, had left the country some years before.

Shortly after the Cambridge bombing, a second bomb exploded in the ladies' cloakroom at John Vorster Square, scaring the hell out of the divisional commander of police for the Witwatersrand, who was blown off a toilet in the adjoining men's lavatories.

Sparg's family was placed on WH11, which noted that after the bombing they had received calls from a public phone booth in Hillbrow. A section under Captain 'Wynie' van Wyngaardt was given the near-impossible task of trying to find Sparg in that high-density area, and at first we were not overly optimistic.

For two days we pounded the pavements, interviewing one caretaker after another. Our feet were sore and our spirits low. Our search parameters were exceptionally wide: recent occupancy by a white woman. All we had was Sparg's photo from our 'terrorist album', a collection of photos of people whom we knew were, or whom we suspected of being, in anti-apartheid structures. Finally, at one of the many blocks of flats we visited, a caretaker reported that a white woman had taken up occupancy during the period we were looking at. She had signed the register, although the caretaker pointed out that her spoken name didn't seem to match her written one. The description we had of her didn't quite match his either, but Sparg had since peroxided her hair. At first, our bosses were reluctant to act on the tip, but I persuaded them that we should at least take a look at the flat.

The place was untidy, and we proceeded with a very hasty search. Before opening the only built-in cupboard, I noticed a hair taped between the opening of the two doors, an espionage trick as old as the hills, designed to gauge whether anyone has searched the premises. Inside the cupboard was a blue kitbag, and the instant I slipped my hand inside I felt the cold steel of limpet mines.

We replaced everything, carefully matching up the hair and the sticky tape, and left, 'Wynie' relaying messages to all and sundry on the way back to John Vorster Square.

At a staff meeting later that afternoon, Colonel Erasmus gave me what he suggested was the 'honour and privilege' of making the actual arrest, which I carried out with Sergeant Elise Pretorius (whose husband was later killed in a shootout with Winnie Mandela's bodyguards).

Other information received was that Sparg may have been accompanied by one Arnold Geyer, an 'international terrorist' regarded as extremely dangerous, as he was rumoured to have operated with the notorious Italian Red Brigade.

Oosthuizen interrogated Sparg in the flat immediately after the arrest and within the hour she revealed that there was another bomb in the toilet just behind the charge office at Hillbrow Police Station, which had not detonated. We relocated to Hillbrow SAP just down the road and disarmed the device in the courtyard.

For the next few days I sat quietly in my office writing a lengthy statement for the Investigation Branch, expecting to appear in court on a cut-and-dried case of terrorism. The state, however, decided that an officer's evidence would carry more credibility in court, so the statements were altered to show that Lieutenant Charles Zeelie had been the arresting officer.

In the follow-up to Sparg's capture, several other suspects were held and I was seconded to interrogation duties, interviewing her accomplices Stephen Marais and Rocklyn 'Rocky' Williams (he went on to become a colonel in the new South African National Defence Force).

Marais particularly was on the receiving end of the wrath of elements within the Investigation Branch. Here was a born-and-bred Afrikaner who had turned on the *volk*.

I was to make sure, demanded chief investigator Colonel A. van Niekerk – and damn sure, at that – that Marais was not going to become another Aggett, so I ignored the usual third-degree methods and round-the-clock interrogations, and simply set out to win his cooperation.

All we required now was his own confession. But with no Radio Moscow at my disposal, I was left with very few options, so I simply demanded a statement from him, handed him a pen and paper, and instructed him to write it over two or three days. Then I would read it and tear it up – after photocopying it without him knowing, of course.

The first statement was three or four pages. I read it, copied it and tore it up in front of him. The second was a little longer, but the same procedure followed. And so it went on until, after several weeks of this demoralising treatment, Stephen was writing 30 or 40 pages, which I then analysed, photocopied and tore up. His final statement was something like 90 pages.

Meanwhile, the SB in East London was insisting that Sparg's case be handled by them, since the Cambridge Police Station had been her first target, and they had identified the suspect. But Colonel Erasmus would have none of it.

Rocky Williams's interrogation, however, posed a different kind of problem. He was difficult from the start and the evidence we had was not quite as solid as was the case with Sparg and Marais. The statement ploy didn't work, because Williams's moods alternated between extraordinary highs, when he was highly communicative and we could discuss a wide variety of matters, and periods of spiralling depression and recalcitrance. We were hard pressed to produce results, but my fellow interrogator, a young sergeant, and I came up with a strategy to break him. We went down to the cells, which were specially prepared with video monitors, Perspex shields over the bars and other measures introduced to prevent suicides. There I asked Williams when he was going to talk, but before he could answer, I slapped him across his face so hard that he stumbled back against the wall. Without further ado, we returned him to his cell. That afternoon, we were notified that we were to be charged with assault, and the sergeant and I reported to Brigadier Quartus Grobler of the Detective Branch.

'What you do now', he told us, 'is you go down at the same time tomorrow, take him out of the cell and hit him again. Repeat the performance exactly. Do it at the same time and repeat exactly what you did the day before.'

The logic was simple: nobody in their right minds would believe that after being charged with assault on one day, we would be so stupid as to re-enact the assault the very next day, and the next and the next.

'If he charges you again, we just keep repeating the performance. If he keeps charging you, it will look like he's trying to discredit you.'

The next day, the sergeant and I were back at the cells.

'So ... you've laid a charge, Rocky?'

'Yes. I'm not taking any shit from you guys.'

The sergeant, a powerful chap, brought his hand down against the side of Williams's face with such force that it sounded like an explosion.

'Now charge us again, Rocky. Please do. We'll welcome it. In fact, here's the paper for your statement.'

We left, watching Williams for a while on the monitor, sitting with his head in his hands, apparently helpless and defeated. On the way back to the tenth floor, we stopped at Grobler's office where he simply instructed us to keep it up.

The following morning at the same time, and after another slap, we left Williams in tears. As expected, he eventually withdrew the first charge against us, and we went and thanked the brigadier.

We were later withdrawn from the case by Oosie, who felt that time was being wasted and that the Investigation Branch could carry on without us. As disconnected from my actions as I was, I parted on what I felt were amicable terms with Williams and Marais, who assured me that it wouldn't be long before they would be out of jail and living in a democratic South Africa.

I laughed. That will be the day hell freezes over. I promised Rocky that if it ever came about, I would pay for the drinks.

I knew how to scare people. I still do – as when I'm on my motorbike and if Dylan and I run into the right-wing guys in town. Fear came from my father. He was a vicious and aggressive person, who terrorised me. Maybe that came from his time in World War II, about which he never spoke. Because I was the youngest I was easy pickings. Getting dressed after a bath, he'd come in and lock the door and brutalise me. My mum, intelligent, a speed reader and an alcoholic, took many blows from my father. He beat the hell out of her, and she often took the blows for me. My mum, who wanted me to have an art career, died the week I started in the SB. The beatings carried on until I was 14. One day I was making a model ship at home and my sister knocked it over. She and I had an argument, and I got clouted by my father. He pushed me back into the sunken lounge and continued hitting me, punching my arms. I was a skinny guy, but I managed to punch him and he fell backwards over a coffee table. I broke his nose. I knew what terror was before I joined the police force.

So when it came to interrogations, slapping, I was made to be able to do something like that. I was sadistic and I could lose my temper. I couldn't do waterboarding, however, and I kept that from my colleagues – I didn't want them to see that it repelled me. In Ovamboland, nevertheless, there were no holds barred with torture. And the translators were bloodthirsty too. One of our translators, Johannes, was always smiling and singing 'London Bridge' and, caught in the middle of this awful war, egged us on, encouraging ever more cruel dimensions to the torture.

Back in South Africa, the country had changed a lot after 1976. We knew that the population was scared of us and it was a great power trip knowing people were so frightened of me. I enjoyed it. I bought dark glasses and loved big cars. Once I had a Ford Fairlane 500 in which I raced around Johannesburg. We at the SB had the chief public prosecutor in our back pocket and had no difficulty getting problems quashed. For friends too. We got away with so much: we could even organise firearms and dish out ammo. We knew that we were licensed to kill.

And so we went back to our recruitment drive, now including white matriculants who had been identified by teachers, headteachers or trusted people in the community. They were given the option of joining the SAP and having all their studies, medical bills and costs paid. That's if they went to university where they would, of course, act as informers or participate in Stratcom operations on campus.

But then came the spiral downwards. We could feel it. It was relatively slow initially, but undoubtedly there. To some extent, it became more evident when we were summoned to the Head Office to give evidence before the De Witt Commission enquiring into the treatment of police officers. We were told that we could speak freely, criticise, say what we wanted and, unbelievably, whatever we said would not be held against us.

It was a fiasco. We were an embittered force, and even when we were on high-level actions such as Operation Jonas – in which the SB 'hijacked' local control of the Pan African News Agency (PANA) and infiltrated the South African Coordinating Development Council (SADC) – or on Operations Olivetti and Golfball, which were spin-offs for the handlers of agents Odile Harington (who was arrested and tortured in Zimbabwe) and Olivia Forsyth (who was exposed as an agent by the ANC and who ended up in its Quatro camp in Angola where she was tortured), we were running on empty.

At this juncture, we were unable to connect with the emotions of the likes of Forsyth, who in private meetings with the SB recounted a few of her experiences at the hands of the ANC. We heard separately that she had been raped, starved and brutalised, but we were not open to bringing her to the point at which she could talk properly about these traumas. Instead, she was paraded before all the major SB units around the country by Colonel Victor McPherson, then deputy commander of Stratcom, as a 'morale-boosting' exercise. There was no meaning in it at all. Forsyth was little more than a shell. Yes, she hated the ANC. Didn't we all? But what had really happened there? What had got her to the point at which she was psychologically and emotionally destroyed at Quatro?

We white security forces were raised to be 'men', to stand up to torture, but when I came face to face with Forsyth's vulnerability and fragility, I realised that I too would have spilled the beans about everything I knew had they brought a spider near me.

At this time, the government was staging brutal SADF raids into neighbouring Zambia, Zimbabwe and Botswana, and the securocrats were ensuring that the military option took preference over diplomatic initiatives. Hearts and minds – psych ops or Stratcom – was thus hit and miss. Then government reimposed the State of Emergency on 12 June 1986, adding ever-more extensive and arbitrary powers of arrest to the security forces. On the night the Emergency was declared, Johannesburg felt like a ghost town.

At Highpoint in Hillbrow, a lone drunk, spotting a group of us heavily armed policemen, shouted, 'The boere have taken charge! The boere have taken charge!'

Emergency regulations superseded all existing laws, so in cases where we couldn't easily gain entry to premises to effect an arrest, we would simply kick the door down, often first spraying tear gas through the keyhole or tossing a grenade through a window.

We firebombed premises rented by the organisations we were monitoring. We hit the homes of suspects. This was like the old days with Omega, but we were much better assisted this time around by Emergency regulations, which had effectively gagged the media – to the extent that even the use of certain words or phrases such as the 'apartheid regime', 'white minority regime', 'riot-torn' and 'draconian' was forbidden. We were thus swift to confiscate newspapers that flouted the restrictions, the most common culprits being the *Weekly Mail* and the *Sowetan*.

We even arrested and detained some of our own agents, the plan being to heighten their credibility. False sources and agents' files containing the names of suspects were left lying on desks, open to be read by other suspects who had been detained and were being processed in that particular office at that time.

Another ploy was to drop the name of an agent in the presence of arrested suspects and receive what then appeared to be a tongue-lashing from a superior, who just happened to be present, or to leave a receipt for payment of source fees within reach of a detainee. In many instances, the signatures on those receipts were my forgeries.

When the enthusiasm of a source waned, which was frequent, we'd smooth things over with lectures and exhortations and the odd threat – or gifts, or financial assistance for a car and a trip overseas. Almost no one was willingly linked to the SB without incentives. There was seldom any actual ideological buy-in.

In April 1987, Dylan made his momentous arrival. After a normal confinement and delivery, he was shown to have been born deaf. Fortunately, surgery could restore his hearing, but he was then diagnosed with mild cerebral palsy – most likely due to being completely deaf for the first seven months of his life.

So began a nightmare of consultations and incorrect diagnoses. At the time, I was studying for the SAP exams. I, considering the circumstances, applied for an extension, only to be informed that my family situation was 'no excuse'. So I got drunk, took my lecture notes and study material, tore everything up and burnt it all in a braai drum.

As the flames grew, I cried out of rage, frustration and remorse about wasted time and my wasted life. I was then given a back-dated promotion to warrant officer, but still every event was set against a backdrop of violence. Such was my existence at the time.

On the announcement of my promotion, a function was held at a safe house in Honeydew, which turned out to be something of a double celebration because Mozambique's president, Samora Machel, had been killed in a plane crash the day before. We all ended up singing, 'When the plane hits the ground and there's k-----rs all around, it's Samora,' to the tune of Dean Martin's 'That's Amore'.

In the ensuing Margo Commission of Inquiry, the regime was cleared of complicity in the crash, although it was most likely the work of MI.

There were so many deaths and disappearances at that time that even we sometimes lost track. Some deaths, like that of the activist Stanza Bopape, stood out more than others.

An excellent NGO source, 'Alice', was troubled by rumours that Bopape had been murdered by the SB. The Black Sash and other organisations created negative publicity for us by asking probing questions and sticking up posters asking 'Where Is Stanza?' all around Johannesburg. I defended the state to the hilt. I had genuinely never heard of Bopape and managed to convince a distraught Alice that this was yet another attempt by the vicious left-wing propaganda machine to discredit the authorities. I asked her, 'Do we, or do I, look like murderers?'

I don't think I knew myself.

Meanwhile, we continued our reign of destruction and terror.

On 23 April 1987, after a shooting incident involving members of the Riot Unit, Cosatu House was raided by a throng of policemen who, having secured the building, handed it over to the SB. What followed was a demolition job, the likes of which were unprecedented and unparalleled. It was as if the accumulated rage and frustration of the police, caught as usual in the middle of the ongoing political conflict, were vented on the building and its contents.

I was placed in charge of the basement and ground floor – I use the words 'in charge' advisedly, as there was no control whatsoever. The Uniform Branch and the SB from surrounding areas soon arrived to join the fray – the whole system seemed determined to destroy COSATU.

Doors were promptly closed, and then filing cabinets filled with documents and records rained down like confetti from the balconies of the ten-storey building, office equipment was smashed, PCs were tossed out of the windows and over the balconies into the courtyard, video monitors and an extensive security system were destroyed, and what wasn't smashed or broken was stolen.

When we started the raid, the operation was surreptitious, but by the end we were brazen. SB members carted heaps of documents, stationery, office equipment and COSATU tracksuits, T-shirts and caps into my domain on the ground floor and then into waiting vehicles.

A uniformed policeman asked if he could have a tracksuit.

'Help yourself, mate,' I laughed. 'There's plenty!'

My personal haul included a car full of tracksuits, caps, T-shirts, a sack of wrapped Christmas presents (which came in handy at the end of the year), calculators, clocks and the *pièce de résistance* – the personal telephone of Jay Naidoo,[14] an expensive imported model that I used for many years. I found COSATU's printing machine in the basement and smashed the plates and control panel. Some hours later I returned to the basement to find that the machine had been completely destroyed, and cars in the basement had likewise been seriously damaged.

SB members started a fire on the eighth floor and, when the Johannesburg Fire Department arrived, firefighters ended up running from floor to floor as they were told that the blaze was upstairs, then downstairs, then out and so on.

From our Stratcom 'kit' containing everything from atropine and digitalis to guns and knives, I retrieved a bag of Jalap – a laxative used in horseracing and one of the most popular items in our arsenal – and tipped it into the instant coffee in the COSATU tearoom. We lost our breath laughing about how COSATU officials were going to shit themselves to death.

At the end of this night's work, the building (or what was left of it) was sealed up and, within days, COSATU had instituted proceedings for about R2.5 million in damages against the SAP. Advocates were thus appointed, and having been 'in charge' of the basement and ground floor, I was among the many members called in to be interviewed.

'Do you know anything about a printing machine in the basement?'

'Yes, sir. I was one of the first in the basement and noticed there was an old damaged machine in the corner.'

'And of course you never saw anyone damage it?' they stated.

'No, definitely not.'

'What about the cars in the basement? There are allegations that there were private vehicles that were damaged.'

'I didn't actually examine them closely at all.'

'Did you see anyone else or allow anyone else into the basement?'

'No, sir.'

And so it went on. Denial of everything. What was indisputable, however, was the devastating damage to the building. The usual ploy of accusing the left of attempting to discredit the police and the state wasn't going to wash so easily with this damning evidence.

Shortly after the raid, I accompanied colleagues on a late-night excursion to Cosatu House to check on the security and, in particular, to find a way back into the building. This was at the request of Colonel Erasmus, ostensibly to plant 'tomatoes' before COSATU could resume activities there.

Erasmus had on an earlier occasion given me and a colleague a tin of specially prepared gas in a police-issue canister for use during such activities, in case we were confronted. We were assured the gas would immobilise our antagonists while we made our escape, with further instructions that we weren't to breathe the gas ourselves as it had undergone only rudimentary testing and could well be fatal if inhaled. I had misgivings, as did other colleagues. Beyers insisted that he would never use it.

Then, a few months later, on 7 May, a massive late-night explosion nearly brought the whole building down. The Stratcom machinery swung into top gear, our business being to spread the word that the blast was the work of a disenchanted faction within COSATU, or of the far-right wing, or even of the Azanian People's Liberation Army (APLA).[15]

THIS ONE EVENT WOULD meet several of our objectives because dissent would inevitably spread among COSATU members and the left in general, giving us a golden opportunity to attack in all directions and providing justification for the continuing State of Emergency.

I never knew exactly which of my colleagues placed the explosives, the need-to-know principle being firmly in place and strictly applied. Our bets were on it being MI, specifically a member of the SADF's elite Reconnaissance Commando. But of course, it could have been our in-house inspectors of explosives.

Shortly after the bombing, COSATU and affiliated union offices were raided or firebombed in Germiston, East London, Pietersburg, Vryheid, Kroonstad and Nelspruit, resulting in a massive loss of documentation and other material, and seriously setting back the federation's activities.

Could anyone believe that this was not a coordinated effort? The Stratcom engine churned out disinformation at an accelerated rate, and COSATU appeared to be splitting from within, with 'militant factions' blamed for the violence and arson.

By February 1988, COSATU had recovered somewhat, only to have further restrictions placed on it and 17 other anti-government bodies by the Minister of Police, prohibiting the 'dissemination of their own or anyone else's views'.

As the year dragged on, the responsibility of watching over my sources at times superseded the demands of my family and one crisis after another that Linda and I faced with our young son. I found the massive workload, the stress of worrying about Dylan's future and the endless stream of medical appointments, in our attempts to get a proper diagnosis, too much to bear.

I would work three or four nights back-to-back, interspersed with 18-hour days. During the respites, I'd be unable to sleep, so I would work on source reports that were soul-destroying in themselves. In one epic episode, I was awake for three days. Sleep was becoming an increasingly rare reprieve. Dreams evolved into nightmares. I was afraid of sleep but also afraid of being awake and of not being able to function. My frustration levels catapulted through the roof. Fear was another factor. A 'terrorist' was apprehended on the East Rand with a list of several SB members' addresses found in the lining of his jacket. My home address was on the list. When I wasn't home, Linda and the children overnighted with family nearby.

While limpet mines were being detonated all over Johannesburg, students who aspired to join the hallowed ranks of the officer corps were to learn on the job about clock detonators and sticks of dynamite. The SB had no choice but to train them while we worked because Oosie demanded that the ideologically sound young matriculants, who'd been hand-picked (or allowed in through nepotism), be integrated into our set-up.

After an especially busy period, I returned home one night exhausted but hyped, only to find our bedroom door locked. With bleary eyes, I opened an envelope pinned to the door.

'Our client, Mrs L.K. Erasmus … proceedings … dissolution of the marriage … support for the minor children …'

My mind struggled to focus on the words, but I knew immediately what this was. Stunned, bewildered, I headed for Dylan's room. For a long time I stared down at his sleeping form, moonlight filtering through the curtain and falling on his little face. I lifted and rubbed his slightly stiff arm, willing it to relax and take an able form, when the room exploded into blinding light.

'What are you doing?'

'I'm sitting with my son. What does it look like?'

Silence. Linda left, and the main bedroom door slammed shut, key turning in the lock. Hatred welled up in my heart, and my throat constricted. I felt an overwhelming rage sweep through me. When I came to, my cocked 9 mm was pointing between my wife's frightened eyes. Our bedroom door hung shattered, ripped off its hinges.

Holding all the power, I roared at her: 'Now we'll talk!'

We did eventually, but only after about an hour, when my fury subsided. I lowered the gun and started crying. I resolved to resign, but still we had incalculable medical costs to consider. How would someone like me, with my professional background, be able to start again? How would I be able to undo the damage I'd done to my wife, our marriage and my family?

I returned the following evening to an empty house. Linda and my life as I'd known it 72 hours earlier were gone. Guilt-ridden and terrified by the prospect of loneliness, I felt overwhelmed, engulfed and without hope. There was no return. Linda's bottom line was that if I resigned, she would consider returning. Our families took her side. How could I explain to anyone what I was really involved in?

Those in the inner core of the SB didn't tolerate weakness of any kind in us – and a wife threatening her husband with divorce would indicate weakness on the part of that member. We'd been told. We'd been trained. Keep it together at all costs. All of it! There would be scant sympathy in those ranks for a loser like me. Only the weak are dictated to by a woman. This was the South African way. Women were regarded as hardly worthy; weak men even less so.

I felt I was on a runaway train, one that never slowed enough for me to jump off.

Because of the gravity of Dylan's condition, Linda and I briefly reconciled. He would need the dedication, love and support of both parents, we assured each other. But it was brief indeed, and not strong enough to keep us together as a couple.

Then came the news that Erasmus and Oosie were to be transferred from John Vorster Square to the Head Office, with Erasmus tipped as the next head of the SB and Oosie taking over the reins at the SAP's intelligence unit.

In a world gone mad, hearing this news, it could only become crazier.

Then, out of the blue, I was approached with a request to obtain a 'useable' quantity of HIV-infected blood, via my contacts at the South African Medical Research Laboratory. A savage period of retribution appeared to be under way using the Vlakplaas askaris, some of whom were HIV-positive. My understanding was that some were being dispatched to have unprotected sex with women identified as lefties. Attempting to spread a virus which, at that time had no treatment, was believed to be yet another means of harming the enemy.

I wasn't able to do this. I was taking a risk, I knew, but I refused. I had done many things in my life of which I was horribly ashamed. I had wreaked indescribable havoc and brought untold despair, but I wanted no part of this evil madness. I ducked and dived and squirmed my way out of sourcing infected blood.

Dear Jesus! This was something else!

By now, I had made a decision to perform at a marginal level, just enough to remain employed with the SB, but, try as I might, it kept pulling me back, reeling me in. In early 1988, I participated in several scouting operations to Khotso House in the Johannesburg CBD, where many anti-apartheid organisations were housed. Finally, one night we eventually found a way into the building from a neighbouring office block.

Several visits by Beyers and others led to the theft of a video machine. So far, so SB, but then, on 31 August, a massive explosion ripped through Khotso House's basement and almost brought the building down.

That operation had been conducted in conjunction with Vlakplaas and was celebrated at a braai at the unit's headquarters on a farm outside Pretoria. The SAP hierarchy, including Police Minister Vlok, was there, and since all such 'hard' Stratcom actions had to be approved by Cabinet, he conveyed to us the appreciation of President P.W. Botha.

In October 1988, I was transferred as a senior operative to the intelligence unit, which operated from a new safe house in Honeydew, Johannesburg. After six months, I was transferred back to John Vorster Square where I was promoted to deputy commander of Stratcom. This was something of a boost for my ego, I have to admit. Upward mobility. At last.

We produced publications such as *The Missive*, a dirty little newsletter that purported to be put out by disenchanted radicals and aimed at activists like Audrey Coleman of the Detainees' Parents Support Committee (DPSC) and Krish Naidoo, both of whom were prominent in left-wing circles. This was just the mild stuff, however – there was much worse to come.

By 1990, I'd earned the sobriquet Mr Dirty Tricks (far too playful a term for what I really did), and was nominated to take a Stratcom course to finally be fully indoctrinated into what Dirk Coetzee called 'the heart of the whore'.

The truth was, though, that not only was I already embedded in the heart of the whore, but I had also been feeding and clothing her for years. We SB foot soldiers were her pimps, working for her owner, the National Party, which micromanaged her every act. I realise now that this was the National Party's version of state capture using Stratcom – everything, every facet of daily life as a South African, hung on the strings of the State Security Council (SSC) puppet. Total and unrelenting control.

Chapter Thirteen

The Battering Ram

South Africa, 1990, and the TRC, 1999

I REMEMBER 12 AUGUST 1990 as an exceptionally bleak Sunday. That afternoon Linda drove me through to the South African Railways Police Training Centre at Esselen Park on the East Rand where 80 of us from the SB countrywide were to begin learning Stratcom methods in earnest.

This was just six months after President De Klerk had unbanned the liberation movements and freed Nelson Mandela – in other words, mere months after South Africans had been lied to about reconciliation. De Klerk and his henchmen were only just getting started. I should know. I was one of those henchmen, or at least one of the henchmen's henchmen.

That Sunday evening we met course leader Colonel Johan Putter and the Stratcom unit commander Victor McPherson, the same man who'd paraded Olivia Forsyth around the country as if she'd been a successful agent for our unit when she was, in fact, a survivor of sexual assault and a horribly damaged individual.

Putter stated that the creation of a formal Stratcom unit in Johannesburg was 'a long overdue necessity' and that the Head Office had great expectations for it. When we began the following morning, we opened with a prayer asking the Almighty to help us overcome the enemy, to whom, we felt, we had drawn closer.

The welcome was by Major General P.J. 'Pietertjie' Viljoen, the same individual who had helped concoct the story about Gavin Andersson when we went looking for information on a made-up idea about Neil Aggett's instability way back in 1982. He then handed over to the Guru, Brigadier Oosthuizen, who explained that the aims of Stratcom were to be structured according to a four-year time scale, by which time it was presumed that the National Party government would be facing the first democratic elections.

There was a premium on time. The various projects had to be seen in the short, medium or long term within the four years. But Stratcom could only achieve the desired results if there was, said Oosie, 'an effective utilisation of intelligence'. The intelligence community, he explained, was traditionally reactive, but Stratcom had to be proactive. Specific areas had been identified, and sources, informers and agents were to be targeted with only this in mind. There was not a moment to spare to do anything else.

Four years – tops.

The aim was incontrovertible. We had to neutralise the threat to the National Party and ensure that it retained power – if not in its current form, then in another that would still benefit its champions and the ruling elite. The overt and covert structures of the ANC, then moving into South Africa after being unbanned, were the greatest enemy it had ever faced, especially now that the ANC could freely mobilise the masses. The movement had already declared its target of 400 ANC branches in 13 regions by November 1990.

As a matter of urgency, Stratcom had to achieve the support of what were considered moderate elements in the ANC's economic and finance units, which were identified by our bosses. We believed that they were talking revolution but had, behind the scenes, already pushed for an economic model closer to the one the National Party wanted. Thus, Stratcom had to play up the shortcomings and failures of the ANC. Our priority was to force 'Mandela' – a collective noun for the ANC at that point – to back down at the negotiating table.

We were also directed to keep a specific Stratcom gaze on the SACP, which was 'exercising a direct ideological influence on the ANC'. Every effort had to be made to make the SACP appear dangerous to the working class and the poor. The party was attracting the nation's workers, and 'nationalisation' – as called for in the Freedom Charter – was its rallying cry. We therefore had to make the free enterprise system seem attractive to black people, the message being that mass redistribution meant mass impoverishment.

Fortunately for us, the ANC was facing a massive financial crisis. So was the PAC, but since it had already indicated that it would not be negotiating, nor participating in a future democratic election if its demands were not met, the PAC was considered a much lesser threat. We could almost ignore it – and so we did. Our focus had to be on entities such as the ANC Youth League, and especially on Peter Mokaba once he became its president. It was the youth power base that was the most important in the country. Mokaba was our bull's-eye.

The ANC's Women's League was another base requiring mobilisation and, likewise, had to be closely watched. For us, it held a fascinating contradiction. Its leader, Winnie Mandela, may have been regarded with fear by some, but not by us in Stratcom. Instead, she did more to inadvertently further the aims of Stratcom than a thousand 'Oosies' could ever have hoped. She was just so easy to target.

More complicated was how much attention we could give to exploiting the divisions within the ANC. Those we labelled as radical militants, such as Winnie Mandela, Chris Hani, Steve Tshwete, Peter Mokaba, Harry Gwala and others, could be played off against the pro-negotiation 'moderate' faction under Thabo Mbeki.

Stratcom had to promote internal strife, a rift that was already apparent. In fact, divisions within the ANC were so integrated into how it operated that we only had to tap these lightly to achieve what we wanted.

It was interesting for us to hear the 'four-year' theory explained on that first day of the Stratcom course in 1990, as this had already been mooted back in 1987 and 1988 when Oosthuizen addressed a meeting of SB operatives at the safe house in Honeydew. He had already then informed us that we had to be 'pragmatic in our approach' because the National Party was set to unban the ANC, release Mandela and enter negotiations. Oosthuizen estimated that by 1993 or 1994, elections would be held. But – and this was the most important 'but' of our careers at the SB – the National Party was not prepared to relinquish power completely. Its intention was only to make it seem so and, in the process, retain power by a coalition of allies, such as Inkatha and others. We were assured that our efforts would, in time, be rewarded, but we were too shocked and dismissive then to take advantage of that promise.

Back to the 1990 Stratcom course: the next speaker was Brigadier André Pruis, who was presented as an expert on the ANC. He had written his doctoral thesis on the organisation and was the SAP representative at preparatory talks between the government and the movement. Pruis explained that the country would go through three phases: pre-negotiations and agreement on the rules of negotiation; actual negotiations; and, finally, implementation. When we were gathering at the training centre in Esselen Park, the government was in the pre-negotiations stage. The aim now was thus to create the perception that it was open to other points of view. There would then be a separation of demands, a process that would appear to be give-and-take, and an ostensible progression to a 'new dispensation'.

The ANC's demands were already encompassed in the Harare Declaration,[16] and the government's response had been to lift the Emergency regulations and release political prisoners. The ANC's successes were gauged by its achievement of international solidarity against apartheid, and the scrapping of financial and other sanctions. But, although the ANC may have seemed to be riding the 'Mandela' wave, it was also grappling with internal failures, among them no actual military victories and, with the collapse of communism in Eastern Europe, the crumbling of its ideological support.

It was undeniable, too, that South Africa's economy had taken too many blows during sanctions. Financially, the country was in tatters. It was humiliating for the National Party and humiliating for De Klerk.

Pruis explained that the ANC 'had to effectively and through coordinated Stratcom activity be reduced to just another political party'. So, there we were, on an official government course, with the knowledge of the Cabinet, plotting against the other players in the negotiations. Plain and simple. This was Stratcom through and through: the 'covert utilisation of influences to further the aims of the "clients", being the [protagonists] of the present status quo, the National Party government'.

Our next speaker came from the Department of International Relations at Wits University. He gave us a hawkish but softly spoken analysis of the near-hopeless prospects for the country following sanctions. To illustrate the turmoil we were going through, he drew a parallel between South Africa and the USSR, the latter suffering enormously when communism was abandoned.

He went on to say that the government had had little choice but to relieve the pressure on the country and work together with the ANC, at least on some levels. Now that it was on that path, though, it was determined to win back as much ground as possible.

There were other problems facing Stratcom too. Neo-Nazis, such as the AWB, were gaining support among whites, and that gradual switch within the SAP to the right wing was starting to gather speed. The SB had to ensure that there was a clear understanding in the force that things had changed – that all South Africans now had the right to their own political persuasions. The Catch-22, of course, was that so did members of the SAP.

Stratcom's job was complicated. We had to protect the National Party, but we also had to ensure a climate in which negotiations could take place. This meant that we had to know our enemy – and our bosses – inside and out. We had to fully discover the ANC's exploitable factors, and then identify and promote factions within the ANC that would upset its left flank. But we also had to boost white morale, as well as morale within our own ranks.

Stratcom had to face up to one fact, however – that negotiations could collapse, bringing about the possibility of civil war. The SB instructed us that, if this happened, we should be prepared to 'go back to basics' and rule, directly or indirectly, with an iron fist. We were ready.

The Cabinet decisions on how Stratcom was to be conducted had to be followed to the letter. First, a Centre for Strategic Research was established as an arm of the State Security Council (SSC), reporting directly to Cabinet. Projects and operations could be instituted only after a direct submission had been made to the President. Stratcom was to be managed by the SB, MI, NI and Foreign Affairs. Our operations would include:

- Project Wigwam: The biggest and most important of all the operations, Wigwam was an umbrella for the 'national objective' (or National Party objective) – to neutralise the threat of the radicals within the ANC, the SACP and COSATU, but also the right wing and any other anti-government factions.
- Operation Romulus: The aims here were ad hoc actions instituted to further the objectives of Wigwam. 'Ad hoc' referred not only to impromptu actions, but also those that couldn't always be accommodated under the auspices of any of the other projects. These included some that were illegal.
- Project Jackal and Operation Aristotle: Coordinated in conjunction with MI, these were directed at white high schools and campuses to 'de-radicalise' students and promote Christian values, the benefits of a free enterprise system, freedom of association and an independent judiciary.
- Operation Einstein: Similar to the aims of Jackal, but directed at coloured educational facilities.
- Operation Cicero: The declared aim of this project was to get all campuses to disaffiliate from Nusas.
- Operation Machiavelli: Aimed at gaining control of student radio stations and publications.
- Operation Bismarck: The creation of front organisations as a source of financing and logistics for other operations.
- Operation Ram (which I later coordinated nationally): Promoted all 'positive actions' at tertiary institutions, thus 'exposing' and discrediting left-wing elements.
- Project Omega: Directed at workers, serving to promote 'national ideals'. It was under the auspices of this project that Inkatha started its trade union, UWUSA.

These were the ten basic enterprises for which Stratcom's machinery was set in place. The vast powers of the SB and the intelligence community had many ways of protecting us: there was the rigged forensic testing option, or bribery, blackmail and poison. And of course, we had the Vlakplaas option, if physical measures were needed.

Millions of rand were still being spent on Vlakplaas, with all the funding having to be approved by Cabinet. Since it continued to operate after 1990, the lies told by F.W. de Klerk, Adriaan Vlok and others – who claimed they knew nothing about human rights abuses within the SAP – disgusted many of us in the SB. They knew. They knew everything. In fact, the first post-1994 Police Commissioner, George Fivaz – appointed by Mandela – surely would also have known, and would have been very much aware of all the Stratcom-era officers who had been reappointed or included in the new 'rainbow nation' SAPS.

There were two types of Stratcom: 'soft', which referred to non-physical, propaganda-type activities, and 'hard', which could involve murder, assassination, sabotage, breaking and entering, theft, planting of evidence, blackmail and subversion – all in the name of the national interest, of course.

We were told by Colonel Johan Putter: 'Assassination is an acknowledged strategic communication technique. All countries perpetrate it, but one of the best examples was Operation Damocles[17] in Israel.

'Assassination techniques have certain requirements that you must follow. If you want to assassinate, you are never in your life going to use a firearm to kill a guy. That's out because you draw an investigation to yourself and, if you have drawn an investigation to yourself, you have bloody trouble … So a better alternative technique is, for example, where a target pulls out of his driveway one morning and a big truck rides, *boom*, over him. An accident. Or the guy has a heart attack.'

The last tactic explained the plentiful supply of digitalis in the standard Stratcom kit.

Putter indicated that we had the full support of Minister Vlok: 'So he will take the pain for that, if it ever comes to it.'

He later denied to the *Sunday Times* – which appeared to have been leaked a tape recording of some of our lectures, including this one – that he had talked about assassination and stated it was 'never [a] Stratcom objective to assassinate, and the police were not committing crimes, but fighting crime'.

Vlok's reply was: 'I cannot even remember Colonel Putter.'

Putter later revealed that 'the politicians all knew exactly what we were doing because anything we did we put before them and it would go through the channels'.

This is why we could only laugh in disbelief when, in February 1995, De Klerk said that he had never been part of any conscious decision to commit crimes. What a liar!

If that were the case, it could only be that he didn't consider what we were doing a crime. Certainly, we were not made to believe we were criminals. A well-known political risk analyst lectured us on the right wing during our course. This analyst was a Stratcom stalwart who worked with the SSC and had helped define the parameters of many of our operations.

The Stratcom staff at John Vorster Square at this time comprised Major Gerrit Bruwer, Sergeant Gert Jonker, Constable Karen van der Schyff and me, a warrant officer. The Intelligence Unit was headed by Major Deon Greyling (known as 'PC Plod' for his slow but methodical approach) and a further two units below him were each headed by a major and came under the joint command of Colonel 'Zirk' Gous.

One of the greatest distractions from actual Stratcom work for us was gossip among the staff about each other – a standard SB discrediting technique. Colonel Nic 'Rooi Pen' Coetzee bore the brunt of much hatred. On one occasion, a '*bokpoot*' – a state-manufactured stink bomb – was thrown into his car parked in the basement, and the following day the words 'Stinky Coetzee' appeared in indelible black ink in one of the two elevators that served the SB offices. No amount of scrubbing could remove this or the open hostility to Coetzee.

One of my first tasks on the Stratcom team was to sort out the kit – a large toolbox bearing, among other items, that strong horseracing laxative Jalap, digitalis for inducing heart attacks, syringes, rubber gloves, paint remover, sneezing powder, tear-gas powder, several medications and preparations, including one that negated the effect of the contraceptive pill, containers of arsenic and strychnine, and several vials of the *bokpoot*. Much of this came from the forensics lab.

We also had an assortment of basic tools such as lock picks, and several steel trunks containing printing paper, ink, A+B compound, resin and catalyst (which we also used to damage cars). Most threatening, perhaps, was an array of what we called '*skelm*' firearms, which couldn't be traced back to us. One of the trunks held personal property and contained an AK47, several knives and bayonets and a mass of ammunition, much of which I pinched over the next few months to supplement my own stocks and supply my friends. There were also a few handguns, which I never examined, and, on the shelves of the ninth-floor strongroom, a few old rifles and shotguns in working condition, which we were told we could use only if they were destroyed immediately afterwards.

WH11 intercepts were increasingly useful to us at Stratcom and, on occasion, provided us with some entertainment.

Joe Slovo regularly dined at a top restaurant in Johannesburg, and when WH11 let us know that he was going to be out of town for a few days, I called the venue pretending to be Slovo's assistant, and organised a function for 25 people, demanding the best food and service the establishment could offer. Its management was hard pressed to comply with my many demands and had to employ extra staff. I added in for good measure that 'Mr Slovo demands privacy' and the restaurant erected partitioning as a result.

I then called COSATU and invited some of its members to join the function, and I did the same with Inkatha, hoping to bring about maximum embarrassment and conflict. And that's exactly what happened – the bill was so high that no one was prepared to foot it. Not good PR for the SACP, or any other of the parties involved.

The higher-ups at John Vorster Square were ecstatic. Good laughs were had by all, and we agreed that if this was what Stratcom was all about, hitting the bastards with everything at our disposal, we were going to have a lot of fun. After all, those kinds of malicious schoolboy antics had been our speciality for a long time. They were an essential part of our skills set.

I followed up this little venture with an absolute gem from WH10: they faked an application from Democratic Party MP Dave Dalling's wife, Katharine Ambrose, to join the ANC. At the time, it was speculated that Dalling might throw his lot in with the ANC too, and here was a perfect opportunity to force his hand. I composed a letter, unsigned and supposedly from 'a concerned and despairing South African', who felt that this matter should be exposed, and delivered it to the reception desk at *The Star*. The following day, the newspaper went public with the revelation on the front page and exposed Dalling, who was attacked on all fronts. Of course, the National Party was delighted that an opponent had been thrown to the lions.

An entirely different situation arose, however, with two community organisations in Alexandra Township in Johannesburg. We stoked the differences between the Alexandra Civic Association (ACA) and the Alexandra Action Committee (AAC).

I created a leaflet and a poster in support of the efforts of the AAC, and agents plastered and distributed these everywhere and, in so doing, increased the violence in Alex. In fact, the conflict continued long after we and our street-level proxies had left.

Some might suggest that this profound split and those bloody fights could be considered a Stratcom success, but I disagree. The people of Alex suffered terribly as a result. I deeply regret this action. We did wrong. We should have left it alone.

Our earlier targets – the lefties and, later, the leadership of the former liberation movements and their allies – were on a strangely equal footing with the SB. We were all in a game of cat-and-mouse. We all knew what was going on. As a result, by the early 1990s, most of our enemies on the left had back-up, support and safety nets. The poor people of Alex had none. We manipulated an entire community into battle with one another.

Examples of the 'even playing field' for Stratcom and its adversaries could be seen in Project Jackal, which primarily used the SMA at Wits University and the NSF at the Rand Afrikaans University (RAU) to further its aims.

One of Jackal's major objectives was to promote Inkatha and distribute propaganda material prepared by the Head Office. A classic example was the SMA publication *The Political Dimensions of the Natal Conflict*, which was published nationally and internationally, including in the United States by the International Freedom Front.

By the end of 1990, Stratcom had joined the NI under a front organisation called Lamont Market Research (LMR), which operated from executive offices in Randburg. It all looked good, but I was battling, both financially and in terms of my health. My take-home salary was R1 300 per month, and Dylan was needing more and more care and assistance with his development. After staying awake for another three-day stretch, I finally sought help and was booked into hospital for five days of sleep therapy.

At a loss because he had no idea what was going on, Bruwer called Linda and demanded that she go to the hospital, wake me up and get me to answer a number of queries that he was faced with and couldn't answer.

One of the serious issues surrounded Peter Mokaba, whom we would later claim to be an SB agent. The code name for the operations concerning Mokaba, the ANC Youth League and the South African Youth Congress (SAYCO) was Gordian, as approved by Cabinet. Operation Gordian intensified after January 1992 when recommendations to speed up various facets of the operation were received from Pretoria.

A second operation, code-named Tutor, was aligned with Operation Gordian, and directed at the South African Democratic Teachers' Union (SADTU), which was gaining mass support and undermining the Department of Education and Training (DET), which oversaw the education of black students. A DET flunky had highlighted problems facing the department, among which were shortages of schools, books, teachers, equipment, sporting equipment and much more. This neglect had been one of the focuses of black agitation and protest for decades. We felt that Stratcom could address some of these issues with the spin-off being favourable to us – and support for the government further down the line. Somewhat, anyway. Assisting the DET to overcome its challenges with SADTU would have been not only a good intelligence source and a propaganda ploy with considerable potential, but it could also deal with some of the real problems facing black schools.

However, instead of thinking along these lines to solve the myriad problems and making sense out of a mess that already existed – to the benefit of the National Party, naturally – Stratcom was directed to 'ensure the SACP [becomes] a millstone around the ANC's neck'. This took up a huge amount of human resources and time. Nationally coordinated action to counter the SACP's influence involved front organisations, the media and the daily management of informers. One of these fronts was the Returned Exiles Coordinating Committee (RECOC), an organisation of disenchanted ANC members, many of whom had been detained and apparently abused by the movement while in exile.

One of the RECOC members committed to paper his hellish experiences in the ANC's Quatro camp in Angola, and Bruwer instructed me to turn this information into a book that the government would publish. I refused. I simply didn't have the time. I had been given a week, unbelievably, to complete the book and the Head Office would pay all the costs for printing and mass distribution.

This didn't matter. Government was already generously supporting some exiles with the approval of both Police Commissioner Johan van der Merwe and Minister Adriaan Vlok.

This was the peak for the apartheid intelligence infrastructure, and the success of our operations was essential to structures such as the SSC. It had come into being in 1972, nearly 25 years after the National Party government assumed power, but not long afterwards took a hell of a knock as a direct result of the SADF's involvement in Angola (Operation Savannah). That horrific exercise in bloodshed and violence had been both dangerous and costly. Around that time, there had also been the uprising in Soweto in which many people died or were injured, leaving the State Security Council floundering. The reputational damage had been intense for its leadership. Things were thus looking bad when Stratcom kicked into high gear in 1990.

Some 15 years before, in the middle and late 1970s, government security experts and advisers had already started to accept that oppressive legislation alone was not going to alleviate the steadily increasing political and socio-economic problems facing the country. Certainly, the Info Scandal didn't help, and the SSC was just not up to the job of continuing to uphold the apartheid project.

The SSC tried, of course. It decided its recruits should up their brainpower and prescribed the works of international theorists like André Beaufre[18] and the writings of the American J.J. McCuen to develop anti-revolutionary strategies. As a result, McCuen's manual, *The Art of Counter-revolutionary Warfare*, originally published in 1966, was reproduced and distributed among strategists and state officials. The basis of his work – 'winning hearts and minds' (WHAM) – contained four primary elements that were deemed suitable for the South African situation.

The first element was to seek out and destroy the relatively few hardcore, trained and committed revolutionaries, and once they were identified and eliminated, effective communications could be restored. In our situation, this was the work of units such as the SAP's Vlakplaas and the SADF's CCB.

The second element was counter-organisation – the taking over or infiltration of existing groups of all kinds, or creating new ones as fronts. Counter-organisation included self-defence, the recruitment and training of local militia to form a bridge between the administration and the masses. Actions taken by the apartheid state in this regard were the secret training of Inkatha members in Namibia, the deployment of '*kitskonstabels*' by the SAP, and the mass of vigilante groups that sprang up in the mid-1980s.

The third element, mobile forces, was exemplified in South Africa by the SAP's Riot Squad (renamed the Internal Stability Unit in 1992), which allowed and even facilitated vigilante groups. For example, it openly backed the Witdoeke[19] as they rampaged through the informal settlements on the Cape Flats outside Cape Town, and in Natal it publicly supported Inkatha militia in anti-ANC activities. In fact, the SAP's gun-running to Inkatha took place on a massive scale, with weapons seized in the Border War in Angola and South West Africa, driven into Natal and used to arm Inkatha militants.

The fourth element, so-called civil education, was about establishing a good relationship between the state and the people by addressing local problems and establishing programmes to train loyal leaders and the youth for local administration. A good example of this was Dr Louis Pasques's Adult Education Consultants (AEC), which concentrated specifically on anti-ANC propaganda sessions under the guise of organising Christian clubs or other seemingly innocent sport and community wellness programmes. Aligned with this was the concept of area defence, which would mean military involvement in public works-type programmes such as building roads and bridges, or supplying water to rural communities.

The state's mechanism for the implementation of WHAM was the National Security Management System, or NSMS, which had Joint Management Centres (JMCs) operating with subcommittees in security, intelligence, communications, and political, economic, social and joint operations. The aim of the JMCs was 'to satisfy the welfare of the masses, change and influence their psychological attitudes and maintain security'.

The NSMS fell directly under the SSC, which was chaired by the Deputy Minister of Law and Order. Then came the Secretariat of the SSC, which included administration, the NI and Stratcom. The chair of the Secretariat rotated annually between the NI, MI and the SB. The next tier was the National Joint Management Centre (NJMC), which presided over the national network of regional JMCs and hundreds of sub- and mini-JMCs spread across the country.

During the States of Emergency in the 1980s, the NJMC was tasked with managing issues on a day-to-day basis. At that time it was chaired by Roelf Meyer (Minister of Constitutional Affairs), who also chaired the working group of the SSC, which was supported by the Secretariat and its Stratcom complement.

These were the people who ensured that the term 'black-on-black violence' made it into regular public use so that the predominantly white police force would eventually be perceived as being less at the forefront of violence in black communities. This is also why black vigilante groups such as the Witdoeke and Inkatha had to be promoted, and the notion of 'tribal differences' and conflict hyped up.

In 1988, responding to a sharp increase in levels of anti-UDF violence in Pietermaritzburg and accusations that the SAP was actively aiding Inkatha, Meyer stated that 'the violence was conspicuously a struggle between moderate organisations and black radical groups, and is a black-on-black struggle'.

Stratcom was conceived and formalised way back in 1984 when an SSC study group identified several problem areas in its own structures. For instance, there were too many projects operating over a very wide front; there wasn't enough funding; and there was a distinct lack of coordination and identification of priorities.

The study group was chaired by Lieutenant-General A.J. van Deventer (secretary of the SSC) and members included generals C.L. Viljoen, P.W. van der Westhuizen, J.F. Huyser (all SADF); Dr L.D. Barnard, A.A. Knoetze of NI; J. van Dalsen and J. Lotter (Foreign Affairs); General P.J. Coetzee and Brigadier H.A. Stadler (SAP); and A.P. Stemmet and Colonel A.A. Kotze (SSC Secretariat).

The following Stratcom projects were approved across the board for a period of five years, and financed from the Secret Fund (in consultation with the secretary of the Treasury) and the SADF:

- The Security Forces Support Committee, which was to counter the Detainees' Parents Support Committee and the Black Sash, in conjunction with the SADF.
- *The Aida Parker Newsletter*, which was for the dissemination of anti-ANC propaganda, and which was also conducted in cooperation with the SADF.
- The *Industry International* newsletter, which was run from London in conjunction with Foreign Affairs.
- The SABC's Target Terrorism campaign, which supplied information on the ANC via the various outlets of the public broadcaster.
- Assistance to the Bantustans and neighbouring states, relating to 'partnerships' between these and the SAP, as well as the SAP and the police forces of Swaziland, Lesotho, Mozambique and Zimbabwe.
- Project No. 319, or 'Radar', a French organisation led by Léon Delbecque in Paris, which promoted South Africa's interests in Europe and at the European Parliament, and countered anti-government propaganda disseminated at the United Nations and the Organisation of African Unity (OAU).
- The West German news service, which placed 'objective' articles in the German, Austrian and Swiss media. Church matters dominated.
- Bringing opinion-makers and decision-makers to South Africa, apparently on an ad hoc basis.
- Providing the finances for local experts recruited for propaganda purposes to attend seminars and congresses abroad.
- Hennenhofer PR, consultants from West Germany, which brought dozens of guests – including politicians, academics, journalists, unionists, industrialists, business people and clerics – to South Africa.
- Aderi, a French PR firm contracted to promote South Africa's image abroad.
- The Institute for Strategic Studies, which promoted South African interests and a positive image abroad.
- The Forum South Africa.
- 'Liaison services', personal agents used by South African ambassadors in the United States, Italy and Japan.

The SADF's specific projects included:
- Alborak, which was to 'involve the entire population in defending the country'.

- Tadpole, which was to promote 'a climate of cooperation' between the SADF and the armed forces of the TBVC states (that is, 'independent' Bantustans).
- Girasol (also known as SAMVO), which was to create 'a climate of opportunity' in which southern African states would enter into a mutual defence pact.
- Becket, which was to promote good relations with the non-communist, or 'free world'.

There were also specific 'motivational' projects, such as:
- Harmonic, for women.
- Dipole, for the youth.
- Honey Ant, for secondary-school principals.
- Gypsum, for teachers of youth preparedness courses.
- Weefspoel, for inspectors of education.
- Watent (wagon tent), for the heads and organisers of propaganda '*veldskool*' operations (compulsory for white South African children).
- Bates, to motivate opinion-makers by facilitating 'goodwill visits' to security force units.
- Cupid, to influence black people through 'plough-and-plant' operations and the supply of doctors and teachers.

International or Africa-driven projects to cultivate 'allies' included:
- Elevate, which gave support to President Hastings Banda of Malawi and his successors to ensure continued cooperation with South Africa.
- Tsafoon, to maintain the morale of whites in South West Africa.
- Canteen, to handle the SADF's involvement in establishing a military base in Gabon in such a way that South Africa's involvement was not revealed and, if revealed, to contain the response.
- Santa, to coordinate and increase SADF assistance to Swaziland and ensure the cooperation of the Swazis.
- Arianne, to promote South African interests in Morocco.
- Flask, to promote and build South Africa's image in Iraq – and vice versa – as trustworthy negotiating partners, and to ensure good relations between the two countries.
- Layer, to promote and coordinate South Africa's military cooperation with Israel.

Among the media projects were:

- Seeppot, to influence existing media organisations or create fronts to 'promote national values' in newsletters, pamphlets and magazines.
- Diver, to utilise TV and film companies to influence opinion.
- Yoyo, to use international experts to gain access to the international media.
- Backfire, to use experts in influencing visitors to and from countries abroad.

Projects aimed at 'hostile organisations' included:

- Babushka, which used campus-based front organisations to counter bodies such as the Black Students Society (BSS) and the UDF.
- Weiveld, which aimed to destabilise the ANC's organisational efforts and deprive it of its conventional power bases.
- Breakwater, which aimed to destabilise SWAPO psychologically, both locally and internationally, to such an extent that its influence on its conventional power bases became ineffective.

Projects to counter resistance movements included:

- Destitute/Yam, which promoted UNITA[20] as a legitimate body to the international community and endorsed its right to participate in the Angolan government.
- Whale, which promoted the image of UNITA's leader, Jonas Savimbi, as if he were a statesman or a political leader worthy of repute.
- Capsize, which promoted the Basutoland Congress Party (BCP) as if it were the movement that had the most legitimate claim to power in Lesotho.
- Drama, which aimed to destabilise the new, independent government, militarily and otherwise.

Projects to counter 'hostile states' included:

- Detach, which promoted Angolan dissatisfaction with the Angolan government.
- Balalaika, which aimed to break down the morale of Cuban troops in Angola.
- Lake, which promoted dissatisfaction with the Zimbabwean government among Zimbabweans.
- Zodiac, which promoted the Reverend Ndabaningi Sithole and his party infrastructure with a view to destabilising the Zimbabwean government.
- Bison, aimed at destabilising Chief Leabua Jonathan's government in

Lesotho and discrediting him in the eyes of the international community and in his own country.

'Cultural and religious projects' included:
- Andante, aimed at influencing English-speaking denominations against revolutionary and liberation theology through the distribution of a newsletter.
- Alkurk I, which aimed to influence German-speaking denominations abroad against revolutionary and liberation theology.
- Alkurk II, as above, but aimed at local German-speaking denominations.
- Anvil, aimed at influencing black Christians against liberation theology through front organisations such as Open Doors.
- Antoinette, aimed at influencing Reformed Protestant churches.
- Cargo, which would expose the 'red' political agenda of the World Alliance of Reformed Churches (WARC).
- Epic, which would counter the revolutionary and political theology of the Catholic Church through the front organisation Total Family Planning, nationally and internationally.
- Frog, aimed at countering the influence of the SACC, the Council of Churches in Namibia, and the World Council of Churches in South Africa.
- Serato, which aimed to discredit revolutionary clerics such as Tutu and Boesak on a national and international basis, and counter their influence.
- Tatelo, used to counter pacifism as propagated by conscientious objectors, and project this pacifism as negative within a context of moral preparedness.
- Wanmeul, which aimed to use the Zion Christian Church (ZCC) for anti-revolutionary activities.
- Werda, used to counter the black and liberation theology of the Alliance of Black Reformed Christians in Southern Africa (ABRECSA).

'Supportive projects' (which partnered with Stratcom specifically) included:
- Flap, which involved the training of selected persons from all government departments in the techniques of white, grey and black propaganda.
- Arbela, specific training of selected persons from government departments and the state's legal machinery in the management of Stratcom projects.
- Guild, which trained people in target groups to act as 'advisers' to specific communities.
- Baffle, which trained the leader corps of resistance movements, political advisers, politicians, government officials, and those in public

administration and the free-market system.

- Warmdoek, which aimed to 'positively influence' residents of the Caprivi Strip, including traditional leaders, teachers, women and children, and the security forces.
- Vaalribbok, which had to 'positively influence' the Himbas (a culturally specific community in northern Namibia).
- Vaatdoek, as above, but aimed at the Damaras in Namibia.
- Wenhuis, as above, but involving the Kavango.
- Calendulas, as above, but aimed at the Ovambos.
- Toctan, as above, but designed to 'positively influence' the Ndebele in the Northern Transvaal.

The following were audio-visual projects:
- Project Bessie used high-powered static radio transmitters to jam revolutionary propaganda from outside and broadcast our own propaganda.
- Patrys, as above, but with the use of mobile transmitters.
- Diamond, which was to promote the 'fighting spirit' of the nation through the performing arts.
- Coffee, to prevent 'exposure of the security forces to negative influences during recreational activity', and so protect their 'cultural values' from collapsing.

And, finally, infrastructural projects:
- Fantail, which involved the creation of a communications network and suitable infrastructure to facilitate Stratcom nationally.

From this extensive list of projects, it is clear that by 1990 Stratcom had dug its roots into every sphere of South African life. Every government department and structure had a Stratcom component carrying out instructions at the request of the National Party government and its SSC.

Meanwhile, corruption in all its forms intensified, either going unnoticed or being covered up as a means of 'protecting national security'. One of the most sensational, and unbelievable, cases emerged from the discovery of the misappropriation of trade union funds by an SB hard man, Michael Bellinghan. Bellinghan was involved in a scam in which WH10 intercepted cheques to COSATU and the National Union of Metalworkers of South Africa (NUMSA), after he opened accounts in the names of Mr C. OSATU and Mr (Nicholas) N. UMSA.

The scam was finally exposed during evidence led at Bellinghan's trial for the murder of his wife, Janine, who was found bludgeoned and strangled to death in September 1991. Prior to her murder, Janine, who was considering divorce, had begun to collect evidence on her husband's SB activities and involvement in the trade union scam. Severe strife arose when she threatened to expose the fraud, but Bellinghan was not about to leave it at this.

An inquest had heard claims that the police investigation had been obstructed, and that crucial evidence had allegedly been tampered with and had gone missing from the police forensic laboratory in Pretoria. Investigating officer Major Willie Steyn – who received several death threats – testified that he had been denied access to police witnesses in Natal. The top brass of the SB were understandably nervous that Stratcom would be exposed in open court if Bellinghan was charged, and there were rumours that fellow operatives had helped to provide him with an alibi and had removed essential documents from his house on the morning of his wife's death.

Bellinghan was found guilty, however, and sentenced to 25 years for Janine's murder. By 1995 he was behind bars, but he applied for amnesty at the TRC in 1999, not only for laundering cheques stolen by the SAP, but also on the grounds that he battered Janine to death for 'political reasons' because she was about to leak information about secret SB operations.

When I try to explain all of this to my son, he just gazes at me in disbelief at the utter madness under which we lived.

Bellinghan told the TRC that his judgement 'may have been slightly affected by the accumulated stress of my work and the fact that it was a desperate situation'. I think many of us read this in 1999 and empathised with his 'accumulated stress' and 'desperation', and few of us would have been shocked by his disturbing detachment from responsibility. Bellinghan had left Janine's broken body for his children to find, yet he told the TRC that he believed 'the maid' would find it first as she 'usually arrived before the children awoke'.

For many of us, Bellinghan's horrific tale, which was revealed at the inquest court, was yet another brutal backdrop to 1994, when most South Africans were preparing to be free. While we were tearing ourselves and our families apart, and calming our bloodied brains with whatever pharmaceuticals we could get just to keep speaking in full sentences, Bellinghan was in New Zealand, trying to escape justice.

In 1990, De Klerk changed the name of the National Security Management System to the National Coordinating Mechanism (NCM) and attempts were made to propagate the idea that he had abolished the NSMS and its security and Stratcom components.

The official *Handleiding: Nasionale Koördinerings Meganisme* (*The National Co-ordinating Mechanism Handbook*), distributed after the change, clearly indicates that the structure remained effectively unchanged, barring the introduction of new titles. On page 22, the handbook states that 'the principles of the application of the full powers of the State in order to resist the revolutionary onslaught [are] still valid'.

De Klerk's new NCM was answerable to the Cabinet and its four committees: Constitutional Affairs, Economic Affairs, Social Affairs and Security Affairs. The handbook further states that the SSC remained in place (it was, in any event, a statutory body) and the ministers serving on the Cabinet committees retained their positions.

The name changes included a Security Committee, in place of the former NJMC, under Niël Barnard. A task group, the Joint Security Staff (JSS), was set up under this committee, and was chaired alternately by the Chief of SAP Operations and the SADF's Chief of Staff. By April 1992, the head of the SAP's Internal Stability Unit (the old Riot Squad) was in the chair. The other name change was to the Secretariat of the SSC, which became known as the Security Secretariat (SS) under De Klerk.

Yet, in 1992, De Klerk stated in Parliament that all secret projects of the NI, the SAP and the SADF had been terminated and these bodies were confining themselves to 'only the line functional tasks entrusted to them by law'. He revealed that control over any remaining secret projects was exercised by a Cabinet committee.

Chapter Fourteen

I'm Sure You'll Be Happy Here

Mossel Bay, 1992, to London, Copenhagen and Cowies Hill, 1994

I HAD CUT MY HAIR. Short top and sides with a long, plaited pigtail held securely out of sight by a very uncomfortable collar. In front of me sat a big man neatly attired in a light suit, the expanse of his desk dwarfed by the beautiful panorama of Mossel Bay framed in the window behind him.

This was Major Herbert Rommel van der Merwe, divisional commander of the SB Southern Cape, an area stretching 300 kilometres in either direction, mostly bordered by the purple Outeniqua Mountains.

'We do everything by the book here. This isn't Johannesburg. We keep pocket [case] books here. We're never late. We hold morning parades. Vehicles are inspected every Thursday morning. I don't tolerate dirty vehicles.'

I shifted my weight from one foot to the other.

'You are privileged to be here,' he said. I thought I was. 'Apart from discipline and my rules, you won't have any problems because here, quite simply, we do everything by the book.'

'Yes, sir.'

'All I want from you is your loyalty. And I expect total loyalty to me.'

He stood up and extended his hand.

'Welcome to Mossel Bay. I'm sure you'll be very happy here.'

I kept my pigtail for some six weeks, but summer was approaching and day by day the stiff collars I was wearing were becoming more and more uncomfortable. After I'd showed it off as a joke to some shocked colleagues, Linda cut it off.

Linda and the children were thriving, as was I. We felt safe, secure and happy. With the onset of spring, the southern Cape is visited by whales and dolphins and we would sit for hours on our veranda, listening to the songs of these incredible animals in the little bay below our home. The sleaze of Stratcom, the SB and the hell of Johannesburg were now distant and each idyllic day passed with more contentment. We felt we had arrived. All our dreams had come true.

The SB offices had a canteen built and financed by members, and here I met many people, not only in SAP circles but also from the Mossel Bay business community – bank managers, business owners and Mossgas personnel from the giant R11-billion state oil refinery, among others.

In this corner of the world, Van der Merwe held sway. After those first few desultory weeks, I began to realise that most of these citizens, like the SB staff members, feared the SAP major rather than liked him. As I got to know my colleagues and the regulars better, I could see that several people hated him.

Snooker cue in hand and double J&B within reach, he would from time to time lash out with a biting, acrimonious statement, usually of a personal nature. Yet his victim would invariably return sheepishly to the bar. I, however, ignored the many warnings about Van der Merwe and the tales about his wheeling and dealing, determined that nothing was going to rock my boat in this paradise. Increasingly, though, I could see how he terrorised the staff.

Constable 'Grobbie' Grobler would have to prepare fishing rods and bait on a Saturday afternoon, and drive Van der Merwe in a police vehicle to some place miles from Mossel Bay, bait up the rods and help him to catch a fish. And Rob Stone of the technical staff would be summoned to Van der Merwe's house on a Saturday morning to start his lawnmower, or at any time of the day or night to set his TV or video recorder. This was how discipline was applied, with total control. I had worked under tyrants before, but this was unbelievable. Over time, I became like the rest of the staff, constantly watching my back.

It was obvious, too, that it wasn't only word of mouth that kept Van der Merwe informed of even our private activities at home. There were clearly other sources, and I began to suspect that we were being monitored.

When I was charged with working with WH11, for instance, I noticed that there was tape recording equipment that could not be accounted for. Later, I established that it was installed in the top right-hand drawer of Van der Merwe's desk and that lines were run from the switchboard so that he could listen in to everyone's conversations from the privacy of his office. In fact, not only were our offices bugged, but also our homes, as were the offices and phones of prominent members of the Mossel Bay community.

In the period preceding the National Referendum[21] in early 1992, I was monitoring a WH11 on a prominent Mossel Bay businessman, Mr A., suspected of AWB activities, who was in contact with a second businessman, Mr B. Standing instructions were that the right wing had to be reported to the CO (being Van der Merwe). These two men were discussing Van der Merwe's political outlook. One called him a *'fokken tweegat jakkals'*, and warned the other to beware of the major as he supported the National Party.

I took this tape to the CO, who later called me into his office and closed the door behind me. He then had me listen to another recording, featuring Mr B., the owner of a big Mossel Bay business. The men were sharing seriously unfavourable statements about Van der Merwe, and I knew immediately that its release had not been authorised by WH11. This was because Mr A. had never been placed on WH11, which meant that Van der Merwe was misusing the system to serve a private agenda.

At lunchtime, the major took me out to the yacht club, and explained that he wanted me to devise and implement a strategy to destroy or discredit Mr A. and other 'enemies'. He said I could rely on his assistance and the unlimited use of technical aids and vehicles, and even finance if necessary. In return, he intimated, he would 'see me right' – a reference I took to mean financially, because he knew that Linda and I were struggling to make ends meet.

Van der Merwe wanted me to start nailing Mr A. by calling him and telling him that I was from the *Cape Times* conducting a survey in the Mossel Bay area to determine attitudes to the referendum. The idea was to draw him out on his political persuasions, and record the conversation. I subsequently made the call, not having much option with Van der Merwe looming over me, but was unable to elicit more than noncommittal replies to my questions. Mr A. was more astute than Rommel had given him credit for.

It didn't end there, though. Over the next few weeks, Van der Merwe badgered me endlessly about Mr A. They had been firm friends but had apparently fallen out over a financial dispute. Under pressure, Mr A. had responded by threatening to expose Van der Merwe's involvement at Mossgas.

There was another edge to all of this. When I showed reluctance to get involved in his private issues, Van der Merwe warned me that the ANC would be privy to the ways in which Stratcom staffers had 'stolen or squandered' millions of rand. He made sure I understood that the ANC would find out that I had been convicted in the Aggett matter, and that this would be held against me.

This, despite the fact that we all knew that information on Mossgas tenders was for sale. Sometimes, I felt that I had gathered enough information to bust Van der Merwe. For instance, he and the head of a private security company were rumoured to be close, with SAP personnel and equipment said to be 'frequently and unashamedly' made available to the firm. This particular company was then awarded a multi-million-rand Mossgas security contract, clearly having had prior knowledge of what other companies had tendered.

I tried to steer clear of all of this. As it was, I had other worries. I'd been experiencing problems with my salary, bizarrely receiving just 11 cents in February and R375 in March. Regulations dictated that an SAP member could not query salary discrepancies directly with their superior, but I approached Van der Merwe anyway.

'Bad luck, pal!' he laughed.

To supplement our income, Linda had opened a school teaching ballroom and Latin American dance, and the prospects seemed favourable – at least, we thought it would enable us to survive until my salary problems could be rectified.

Nonetheless, my situation at work was becoming intolerable. When I was warned by colleagues that Van der Merwe had instituted WH11 at my house, I became more fearful that he would act against me in some way. I finally had confirmation of some sinister intent when, intoxicated, he remarked on a personal situation Linda had privately discussed with a family member on our phone.

And so I took leave. I couldn't believe that I was once again facing a personal hell at work over which I had no control. I had thought Mossel Bay was the answer.

In June 1992, the Mossel Bay second-in-command, Major Dennis Schley, was summoned to a meeting in Cape Town. When he got back, he gathered us all together to inform us of certain changes taking place in what was now known as 'the new' South Africa. He explained that mechanisms had been introduced so that members of the force who found it 'difficult to adapt' could seek professional help. This, we were told, would include the services of a psychologist appointed by the SAP in Cape Town. He said that we could discuss our individual situations, even with General Johan van der Merwe if needed, and those of us concerned about our past involvements in what he called 'contentious' matters, such as Stratcom, would also have the opportunity to talk about that – and apply for indemnity. This programme was later dished out to hundreds, if not thousands, of security force members by De Klerk and his government just prior to the April 1994 elections.

Van der Merwe was on leave at the time, and Schley suggested that in view of my Stratcom background, I should discuss the situation with the boss when he returned to work. Van der Merwe, however, flew into a rage when I approached him.

He told me that he was not going to listen to 'any Stratcom stories', and would not allow anyone on his staff to sully the name of his branch by 'running to the Head Office' and applying for indemnity or counselling. Anyway, he had 'done more' during his years at the SB than any of us could imagine, and he didn't need any help or indemnity. Then he banished me from his sight, and was openly hostile to me from then onwards. On every occasion he could, he would make some cutting remark about 'cowards' and snide references to Aggett – many of the details recorded in my personal file of course.

There were three former members of Vlakplaas on the Mossel Bay staff and, as far as I know, they were refused permission take up the offer of counselling and indemnity (however, one of them, a former askari, was given a golden handshake of R250 000, and he left the SAP the same day that I did).

I was devastated by Van der Merwe's actions, realising that I now had absolutely no recourse to higher or other authorities. He'd intensified his boasting about his influence on the general staff and his friendship with Generals Basie Smit, Krappies Engelbrecht and other big shots. I found myself growing increasingly depressed and so I decided to seek outside counselling. I was uncomfortable with trusting the counsellors offered by the SAP, in any case, even if it was the first time in my career that such a need had been recognised.

My impending sense of doom was exacerbated over the following few weeks when I wasn't contacted by any former commanders or senior officers with whom I'd been associated at Stratcom. None had applied for amnesty, despite De Klerk, Vlok and others trying to shove this option down members' throats.

So it was that I consulted a private psychiatrist who hospitalised me for stress. After this, I was told that I was fit for work, but the moment I went back I was confronted by Van der Merwe, who informed me that I was 'finished' in the SB. I was to hand in my vehicle immediately and, most hurtful of all, was told that I was to go on an advanced bush and riot training course at Maleoskop Base in what was then the Transvaal. Van der Merwe said that he would not tolerate having a 'mad person' on his staff, and that my mental state was unacceptable.

I was readmitted to hospital after just one day back at work and never returned, being finally declared unfit for further service at the beginning of 1993. I was medically boarded in May of that year. During this time, my file and medical reports were mysteriously mislaid, I went onto half-salary and then no salary, and Linda and I had no choice but to close the dance school and sell off everything just to get by.

There were times when we didn't have food and I applied for financial help from the SAP's assistance fund. Despite having paid into this fund for 18 years and the request being endorsed by a police welfare worker, my application was turned down by the Head Office. In desperation, I finally contacted Van der Merwe. His response was that my family and I should eat 'mealie meal and lungs'.

I subsequently heard that Van der Merwe had used his contacts at the Head Office to ensure that I would receive no payout from the fund; even the social worker could not believe that her motivation had been denied. I had to concentrate later to examine the trajectory of events.

In February 1993, I'd sent a fax to SAP Mossel Bay and Head Office in Cape Town, setting out the prevailing circumstances and making a request for indemnity. There was no acknowledgement of receipt.

Between bouts of hospitalisation and many sessions of therapy, I reported repeatedly to the Head Office, the Guru, the head of CIS and, later, Legal Services. Prior to being boarded, I had instituted proceedings against the Minister of Law and Order for the loss of my career, and an article about this appeared later in the *Sunday Times*. As a result of this article, the Police Commissioner ordered an investigation into the claim that I had been run out of John Vorster Square by a former CO.

The Guru told me that the Commissioner was simply concerned about my well-being. I knew, though, and was warned, that the real reason for his 'concern' was to determine how much I was able to reveal – especially about Stratcom. The aim of the investigation into me was no more than damage control. Ex-colleagues said that I was perceived in certain SAP circles as a traitor, and that former colleagues from the SB at John Vorster Square were on their way to Mossel Bay 'to sort me out'.

Word had circulated that I'd received a golden handshake of between R300 000 and R600 000, presumably to inflame the anger directed at me by my ex-colleagues. Indeed, I became persona non grata and lost many of my friends in the police. Many – understandably, I suppose – were afraid of being compromised or linked to crime. Many colleagues had been deeply involved in what was called 'Third Force' activity.

In February 1993, our home in Herolds Bay was entered and searched, and Linda and I began to receive a number of death threats. I was once talking on the phone when Linda interrupted the call. She had a strange look on her face. The children had gone to school without lunch. We'd been surviving on charity and the odd handout. My wife had simply had enough. While I was trying to wrap up my conversation, she told me that she was done.

I bolted down the stairs when I heard her starting the car. I tried the car doors, but she'd locked herself inside. The engine was revving and Linda was slumped over the steering wheel, sobbing. The next moment, the wheels spun and she raced out into the road with me running frantically alongside the car. I watched hopelessly as she disappeared into the distance.

I raced down the road to friends, and an hour later managed to get a lift into George, 20 kilometres away. I found Linda at Candice's school, slumped on the ground next to the car, still wailing. Other parents were looking away in embarrassment. Children were staring and Candice was crying.

I eventually managed to get Linda back into the car and drove her to the psychiatrist, who hospitalised her immediately. The next day I borrowed some cash to buy basic foodstuffs, and then headed to the hospital. She told me that she would be taking the children to stay with her mother for a while. The SAP and I were destroying them, she said. She couldn't bear my supposed loyalty to the police any longer, especially not after the way the SAP and my former colleagues had turned on me.

I had no choice in the matter. She promised they might return once everything was safe.

That very day, I had to go to the SAP district headquarters in George to receive documents relating to my discharge from the force. There I came face to face with Van der Merwe on the stairs, and he stopped and smiled as I went past. It took every ounce of strength not to smash my fist into his face. But then he laughed, and mumbled: '*Fokken mal donner*.'

I stopped. Rage welled up in my throat when I heard his sniggers as he carried on up the stairs. Now I would fight. I resolved to fight to the death if necessary. I would never give up or back down.

That night after putting the children to bed, I opened the safe and took out a 9 mm Beretta and an R3 assault rifle and got ready to hit the road to Mossel Bay. I was consumed with a raging hatred. I think I was in shock.

I sat in the car outside Van der Merwe's home in Maroela Street, my weapons at the ready, for what seemed like ages. Gradually, a sort of peace settled on me, no doubt brought on by the copious amounts of alcohol and tablets I had consumed. For the umpteenth time, I lifted the rifle and tried to focus through the telescope, but I couldn't stop shaking. So much adrenalin. I wanted this enormous, crushing burden off my chest. I wanted to slowly kill a man whom I regarded as an animal and then, God willing, I'd kill all the others who had allowed this to happen. I had also learned that De Klerk was to visit Pacaltsdorp in George and, for good measure, I'd put a bullet in his arse too.

I would be caught, of course, and possibly committed. Either way, I would be taken away from Linda, Candice and Dylan. What would I do without my family to whom I owed so much? We had to stay together. We had to recover. There had to be another way. Somehow, there had to be justice.

With a heavy heart, I drove back to Herolds Bay, struggling to keep awake, thinking of Linda in hospital, and of my children, who were both confused and scared.

Linda responded well to therapy, but we were forced to sell our home and move to Cape Town to start over, with fresh objectives in mind. With my gratuity from the police, we bought a ski-boat and earned our skippers' tickets and international radio licences. We enrolled Dylan at the Vista Nova School for special needs children in Rondebosch and gradually our lives returned to some semblance of normality. We'd resolved to put as much of the terror as we could behind us, and spend our working time selling deep-sea charters and scuba-diving trips.

Later that year, Nannie Beyers called me up out of nowhere – I'd changed my contact details and was trying to live in relative obscurity – to tell me that there had been a renewed bid to shut me down, so I wasn't entirely surprised to receive a call from Bruwer later, who was evasive when I asked him how he'd got my number.

A week later, I'd just got home from Hout Bay where our boat was moored and found Linda in tears. There was a stream of messages on our answering machine: 'Fucking bitch!'; 'Whore wife of a traitor!'; 'If Paul talks, we'll kill your fucking children!' There was also a warning that my lawyer was reporting to the SB Head Office, which I didn't quite believe, but still Linda and I felt that we had no choice. So we packed up and moved again.

Enraged, I made contact with Carl Niehaus of the ANC, who I felt might have an interest in what I had to say. I wasn't prepared to reveal any state secrets, though, and so the contact fizzled out. I then – unsuccessfully – tried to seek an audience with members of the opposition in Parliament. After moving back to Knysna, Linda, who had found a new resolve, sent a fax to a National Party spokesperson, Hennie Smit, but he was not interested.

Early in March 1994, I read in the papers that there was speculation as to the identity of a person code-named 'Q' who had opened up to the Goldstone Commission[22] on Third Force activities. A week later, I got information that I had been implicated regarding Stratcom. Finally, after three days of terror in which I expected to be arrested at any moment, Linda and I came to a decision.

Why wouldn't these people leave us alone? What did I have to lose anyway? There wasn't much left that they hadn't taken.

Although I believed the Goldstone Commission was yet another National Party set-up, it was at least an option – one way to try to save my family. In fact, there was no other. Linda picked up the phone.

'Is that the Goldstone Commission? I am Mrs Linda Erasmus and my husband Paul was a member of the SB for 18 years ...'

And so we embarked on a new road. Within a short time, I would have yet another label: Q4.

Within a day of Linda's call, Advocate Carl Koenig and Lieutenant-Colonel Frank Dutton of the Goldstone Commission arrived at our home in Knysna.

Dutton had sprung to fame when, as a captain and despite pressure from above, he had persisted in an investigation into the December 1988 massacre of 11 men, women and children at a home funeral vigil in the rural community of Trust Feeds, near Hanover in Natal. He subsequently proved that the local SAP commander, Brian Mitchell, and members of Mitchell's staff were responsible. Mitchell was tried and received 11 death sentences for ordering the massacre. The fearless Dutton earned a promotion for his dedication.

I presented the pair with a few documents as an overview of my career in the SB, and told them that the rest were in Australia and Britain for safe-keeping with lawyers who had specific instructions to release them to the media should either Linda or I come to any harm. We'd been using this little deception since the problems in Mossel Bay, and I believe it saved my skin.

Dutton and Koenig left after taking copious notes.

Koenig phoned the next day and told us we were to go to Johannesburg for two weeks, during which time I should cooperate with them, presumably to save my backside, after which we'd be able to return home to Knysna. I felt that this would be a fortnight in which I could sell my friends down the river and trade my freedom.

'Don't worry,' they said. 'We just want to know your story! Your friends won't be prosecuted. We'll look after you. The Goldstone Commission is not a body that institutes prosecutions; we just want to know about the Third Force.'

That same evening, Koenig and Dutton returned to Knysna to tell us that not only would we be leaving for Johannesburg the very next morning, but also that we would then go on to London. We were now on the witness protection programme of the Goldstone Commission.

On the following Saturday, we were ushered through customs by an efficient NI team and, three hours later, departed South African airspace. A huge weight lifted off my shoulders. I'd told Koenig and Dutton before we left that I had more documents with me, but would only reveal the whole truth once I had their promise that there would be no prosecutions.

We landed at Heathrow Airport the following morning and, apparently due to some mix-up with British Intelligence, I was the only one who was thoroughly searched.

We drove through London in convoy, and at one point the otherwise silent British cops asked me to lie down on the seat and put a pillowcase-type bag over me. Linda's continual demand to have a cigarette was finally agreed to, and we stopped. When I was eventually allowed out of the Land Rover, I could see Windsor Castle in the hazy distance. We eventually arrived at a beautiful stone house surrounded by a field of daffodils. Unbelievably, this was our safe house on a farm in Bristol, where strict security measures were applied by British Intelligence.

I spent two days sorting out documents and diaries before being told that I was to travel to Denmark to give my evidence to Goldstone.

In addition to the dozens of questions I faced from the South African contingent, I also fielded some from the Brits. They showed particular interest in the information I had about Winnie Mandela and the murder of Stompie Seipei. They wanted to know whether the SB had any prima facie evidence that Winnie had been there when the child was killed. The Brits were well apprised of the situation in South Africa, although their focus seemed more on incumbent political leaders than on whom I might implicate in a crime.

Leaving Linda and the children behind in England, I was soon en route to Copenhagen. Dutton told me that other witnesses, also Qs, had already arrived and, yes, they had been asked about Stratcom and, yes, they had given my name. This made me feel that I had made the right decision to go to the commission.

On the morning that I was to give evidence, I met the other three individuals: Brood van Heerden, Willie Nortjé and Chappies Klopper. I had never met Chappies before, but I knew Brood from John Vorster Square and had last seen Willie in Ovamboland way back in 1981.

I told my story over a period of three days. Although I felt that to provide full details would have taken a week, at least I was able to give the commission a solid outline. Koenig had prepared the questions and led the evidence before Goldstone who, from time to time, also put questions or asked for further explanations.

My concern at the time was that the commission's report would be covered up by the De Klerk government, and I voiced my reservations. Not unsurprisingly, the other Qs had similar misgivings and, after giving evidence, I considered going public by calling a press conference in London. My casebook notes of the Stratcom era reflect this concern. Although De Klerk had appointed the commission, Stratcom officers were actively engaged in discrediting both him and the Goldstone Commission.

I wanted to reveal the duplicity of the National Party in continuing with Stratcom operations after the release of Mandela and the so-called levelling of the political playing fields by a glib De Klerk. But this was never going to run smoothly and, after it was confided to me that I was now persona non grata in Britain too, Linda and the children were brought to Denmark. This news was a lie, we later established, but for us it was a continuation of the humiliation and doubt. I knew, more than ever, that all the doors were closing behind me.

For several days, we had the opportunity to sightsee in Denmark, escorted everywhere by the caring and very thorough Danish Security and Intelligence Service, who went the extra mile for us. Linda and I were astonished by the orderly way of life, the cleanliness of the towns and the visibly relaxed people. Like those who taste forbidden fruit, we were hooked on that sense of freedom.

The Danes who sat in on the Goldstone Commission as observers couldn't believe some of the revelations of how we, as police officers, had protected the monstrous, evil system. At that stage, all the Qs agreed: we had been misled. No, deceived. No, betrayed.

We returned to Britain after a week, and were accommodated in a luxury penthouse in the West End with Dutton's wife and his son. Like us, his wife found it hard to be removed from everything she knew and placed among strangers in a strange country.

We felt very sorry for her. At the same time, there was speculation about how South Africa was going to become a bloodbath with the first democratic elections just a few weeks away. With the continued tension on all fronts, it was a very uncomfortable time for all of us.

The Duttons returned to South Africa before the elections, but the Goldstone Commission decided that it would be unsafe for us to go back at that point. Besides, representatives of the Department of Justice were coming to see me in London, to take a statement and discuss certain issues.

The meeting was scheduled to be held at the Horse Guards Hotel in London. I met Assistant Attorney-General Antoinette de Jager and, despite my reservations, General Martin Nel of the SAP. I was assured that, as he was head of the SAP's commercial crimes unit, he wasn't tainted by the SB. This was apparently why he was brought into the Goldstone Commission.

The meeting was fraught, though. A sworn statement was taken regarding the AK47 deal between me, Bruwer and Beyers in which we had claimed a R6 000 reward. I reminded them that I had been promised that no charges were to be brought against, especially, Nannie Beyers. Were they going to renege on this promise? I had stood firm that I would not implicate my colleagues, but I sensed that Nel really disliked me, especially when he demanded to know how I came to be in possession of a document authorising the top-secret Stratcom RECOC project, one that bore the signatures of both Adriaan Vlok and Commissioner of Police Johann Coetzee.

I could now clearly see that they were going to charge all and sundry, but De Jager insisted that Beyers would not be held accountable. What horrified me, though, was that Stratcom, and the mass of illegal actions we had carried out at the behest of the National Party government under De Klerk, were being overlooked and skilfully sidestepped.

Nel asked – in a way that I found confrontational and threatening – whether I was aware that the Kahn Commission had reported on all Stratcom activities to De Klerk and, on presentation of that report, no further steps had been contemplated by the government. I hadn't heard of the Kahn Commission, but I couldn't accept that, if it had really been independent and heard everything about what we had done post-1990, it wouldn't have recommended legal steps be taken.

Regarding what he referred to as 'the Aggett incident', Nel said the SB Head Office had given me the maximum fine specified by the law and, as such, there were no irregularities.

De Jager seemed more sympathetic, but Linda and I just wanted to go home. On several occasions we were told that we would be relocated, given new identities and set up in business in a foreign country where we could get on with our lives. Meanwhile, our children were not at school, and there was no therapy for Dylan.

We continually expressed our fears about our home in Knysna, and were told not to worry. All would be taken care of and we should take the opportunity to enjoy London – a time we would never have had if it weren't for the Goldstone Commission. We didn't feel the same, however. Our allowance was barely sufficient to live on, let alone behave like tourists, and on one occasion, when we received no money for nine days, I had no choice but to tap into our bank account in Knysna. British Intelligence wasn't happy about this at all, as we could have revealed our whereabouts and compromised our safety.

We voted on 27 April 1994 at South Africa House on Trafalgar Square, and there were so many SB suspects there that it was difficult for me to hide in the crowd. Linda and I marvelled at how the situation had changed. I had spent the best years of my life trying to destroy many of these people, and yet here we were, standing shoulder to shoulder in a festive atmosphere, waiting to cast our votes. I succumbed that day, and bought a small ANC rosette that Candice liked. Within days, it was announced that the party had won the election by a considerable margin.

After a visit by Dr Torie Pretorius of the Justice Department, we were more than determined to go home and carry on with our lives. He told us that behind the scenes Eugene de Kock had been arrested, and that we Qs were therefore safer – as if De Kock had run the Third Force all on his own and there were none of his other operatives out there. We were thus really disappointed when we were told that we would not be able to return to Knysna; the new NIS had done an appraisal and advised against it because the whole town now knew of our status. We had been compromised by members of the Goldstone Commission. In the end, we had only a few days in Knysna – a deeply miserable time – feeling terribly betrayed.

A neighbour popped in to see if we were well, and asked Linda whether I had been brainwashed by the commission. Former friends from the boat club were openly hostile, and from Mossel Bay, 100 kilometres away, I heard that I was seen as a traitor, not only by my colleagues at the SB in Mossel Bay, but also by white South Africans in general.

Linda and I subsequently found a house in Cowies Hill, Pinetown, in KwaZulu-Natal, an area sanctioned as safe by the commision and our safety officer, Dr Torie Pretorius – this despite Pinetown and environs having, at the time, the highest crime and associated political incidences in the country. Because we were on the commission's witness protection programme, the house had been rented in the name of the Goldstone Commission, as were the electricity and telephone accounts. This was incompetence on a grand scale. Our personal safety was being compromised. We decided that we would have to knuckle down, though – we would pick up the pieces and somehow start again. That was 1 July 1994.

Promises of financial assistance never materialised either, and on our own initiative and with the last of our resources, Linda and I started an import–export business. This proved to be a nightmare, however: we were compromised once again, this time in Mozambique by a man who told all and sundry about the Goldstone Commission.

The owners of a pub and restaurant down the road in Cowies Hill were also informed about our status. Their son, aged 11, asked our daughter Candice why her father was on a witness protection programme – was it because I was in the army, the SAP or the AWB? This upset her terribly – the Goldstone Commission had been her best-kept secret, and she had never discussed our situation with anyone other than me and Linda.

I have no doubt that the maintenance of security was not a priority among all members of the Goldstone Commission, some of whom were seconded to the Investigation Task Unit (ITU) in KwaZulu-Natal to investigate Third Force activities there. When the commission closed at the end of September 1994, commission documentation and dockets – including sworn statements from other witnesses, revealing their addresses and identities and other sensitive information – were left in our garage together with a heap of SAP case dockets.

On the closure of the commission we were confirmed as still being on the witness protection programme, but nothing was going well. In a conversation in February 1995, our contact at the ITU told us he believed that relocating us to KZN had been 'a grave mistake' because elements of the IFP would stop at nothing to silence commission witnesses. At least two had already been murdered, so our fear now extended beyond my former SB colleagues.

We reported all these indiscretions and irregularities to Pretorius, including attempts by the ITU to convince us that we shouldn't trust his department. We were confused. Weren't we supposed to be on the same side now?

Members of the ITU continually vilified Pretorius and exhorted us not to trust him because he was an 'NIS agent'. Our worries thus mounted. We were trapped in a vacuum of insecurity. The people around us were making up the rules as they went along, with all guarantees and glimmers of resolution being dashed.

'You're a key witness in the TRC.'

'You'll be given a position overseas.'

'You will be able to work for National Intelligence.'

And, unbelievably, 'How would you feel about going back to the SAP?'

The days dragged on with no end in sight. We were in a place we didn't like, 1 200 kilometres from Knysna, in what we increasingly saw as a hazardous situation. The Department of Justice then confirmed that the largest part of our claim – that being compensation for our boat – would not be met. The bulk of our future was still in Knysna, but we eventually gave up and sold it at a loss of R28 000.

Linda wanted to teach dancing again and went for an audition at a local studio but had to resort to a feeble excuse when the owners asked her to sign a contract. She came home in tears. One of the only things she was able to do under the circumstances was being denied her. She was again succumbing to depression, and in my usual clumsy way I tried to assure her that all was well. It came as no surprise, however, that Linda was nearing breaking point again, and finally she consulted a lawyer with the intention of instituting divorce proceedings, primarily to ensure the children's safety.

At about midnight on 23 March 1995, I heard our dogs barking. I crawled out of bed and made my way down the passage, through the front door and security gate and into the darkness. After inspecting our yard and finding nothing amiss, I went back into the house, switched off the lights and lay awake, all senses alert.

Crash!

Linda was out of the bed ahead of me.

'Get down, get down!' I shouted. The children, the children! Linda grabbed and dragged them down the passage, Dylan crying out. I fired through the curtains onto the balcony. Two, three shots. 'Go! Get to the kitchen and lie flat.'

Heading out of the front door, I ducked behind the wall and shot two bullets to the left from where the sound of the barking came. I thought I could make out a hand grenade in the darkness. I opened fire in the exposed area of the front yard. Left, right. Four, eight, ten shots. I ducked behind the wall again.

By this time, my magazine was empty, and I was deaf from my own shots.

Linda telephoned the emergency number and, minutes later, our yard was swarming with policemen and neighbours, and a photographer. One cop had to wash his hands in our kitchen sink because they were burning from the acid that had been thrown over our cars. Another saw a white car with Gauteng plates, its occupants concealing their faces as they raced by.

So much for witness protection, I thought. I finally managed to get in touch with our contact there, some eight hours after the incident.

Linda was raging and unstoppable. She phoned the Danish Embassy and explained our situation, and contacted the *Sunday Times* to give them her story. She stated that if anyone had anything they wanted to get off their chest, they should rather flee while they could, and avoid any so-called witness protection and promises that would inevitably be forgotten.

Linda wanted to raise money to leave the country, go where nobody knew her identity or those of the children, and said that if I wanted to come it would be wonderful, but if I wanted to stay loyal to the system, well, I could stay and get myself killed. The children came first.

I was in a dilemma.

211

I realised, too, that when the *Sunday Times* published Linda's story, my identity as Q4 would be revealed and, on impulse, I called Harvey Ward and some of my other former agents. Ward and I spoke about the old days, confirming all that had happened. Although initially reluctant to talk on the phone, he eventually brought me up to date and told me that he was continuing with his activities against the ANC, although, he said, certain elements in the National Party had now also become targets.

I then expressed an interest in picking up on Stratcom activities from where we had left off in 1991, ostensibly on behalf of 'a right-wing party', knowing that Ward was in contact with an old agent of mine. I'd heard that the agent had continued with Stratcom activities too, but now on behalf of the Freedom Front.[23] I requested the names of people who could be effectively used for this purpose.

According to another contact, British MP Andrew Hunter was apparently in a position where he might resume contact with me directly. There were other members of the British Parliament who might, my contact claimed, be 'prepared to assist' too, including Gibb Stuart (Ward's former partner in the publishing business), Lord Sudeley, who was president and chairman of the arch-conservative Monday Club for 17 years, and M. Walsh of the Truth about Africa League, a subcommittee of the Monday Club.

Ward also ventured that, in the United States, there might be interest from Slimp, among others, and suggested a face-to-face to brief me on 'the old network', which was still 'firmly in place'. He had been advised to dispose of a lot of data and urged me to maintain security at all costs.

Then suddenly Ward died – five weeks after our conversation, having collapsed while playing bowls.

I travelled to Pretoria where I handed over a 57-page statement on our compromised position to Torie Pretorius. An angry confrontation followed with Attorney-General Dr Jan D'Oliveira. The final blow came when D'Oliveira said that he had inherited us from the Goldstone Commission and had had no choice but to include us on his witness protection programme. Promises made by the Goldstone Commission that could not be met were, therefore, not his responsibility. In a subsequent response to the *Sunday Times*, D'Oliveira claimed that all our 'grievances and complaints' had been 'satisfactorily attended to', and I was hard pressed to prevent Linda from issuing a public rebuttal, not wanting our situation with D'Oliveira to deteriorate any further.

After the attack on our house, we once again relocated – but this time on my terms. Nobody was able to contact us, except on our mobile phones, and the lease agreement, utility accounts and other formalities were arranged according to regular intelligence practices. In the meantime, however, the Department of Justice had made it quite clear that our participation on the witness protection programme would stop around the end of June 1995. We would also not be reimbursed for any of the losses we had incurred.

If I had been putting off seeing this fact, or had been pretending that it wasn't so, this was the moment I knew for certain that I was expendable – that our being compromised so regularly was more than just the department's lack of experience. Once I'd come to some sort of acceptance of this fact, and dealt with some of the emotions that came with this realisation, I began to think that this was not (only) a personal thing and that there could well be a more sinister motive.

Unlike the other Q witnesses, my evidence concerned not only the criminal activities of individuals but also centred on how these actions were condoned – if not directly sanctioned – by the National Party governments of Botha and De Klerk.

At the opening of the proceedings and under oath, I was made aware of my rights by state advocate Koenig and told of the guarantee that anything that I said could not be used against me in any criminal proceedings, with Goldstone himself interjecting that this guarantee included both criminal and civil proceedings. This entire section had been omitted from the transcript, however, and further swathes had been swapped around or not transcribed at all.

On one tape, the transcription stopped when I began to explain the discrediting of Winnie Mandela using the disinformation regarding an affair between her and Chris Ball, and how this was a classic Stratcom tactic. The same happened with the explanation of Stratcom clients and the involvement of the apartheid Cabinet, with the exception of Kobie Coetsee. So too with a reference to Pik Botha and the four-year plan to reduce the ANC to 'just another political party'.

A whole side of one tape had been wiped and, according to the transcription, the other side was blank. On checking if this was indeed so, I found it perfectly audible; it contained masses of detail I had given on the local and overseas operations, including the cover-up of a sexual assault in Mossel Bay and the bugging of the ANC, which continued until I left the force in 1993. Details of the further discrediting of Winnie Mandela and the involvement of British parliamentarians, as well as the top-secret creation of a 'new' political party, were not recorded in the transcripts.

I was stunned.

Two tape recorders do not break down at the same time and, considering the gravity and political ramifications of the evidence I had given, I could not accept that mistakes like this could be made.

Other Goldstone evidence had been released earlier to the *Sowetan* newspaper by a policeman working for the Department of Justice. Meanwhile, former UDF activist Shirley Gunn had instituted criminal and civil proceedings against Vlok, who had implicated her in the bombing of Khotso House, alleging that she had carried the explosives into the building. Gunn was heavily pregnant at the time.

By now, I was concerned that Stratcom victims might be able to institute proceedings against me. Even Nelson Mandela might have had a claim. My stress levels were again reaching epic proportions and my thoughts continually turned to the words of our priest from two years before: 'Paul, the truth will set you free from this bondage.' And from a psychiatrist: 'You cannot defend an evil system. Get it off your chest. The catharsis will set you free. You'll be able to come to terms with yourself, and what you have done.'

The Department of Justice, however, could give no assurances, and I was told that only a court could grant indemnity. Goldstone's promises of indemnity were worthless babble. On top of that, the Department of Justice had no explanation for the irregularities in the transcriptions.

I was now up against the behemoth with two heads: one, a National Party that I knew only too well, and the other, a National Party that had realised it was losing badly to the ANC and would never regain its political ground.

Chapter Fifteen

Mr Dirty Tricks

Johannesburg, 1995

IN EARLY JUNE 1995, a meeting was arranged with the *Weekly Mail* editor, Anton Harber, and I drove 300 kilometres from KwaZulu-Natal to meet him at a restaurant in Harrismith, halfway to Johannesburg.

I wondered how he would react to me. I had not only been – and still was, in many respects – the enemy, but also someone who had had the opportunity and the brainpower to see that what I was doing was wrong but continued to do it nevertheless.

For a long moment, Harber and I looked at each other.

'You're lucky to be alive,' I said, giving him my broadest smile.

We shook hands tentatively and then began. Harber seldom commented.

The next week the newspaper carried a banner headline, 'Mr Dirty Tricks …', and I immediately found myself in the midst of a storm, with dozens of requests for interviews and information.

'Were you involved in the death of my brother at Derdefontein?'

'Was the head of the South African Communications Service (SACS) a Stratcom agent?'

'Did Stratcom target Chris Hani?'

'Is Winnie as bad as we've been led to believe? Did she kill Stompie?'

'Which ANC parliamentarians were Stratcom agents?'

'Who is paying you to destroy the National Party?'

'Are you a member of the ANC?'

'Do you know that the right wing is ecstatic at your revelations because they will pick up votes in the next elections?'

'How much money are you making out of this?'

I summarised my story as best I could, over and over again: the National Party under F.W. de Klerk had been double-dealing in the negotiation process, as we had only been trained formally in Stratcom in August 1990, six months after the release of Mandela; Stratcom had not only continued, but also accelerated after the signing of various accords between the National Party and the liberation movements; and the SB had continued monitoring National Party opponents until at least 1993.

Calls came in from all over the world. One of my most memorable interviews was on SABC Radio with former detainees whom I had interrogated, Rocky Williams and Stephen Marais, as well as 'dirty tricks' victim the Reverend Rob Robertson on the line from the United States.

There were other examples of this kind of interview, with some former targets being conciliatory, while others publicly attacked me. I found it very difficult to know, even within myself, whether my intentions were to save my reputation or my life.

Vlok was unavailable for comment throughout. He had previously had an onset of what appeared to be selective amnesia when the *Sunday Times* claimed that it had the tape recording of the moment during that 1990 Stratcom course when assassination was discussed.

The former Commissioner of Police, Johan van der Merwe, said my revelations were 'total rubbish'.

After two weeks, I released the final Goldstone Report – which I had pinched from our safety officer, Torie Pretorius – described by the *Weekly Mail* as a 'hot potato' that no political party wanted to touch. This was because the 'depraved police leadership' of the past could sully the political parties' 'understanding' with each other. But of course I had known this all along. I saw this all very clearly, long before I decided to share the report. By the time I did this, I was so utterly disconnected from everything that all I wanted to do was clear out my boxes, shelves and cupboards, and get rid of all the clutter, mess and hoardings that I would otherwise drag with me into the next stage in my life.

The report implicated members of the SAP in multiple illegal activities, including murder, the supply of illegal arms and ammunition, fraud, blackmail and political disinformation. A large number of senior police officers, including the Commissioner, were not only aware of these criminal activities but also must have approved them and the funding that made them possible.

The report also clearly pointed to the involvement of Vlok and a host of Third Force activities.

Justice Goldstone's comments in the report included this reference:

> We would draw attention to the fact that Erasmus has opened only one window into the frightening operations of the Security Police.
>
> Their involvement in violence and political intimidation is pervasive and touches directly or indirectly every citizen in this country. The documents we have been given by one Warrant Officer can be but a tiny sample of the whole.
>
> The whole illegal, criminal and oppressive system is still in place and its architects are in control of the SAP. It cannot be coincidence that in the most senior ranks of the SAP there is such a predominance of officers who have led the SB over the past couple of decades.
>
> It is a bleak prospect that this country enters its first democratic election with this security structure in place. Appropriate steps are necessary and urgent to attempt to neutralise the effect of it before the election and to cut it out root and branch at the earliest possible time.
>
> Perhaps the worst feature of this investigation is that members of the Commission and its staff fear for their lives. So too, obviously, do the people who have given testimony to the Commission. This feature illustrates the depravity of the leadership of the SAP elements within it.

Goldstone recommended that urgent and immediate steps be taken, and that the leadership of the SAP, including the Commissioner, be effectively relieved of their positions as they were 'patently unsuited' for these. He said that one of the first acts of the new government should be to establish a commission to expose the system that 'caused so much misery, death and destruction of people and property', to identify victims of that system and to pay the appropriate compensation to them.

Adriaan Vlok responded, 'it is total nonsense that I had known about any such operations'. Police Commissioner Johan van der Merwe was also in denial and added that, should the report in fact exist, 'the way in which the allegations were handled' by the Goldstone Commission was 'shocking and showed a total ignorance of justice, democracy and transparency'.

Johann Coetzee, former head of the SB and a SB career policeman himself, suggested that the Police Commissioner should not venture to talk about 'justice, democracy and transparency' when he had been part of everything that ever happened in the SB.

Van der Merwe then stated, 'the people involved' in releasing the report were guilty of an offence and liable for a R4 000 penalty. I invited him to charge me for the offence.

Then came De Klerk's seven-page statement in which he claimed that Stratcom and Third Force activities conducted after 1990 were the work and responsibility of 'renegade elements' within the security forces, who 'could have been involved in illegal actions aimed at promoting their own political and even criminal agendas'.

The leader of the Democratic Party, Tony Leon, summed it up when he said that it seemed as though the National Party was turning its back on the foot soldiers who, encouraged by their political leaders, had committed acts of terror against the South African people.

Johan van der Merwe later turned on his former masters and admitted that De Klerk had, indeed, been briefed on all secret projects during the last four years of his government. Van der Merwe had, however, set himself up against former members of the SAP too, by putting his name on the indemnity list of 3 500 police officers whom De Klerk had approved just before being replaced by Mandela in the April 1994 election. As an expression of solidarity with the SAP of his era, De Klerk had placed his own name on that list too.

When it was reported that De Klerk, some ex-ministers and generals involved with the old State Security Council had already met on three occasions and were planning a fourth to prepare themselves for what must have felt like the coming onslaught of the TRC, I felt that old fury burning bright as ever inside me. Surely the concept of a truth commission was that each individual go before the commission and tell their story alone, because that is what they chose to do – for whatever reason.

What preparation did they need? If the National Party leadership, old and new, was plotting before they approached the commission, surely apartheid security force members should also get together and plan what they would tell the TRC?

We, the foot soldiers, were embattled, not so much by our consciences, but by the fact that we had been disregarded and discarded, thrown away by those who represented a government that had employed us to kill, maim and torture. This is the truth. We simply couldn't get over it. And the fact was that this time there was no way of threatening our way back in, or of utilising contacts we may have made, or of appealing on the basis of race or history – this time we were finally beaten.

I – and probably all of us – properly understood what had to be done at the TRC: it was each man for himself. Survival of the fittest. It wasn't going to help me, Paul Erasmus, to connive with others when I knew full well that we had been trained in the SB to betray one another. Fuck '*Volk en Vlag*'!

Of course, there were many times that we were called to order. Individuals such as the Reverend Frank Chikane of the South African Council of Churches (SACC), whose name I had once placed alongside that of other anti-apartheid activists on the SB list for what we called 'permanent removal', told me that his first concern was for my wife and children and our safety. He said that he and other SACC members had being praying for this as soon as I went public. This is the same man who was poisoned by the SAP with an organophosphate pesticide called Paraoxon.

Chikane told the media that, for the sake of the country, he hoped more people would join me. 'We are all prisoners and victims,' he said.

I thought about this when a Dutch journalist arranged a meeting between me, Winnie Mandela and Peter Mokaba. I agreed, although I felt numb at the thought of meeting them face to face, especially Winnie.

This meeting was also linked to the *Weekly Mail*, which had run its incendiary headline, 'The Trashing of Winnie', the week before we were to meet. The article itself contained a lot of Stratcom detail about the actions against the Mandelas, especially Winnie. I had been on the team that had toiled to make the world believe that she was an evil murderer and hell-bent on killing whites; and that she engaged in drunken orgies with young activists. How was she going to react to me? As it turned out, I had now become a victim of my own propaganda.

Naturally, when she walked in, I was as entranced as almost every other person who met her. She did, indeed, have an aura about her, one that writers, poets, songwriters, artists, even politicians, have described so well. Standing there, I didn't know whether I was in awe or terror.

Winnie was friendly, but not effusive: 'Good morning, Mr Erasmus. Thank you very much for coming. How are your wife and children? Are they safe?'

Her eyes never left mine. If I had missed every other opportunity, I wasn't going to miss this one. The Goldstone Commission, the interview with the *Weekly Mail*, other media conversations – none was as pivotal as this one. Idiot that I might have been at other times, I seized this chance to try to get it right.

I told her that I could substantiate, with documentation, what she had read in the *Weekly Mail*.

Often, when we met after that, I sensed an overwhelming sadness in her, and even in that introductory meeting, Winnie intermittently dabbed at her eyes with a tissue. At the end, she put her arm around my shoulders and thanked me.

In July 1995, I was at Johannesburg International Airport, reading a newspaper while I waited for my flight to Durban, when someone flopped into the seat opposite me.

'Hello, Paul!'

I was startled when I recognised one of my former Stratcom unit commanders, who was immediately joined by a second senior police officer. An acrimonious exchange followed in which I was warned that if I revealed the name of 'just one more Stratcom agent', I could be 'hunted down'. But they switched as readily from their sinister warning to imploring me to stop because I was 'throwing a spanner in the works' of what senior colleagues were 'planning to tell the TRC'. They calmly told me, too, that De Kock – who was then on trial – would 'not see October'. As it was, he had fallen seriously ill that April and family members feared that a near-fatal blood clot he'd suffered might be the result of an attempt to poison him.

Nannie Beyers said he had heard that the plan was now to implicate me in the death of Stanza Bopape, who had been shocked to death on the tenth floor of John Vorster Square in 1988.

It wasn't a good time for Beyers when he called me about the rumoured Bopape cover-up He was trying to contend with his own demons, two significant ones being a reprisal bombing by the SB of a gay nightclub called the Why Not in Hillbrow, and the poisoning of the Reverend Frank Chikane. He had refused to apply for amnesty and, worse, refused to submit to any form of therapy for his PTSD. He had resigned from the police around the same time as I had, whereupon he had been summoned to General Gert Erasmus's office and told that he would be promoted immediately to lieutenant if he would retract his resignation.

Beyers's wife told me a few years later, after his death, that she was convinced the SAP – or former members of the SAP – had killed him. I had taken Nannie to Shell House for tea with Winnie and she listened intently when he told her about the abuse of conscripts by elements in the SADF, the Noord Street bombing and how a select few like him and me were regularly given orders to kill people. He also outlined the events that led up to the poisoning of Frank Chikane. Beyers and I had been tasked with the preparatory work leading up to the application of the poison on the reverend's luggage.

Linda and I decided to go back to George in 1996 and bought an old house. Yet, although I tried, I couldn't avoid the news about the imminent TRC hearings. I eventually sat down to write my amnesty application.

Judge Richard Goldstone and the Department of Justice had, of course, repeatedly told Q witnesses that if we cooperated fully, there would be no prosecutions. Yet, the Attorney-General's office still indicated that I should apply for amnesty as the new Promotion of National Unity and Reconciliation Act, No. 34 of 1995, had come into effect. The rules were simple: full disclosure and being able to substantiate that the activities in which I participated were for 'a political reason'. The primary issue with full disclosure, of course, is being able to remember enough to give a truthful account of circumstances that might have occurred two decades earlier.

Naturally, there would be discomfort in having to reveal who else was present during the events and describing their role in these. If one did not remember an event, or the details surrounding it, with complete clarity, there was a danger of mistakenly including people at the scene of a crime – or, indeed, being wrongly implicated by someone else during their testimony.

A comparison of evidence from various witnesses could result in terrible confrontations – a nightmare of counter-accusations and bitterness. I decided to go ahead anyway with what I remembered. There wasn't going to be another time, another opportunity, like the TRC. This was my only chance.

Contrary to instructions, I had never handed in a personal casebook to my superior officers, and while relatively few of the illegal activities in which I had been involved were recorded there, even oblique references were a great help in building a chronological account. I also had a mass of official documentation. My full set of casebooks contains details of over 11 000 SB investigations. I thus wrote my amnesty application using the casebooks as a guideline and was horrified – as was Linda – when the tally of serious offences came to over 500 in the context of 80 incidents. I was told by a TRC commissioner that this was a South African record.

This wasn't me, I thought. This was a monster!

I fell into a hellish depression.

Chapter Sixteen

'I Have Stompie'

Johannesburg and Nairobi, 1998

I WAS SITTING IN CHURCH when another congregant engaged me in a conversation I shouldn't have had. Chatting about Genesis 9 and the story of Noah, we wound our way to a popular topic for conservative Christians: the ark-builder's 'bout of sudden drunkenness'.

The man became animated. He said that this could be explained from an environmental point of view because there had been increased levels of ozone prior to the flood, which could have caused a fermentation process in the grape juice Noah had been making to take on his trip. Noah had unwittingly got drunk when he consumed the juice.

The man became quite swept up by his theory, insisting that the altered carbon dioxide levels of the atmosphere described in the Old Testament had led to a remarkable discovery. Cancer and other potentially fatal illnesses 'could not survive in the presence of higher oxygen levels'. His conclusion? If a person of our times drank watered-down hydrogen peroxide, it would have the same effect – killing off viruses and bacteria in the body.

Not only that. He told me that there was a group in Rosettenville, a suburb south of Johannesburg, that were treating and curing not only cancer, but also AIDS, using adaptations of ancient and biblical knowledge combined with modern science.

I argued at length with this man. This had to be a scam. But then – perhaps from a twisted need to be privy to something secret that might later reap dividends – I became friendly, or so I thought, with the owner of the clinic where these studies were being conducted.

The particular 'snake oil' peddled by Shawn Stewart, who ran the Genesis Research Centre in Rosettenville, was in fact 'technology' developed by a criminal, Basil Wainwright, who claimed to be a former developer of nuclear weapons. Wainwright – who liked to be called 'Dr', as well as being a wanted man in Kenya, among other places – claimed that his 'polyatomic apheresis treatment' resulted in HIV reversal, or what he termed 'HIV inactivation'.

Certainly, there were some sophisticated-looking pieces of equipment at Stewart's clinic. Simply put, the treatment involved withdrawing a non-threatening amount of blood from a client, exposing it to a gaseous ozone-oxygen mixture, which was supposed to inactivate any infectious organisms such as viruses and bacteria, and then 'reinfusing' it into the client.

Stewart was passionate, fervent in his belief in the efficacy of this treatment. According to him, every time this was done, the viral and bacterial loads in that amount of blood were wiped out. Performed over a period of time, the treatment could totally eradicate viruses and cure clients.

There were two basic types of oxygen therapy: ozone blood infusion, and the absorption of oxygen water (hydrogen peroxide) in very low concentrations. Stewart was so inspired by Wainwright, who turned out to be a conman of note, that he believed – or perpetuated the idea for his own profit – that it was acceptable to run an unregistered clinic and trick desperate, often dying, people. Also disturbing was that Stewart was a devout Christian who was reluctant to treat clients who were not 'born again'.

I approached an acquaintance, journalist Andrea Vinassa, and tried to convince her to meet Stewart. This was in 1998. I wanted to make this therapy 'real', will it to life so that it could cure people of what was then a killer virus, and so that I could be a part of this. Mandela had yet to focus his attention on HIV and AIDS, and at the time South Africa was far from an ARV rollout of any kind. The number of people contracting HIV was escalating, and thousands were dying.

I honestly hadn't cared that much about other people my whole adult life. I had no idea of how to live in a world where I could contribute in some humane way. A part of me had to prove to the world that I wasn't the monster I had become. I had to reach Jesus' outstretched hand. The quackery gave me a bizarre kind of focus on something other than my chaotic life. Maybe, just maybe, there was a possibility that this therapy could reverse HIV. Or was Stewart exploiting people as much as I was pretending?

Then I made a mad decision.

I persuaded Stewart that Winnie Mandela's support was the way forward. He was sceptical and nervous, but after I had made the requisite overtures to her, she agreed to a briefing on how the treatment worked. He introduced her to some of his clients and showed her 'medical reports', including from supposedly respected sources, among them doctors and pathologists.

Winnie then brought her own doctors into this toxic mix on her second visit, and those doctors claimed to be equally amazed, or flummoxed, by what they saw. Things were hurtling out of control.

Winnie said that she wanted to approach the inventor of this 'wonder cure', and, if possible, bring him to South Africa. Of course, this couldn't be done – Wainwright was unavailable, in Kenya, where he lived as a fugitive, a wanted man. Then, within a few days and after plenty of drama involving money, plane tickets, and the question of whether this was an officially sanctioned visit or not, we were on our way to Nairobi.

The status of Winnie's visit was changed to official while we were in the air, although she told me and Vinassa – who had come with us – that she was in serious trouble with almost everyone in the ANC, from the president down. She had told ANC officials and others in her circle that while there were people suffering, she would not be dictated to by protocol. This was a disaster in the making.

We only realised the extent of the storm that had erupted when we touched down in Kenya. The Kenyan government did not really want to deal with this, but agreed to host us at a luxury guest house before meeting Wainwright. He was seen as a charlatan by many Kenyans, who wanted him kicked out of the country.

Despite this, we were introduced to people who had supposedly been cured of HIV. We saw the apheresis machine at work, with dark, venous blood being tapped out of clients, running through the machine, and being reinfused as bright red arterial blood.

Winnie made a huge impact and carried herself with authority throughout. She prayed for us at breakfast, imploring God to make this fact-finding mission a success and a 'blessing to so many suffering people'.

I had only just got custody of Dylan, and Winnie became something of a grandmother figure to him while we were in Kenya, admonishing me when she felt I was setting the wrong example or when I was behaving towards him in a way she didn't like.

Wainwright lived with armed protection, compliments of the authorities, in Kenya's Karen Estates. But there was ambiguity in the government's response to him. We were whisked off to a state banquet and then for a private meeting with President Daniel arap Moi, only to be excluded from the meeting at the last minute, much to Winnie's disappointment.

Finally, when Wainwright expressed reservations about supplying his machines to South Africa, it dawned on us that the deal was not completely legitimate. We were all disillusioned, especially as a war was now raging around the topic in the media in Kenya and in South Africa. Some international media had even picked up on it. I could no longer control this kind of response – it was well out of my league now. And so, unable to melt back into the ANC's collective embrace – political, ideological or historical – Winnie bore the brunt of the fallout.

Winnie's view was that if we were being conned, she would be able to accept that, but if the treatment was genuine and we hadn't done our best to deliver it to people, we would, she said, never be able to live with ourselves.

Fortunately for me, Winnie came to represent so much more in my life than just this insanity on my part. That Kenyan experience is symbolic of my complete lapse of reason at that time – how I tried to use my old manipulative skills to twist a good person into my knot. Not only had I become enmeshed in a bogus scheme, but, worse, I had continued darkening Winnie's reputation – already horrifically damaged by Stratcom.

Winnie was rather depressed when we all flew back to South Africa, but if she was wounded, she certainly wasn't defeated. She even had the grace to describe Stewart as possibly being 'a scarred genius' – this even though we arrived back to a frenzy of allegations and warrants of arrest for Stewart and me for practising medicine without a licence. Genesis was subsequently raided under warrant and Stewart's machines removed.

This was all happening against the backdrop of another major AIDS cure scandal – the Virodene project – for which Health Minister Nkosazana Dlamini-Zuma, an early booster of the toxic compound, was somehow forgiven.

The ANC hardly batted an eyelid over the Dlamini-Zuma Virodene debacle, but Winnie faced the full force of its wrath over oxytherapy.

That I was attacked for wanting to 'inject bleach into people's veins' and trying to syphon cash off people frantic to save their children's lives was upsetting, but I was equally perturbed about having severed the one connection I cared about: that with Winnie.

The fallout for Winnie from the oxygen therapy 'cure' was catastrophic. When I saw her again at Luthuli House, she was in tears, roundly condemned not so much for believing in this lunacy of an AIDS cure, but for allowing herself to be led by the nose by a dangerous ex-SB cop – me – who was trying to damage the ANC. These were among the allegations levelled at Winnie and me.

'There is no chance of redemption for people like you and me,' said Winnie during a tearful meeting we had some weeks later. 'I have Stompie and you have to live with what you did as well. We will never be allowed to find peace.'

Chapter Seventeen

Testimony

Transcript of the testimony of the former Security Police and Stratcom operative, Paul Erasmus, to the Truth and Reconciliation Hearings on the Mandela United Football Club, 28 November 1997

PIERS PIGOU (TRC INVESTOGATOR): 'I ... want to refer you back to your statement ... where you refer to President Mandela as being an obvious target, due to his impeccable integrity. The next sentence, I just need that to be explained to me a little bit more.

'"I/we put out the message that he had little control over the radical ANC cadres and SDUs [self-defence units], there was a power struggle within the ANC hierarchy, he was going senile", and this is the point that I [would like you to] perhaps explain to me: "... And had little control over his wife who was running rampant in the townships with her Football Club, who were inter alia intimidating the local population."

'Now the subject of much of the discussion for the course of this week has been about his wife who was running rampant or alleged to be running rampant in the townships with the Football Club who were inter alia intimidating the local population.

'Were you spreading disinformation about the Football Club and Mrs Mandela as to what they were doing in the townships or were you spreading information over the fact that he [President Mandela] had little control over his wife who was running rampant in the townships?

'Do you understand the difference that I've got here? I just need you to explain that to me.'

Paul Erasmus: 'I find it a little bit difficult to distinguish between the two. I would answer "yes" to it. As I've explained and I think my former colleague and unit commander [Vic McPherson, who took the stand with me] explained, Stratcom operated on a mixture of, or various aspects of, intelligence gleaned, some of it intelligence reports, media reports, rumours, hearsay or whatever ...'

Pigou: 'And factual information ...'

Erasmus: 'And factual information.'

Pigou: 'So what I'm trying to establish in the course of the Mandela United Football Club activities [is this]: Was the information that you received about this factual, or was this information that you spread as disinformation, that it wasn't actually information that was actually happening at the time, or were these factual reports that you were receiving?'

Erasmus: 'Some of the reports were factual.'

Pigou: 'Could you give us a sense, Mr Erasmus, because you seem to have been quite close to this process, although I know you became only full-time in 1990 from my reading of your statement of those particular things?

'Sorry, I'm mixing you up with Mr McPherson.

'Could you give us a sense of how much of the material that you were receiving around the Football Club was factual information and how much was actually stuff that you had to rework, so to speak?'

Erasmus: 'I think I must maybe just explain that Mrs Winnie Madikizela-Mandela, and after the President's release, were obviously the most heavily targeted people in the Security Branch in the Stratcom sense in the country.

'Mrs Mandela, all the years, I'm very aware of it and I'm on safe ground if I say, was under 24-hour surveillance. The telephone was tapped, the house was bugged, her movements were monitored on a 24-hour basis and I cannot think of any other circumstance or situation in the South African Police Security Branch where more attention was given to anything than Mrs Winnie Madikizela-Mandela's situation.

'Now, with the advent of Stratcom in Johannesburg, to get to your question, I began to receive intelligence reports, and especially after this international capability that we had, had opened his [President Mandela's] doors to us, I began to receive reports, but not on a regular basis. There was some bureaucratic bungling or whatever, but I received reports on an almost daily basis sometimes about the goings-on within the Mandela home.

'These reports were incredibly accurate. What time the President got up, for example. Literally, what he had for breakfast. What Mrs Mandela was doing. A lot of it was absolutely innocuous, which wasn't of value to me in a

Stratcom sense, although I was exhorted on a day-to-day basis and given these reports and [told] 'do something with it' as if I was a machine that could turn out a dirty trick for every occasion.

'I wasn't able to do it. [Although] I also received verbal reports about [it], I had never specialised [in] and had little knowledge of the Mandela United Football Club. [The verbal reports came in] Stratcom seminars and at meetings and at braais, and with regular contact that we had with people in Soweto ...'

Dr Alex Boraine (acting TRC chairperson): 'Mr Erasmus, can you just make your replies a little shorter and little more precise, please?'

Erasmus: 'I am sorry, but I am just trying to put things in perspective. I did receive information about the Mandela United Football Club, as mentioned here, for smoking dagga or marijuana, the glue-sniffing kids and [that they] were uncontrollable, intimidating other residents in Soweto and so on.'

Pigou: 'Could you tell us, I just want to get this clear, according to a press release that I have a copy of here that you made on the 9th of September 1990, it says that, "One of the major Stratcom operations, code-named Romulus, included in this definition many ad hoc activities aimed at the ANC–SACP–COSATU alliance, and from 1990 onwards, I headed the application of Operation Romulus in the Johannesburg area on a full-time basis ..."

'You weren't working on Romulus on a full-time basis during the period which has really been under question here – end of 1988, or shall I say 1987. I think we've been listening to cases today through to mid-1989. We're mainly looking at disinformation. You were talking about disinformation from 1990 onwards. Is that correct?'

Erasmus: 'That is correct.'

Pigou: 'And the nature of the allegations that you seem to be talking mostly about are matters which don't fall within the purview of this Commission. Is that correct?'

Erasmus: 'That is correct.'

Pigou: 'What we are very interested in is the so-called "rampant running around in the townships" of the [Mandela United] Football Club, and the reaction to that by the Security Branch. Now, you've indicated that there was heavy surveillance of Mrs Mandela ... her residence, physical surveillance and telephone tapping, and so forth.'

Erasmus: 'Correct.'

Pigou: 'Would it surprise you then that criminal activities could go on inside the Mandela household, or emanate from the Mandela household, and nothing would be done about them by the local police, Security Branch or other policing structures?'

Erasmus: 'That wouldn't really have surprised me.'

Pigou: 'Why not?'

Erasmus: 'I think at the time, during the latter years anyway, Mrs Mandela, although she was under heavy surveillance and so on, was almost feared by the state. Any move against her would really have upset the political apple-cart.

'There were many times that we questioned why Mrs Mandela – I think the Security Branch questioned – why legal actions weren't or prosecutions weren't taken against Mrs Mandela. But the general feeling was that she should be left alone as far as possible, and that after statements like the necklacing thing, she would be digging her own grave anyway and counter-productive to the ANC ...'

Pigou: 'Thank you. Would you say it was also quite useful for the Security Branch to have the kind of activities that were emanating out of the back yard in Soweto from Mrs Mandela's house? That this was actually very useful propaganda material for you?'

Erasmus: 'Most definitely.'

Pigou: 'So, would you be saying then that much of the information, or some of the information, I don't want to put a figure on it, or a percentage or whatever, proportion of the information that came out about the activities of the Football Club, was indeed factual then. It was actually happening. It was happening out of that back yard in Soweto?'

Erasmus: 'A lot of the information, yes, was correct [although] I never specialised [in it]. I must just point out, Mrs Mandela – even at the height of these activities – was one of many people that I dealt with. I didn't have the time or the opportunity, or in fact the capacity, to make a full study of a given situation. My workload was just too heavy to do it.'

Pigou: 'Thanks. Are you aware of any, well within Operation Romulus, because I am not sure if there were any other operations ... perhaps you could tell us, were there any other Security Branch Stratcom operations against Mrs Mandela? Were you aware, or to your knowledge, was Operation Romulus used to intervene in criminal investigations in order to falsify information or evidence to involve Mrs Mandela in criminal activities such as the Stompie Seipei killing and the kidnapping?'

Erasmus: 'Well, I think what I said about just "the use of dagga" is a clear indication of that type of ... evidence.'

Pigou: 'Yes. I mean, we are talking now about falsifying evidence which could be used for criminal prosecution.'

Erasmus: 'No, I am not aware of that.'

Pigou: 'Okay. Returning to your document very quickly ... you refer to

Sergeant Pretorius as the handler of one Jerry Richardson. Would that be the same Sergeant Stephanus Pretorius who died in Jerry Richardson's house on 9 November 1988?'

Erasmus: 'That is correct.'

Pigou: 'I just want to talk briefly now through some of the reactions that we had during the course of the in-camera Section 29 hearing. This is 1989, so you may not have had direct knowledge as you weren't working full-time on these Stratcom operations, but you may well have had insight into these kinds of things. So we will appreciate whatever information you can give us about this.

'We have been referring in the last couple of days to a Mandela Crisis Committee document which was sent, according to the Crisis Committee members who sat here, to Lusaka [the ANC's headquarters in Zambia when it was still banned] in early 1989.

'During the course of our in-camera hearing, Mrs Madikizela-Mandela, when asked about this document, basically said that it was "a Stratcom", or she had been informed that it was "a Stratcom document".

'I beg your pardon, do you have any knowledge as to whether this was "a Stratcom document"?'

Erasmus: 'I have no knowledge whatsoever. At that time my involvement with Stratcom, if I can just point out, was very much limited. There wasn't, as I have mentioned in my statement … a formal unit in Johannesburg [yet], although there were people that were given certain Stratcom or "strategic communication" tasks.'

Pigou: 'Thank you … Are you aware of the statement issued by what was then called the Mass Democratic Movement [MDM] and reported in the press on the 17th of February 1989? [When this question was posed previously to Winnie Madikizela-Mandela by another TRC commissioner, the answer was], "Yes, a statement was issued by Murphy Morobe as part and parcel of that Stratcom exercise."

'Are you aware whether the MDM statement was a part of a Stratcom exercise?'

Erasmus: 'I have a vague recollection of the statement, but I have no knowledge of whether it was a Stratcom exercise or not.'

Pigou: 'We then follow it up in saying, "We asked Mrs Mandela whether Murphy Morobe is part and parcel of the Stratcom operation," and the response was, "What we subsequently established was that from the very onset when the so-called Stompie affair broke out, the media had, amongst its fraternity, reporters who were working for the system at that time.

'"You have all seen the media presentations that have been made to you. My subsequent information throughout the years has been that the first reporters who broke the so-called Stompie affair ... and I am not going to name the names, I am going to withhold those ... were in fact part of the informers who were planted in the media, and that statement to my information thereafter was that it was part of the exercise that was influenced by Stratcom."

'Are you [Paul Erasmus] aware at the beginning of 1989 whether the first stories and subsequent stories ... but let's confine ourselves for your answer now to the first stories, the initial batch of stories, that came out around the Stompie Seipei incident. Do you have any information as to whether these were part and parcel of a Stratcom exercise?'

Erasmus: 'The only information that I can give you, chairperson, [is] that the media were obviously heavily targeted by the Security Branch. I personally handled agents [in the media] and had contact with the media over the whole duration of my career. But I have no specific knowledge of the situation regarding information being given to the media in the Stompie case.'

Pigou: 'So, once again, that would be a situation, would it [be] that the information, factual information, would come to you and there would be something that you could utilise at a later stage or was utilised at a later stage?'

Erasmus: 'At a later stage. That is correct.'

Pigou: 'Were there any other Stratcom operations related to Winnie Mandela?'

Erasmus: 'Not that I am aware of.'

Pigou: 'Who did you deal with in Soweto? Who was your contact person in Soweto in the Stratcom unit there? Who were you receiving information from?'

Erasmus: 'It was a Sergeant Badenhorst that gave me information from time to time and I had quite a lot of contact with the unit commander, or the most senior person involved with Stratcom. That was Colonel Louis de Jager, or Colonel "Tickey" de Jager.'

Pigou: 'Were the intelligence reports that you received complete? In other words, were the transcripts of the telephone-tampering covering 24 hours every day, or were you receiving just snippets as to what Soweto or other units in the Witwatersrand would want to give you?'

Erasmus: 'From time to time, I did receive full intelligence reports, when and if Sergeant Badenhorst or Colonel De Jager, whoever at Soweto, thought it might be of use. As I mentioned before, a lot of the information was useless, absolutely useless, to me. There was nothing that I could do [with it]. Sergeant Badenhorst also gave me information telephonically, and from time to time just brought me up to date by virtue of an intelligence report that gave me something of an overview of the situation.'

Pigou: 'You've talked about informers in the Football Club. Do you have any concrete information about informers inside the Football Club?'

Erasmus: 'I don't. It was never Security Branch policy [to share information about their agents], although we always used to, within our own ranks, play "spot-the-agent"-type of stuff. It was just curiosity to try and deduce from reports who the agent was, and it was something of pride that you could see a colleague and say, "I know who your agent is," or "I figured it out," or whatever.'

Pigou: 'From your lengthy experience inside the Security Branch, would you be surprised if the Security Branch in Soweto did not have informers inside and around the Football Club or the youths that frequented the Mandela household?'

Erasmus: 'I would have been amazed if that was the case.'

Pigou: 'Could you just tell us one last question now … What was the reason that you, who were based at John Vorster Square, carried out Stratcom operations directed towards people living in Soweto?'

Erasmus: 'As I mentioned before, it was because of the international capability that I had with agents in Britain, and the agent network that was set up in Britain, that I was given that type of information.'

Pigou: 'No further questions, chair.'

Boraine: 'Thank you very much. Mr Semenya?'

Ishmael Semenya (Mrs Mandela's lawyer): 'Thank you, chairperson. I have just heard something to this effect, that "would you be surprised that there were no informers within the Mandela Football Club" … As a matter of fact, I don't know whether the TRC …'

Pigou: 'I think, Mr Semenya, I said "would you be surprised if there were no …"'

Semenya: 'Ja. But on what basis do you put the question?'

Pigou: 'I am putting a theoretical proposition to him, that, on the basis of his experience, when you have someone like that in that situation, would it be surprising if there weren't informers being used around?'

Semenya: 'But, chairperson, my difficulty is this: I am surprised that a TRC official does not put the question, "Would you be surprised that there were informers?" Every time, why state it in the negative? I mean, it represents a particular position, and I think the responsibility is to be as neutral as possible.'

Pigou: 'I think we have tried to demonstrate that today, Mr Semenya.'

Semenya: 'Mr Erasmus, you say in your report, in your statement, rather ... "This agent has a mass of conservative contacts internationally, including politicians" ... And you go on to say, "Almost [all] senior journalists, media representatives, intelligence contacts and so forth, almost immediately [receive] dirt on the ANC ... including matters relating to Mrs Mandela's activities, and other relevant matters began to appear in the international press. Of greater importance in the Stratcom sense, [these] were forwarded ultimately to *inter alia* Conservative Party members and the British Prime Minister."

'Now, we know that Emma Nicholson[24] was a member of the Conservative Party in the UK. Do you know if she was one of these "Conservative Party members" in Britain?'

Erasmus: 'I cannot recall. I have a list of names that I received at that time from the agent – a faxed list which I have given to the TRC, and which is, I believe, in the TRC offices in Cape Town. I cannot state with any certainty if Miss Nicholson's name is on that list or not. I cannot remember all the persons on that.'

Semenya: 'Chairperson, again, I am going to have [to ask] for this list which has been given to the TRC, and which may be of assistance to our task, and we are not getting it. And maybe I must request that, really, we be furnished with all documents relating to these hearings. It becomes very difficult to execute my mandate.'

Boraine: 'I note that. What I'd like to say to you doesn't help you very much, but you are in very good company. I haven't seen it either. We will make the necessary instructions. Thank you.'

Semenya: 'Now are you [Paul Erasmus] able to help us with the concept of informers? Now we know that Jerry Richardson was an informer within the Mandela Football Club ...'

Tony Richards (Jerry Richardson's lawyer): 'May I object there? It must be recorded that Mr Richardson denies and disputes that he's an informer, and it has not been proved. For my learned colleague to make an assertion of fact is most irregular.'

Boraine: 'Do you want to rephrase that?'

Semenya: 'I will rephrase it. Now we know, according to the information of the national Commissioner of Police ...'

Richards: 'The national Commissioner of Police has offered no proof whatsoever, and, again, it's an over-statement and a misrepresentation to which I object.'

Boraine: 'Mr Richards, would you please conduct your enquiries through me rather than directly to your learned colleague?'

Richards: 'I apologise, Mr Chairperson.'

Boraine: 'Thank you. Please rephrase it.'

Semenya: 'The national Commissioner of Police has told the Commission that he has information that Jerry Richardson was paid R10 000 as a police informant. Now, if that information is correct, how would he handle the information he has with his handler?'

Erasmus: 'I think each situation regarding an informer was unique. You had different categories. I must first, maybe, just point out to you we had two ways of recruiting informers, two basic ways. Firstly, a direct approach, where I would, for example, approach somebody and say, "I am from the Security Branch, I would like you to work for us." That would be the one type of scenario. We also made wide use of a tactic which was known as false-flag type of operations, where you would pretend to be somebody else, and then approach somebody, and that person would be the unsuspecting victim of giving information to a person that wasn't what they believed that person to be.

'And then, on the informer network itself, I cannot comment on a sum of R10 000. It sounds a lot of money to my experience. Our top agents during the time that I was involved in Stratcom received expense monies, and the highest salary that I am aware of is the one offered to the principal agent in Britain at the time when we brought him to South Africa, and that was R6 000 a month, apart from his expenses.

'I cannot comment on why somebody would be given R10 000. I really cannot make an assumption.'

Semenya: 'Yes. The assistance I was probably aiming to obtain was, if an informer has information that an offence, particularly an offence like murder, is going to be committed, how would you expect that informer to handle that information?'

Erasmus: 'He would give that information obviously to his handler, and be rewarded accordingly.'

Semenya: 'So if it turns out that Jerry Richardson knew that Dr Abu Baker Asvat[25] was going to be killed, it is reasonable to make the inference that he [Jerry Richardson] would have given this information to his handler?'

Erasmus: 'I am quite certain, with a serious matter, I mean, information like that, would have been conveyed to his handler … Although, I don't know. I must just add I don't know anything about that particular murder or the situation.'

Semenya: 'Yes. I am clearly soliciting what I would later state to be reasonable probabilities. Would it be a reasonable probability that if he

[Richardson] had committed the murders, like that of Stompie, he would have reported those types of things to his handler?'

Erasmus: 'I'm quite certain he would.'

Semenya: 'And if he committed the type of murders that I am told he is applying for amnesty for, he would have reported those types of things to his handler?'

Erasmus: 'I should imagine so.'

Semenya: 'Now, one of the activities of Stratcom was to disseminate a lot of pamphlets. Is that correct?'

Erasmus: 'Pamphleteering was a major part of Stratcom activities.'

Semenya: 'And we recall one dissemination of information depicting Mrs Madikizela-Mandela hugging with the chairperson of the TRC, Archbishop Tutu, where it was suggested that there was a romantic relationship between Archbishop Tutu and Mrs Madikizela-Mandela. Would that have been a typical Stratcom activity?'

Erasmus: 'That type of action would have been a typical Stratcom activity.'

Semenya: 'I have no further questions, chairperson.'

Boraine: 'Mr Richards.'

[After putting it to the Commission and me again that I was not directly involved in Soweto Stratcom activities, Jerry Richardson's lawyer, Tony Richards, continued asking me questions.]

Richards: 'Would you agree that your information was a matter of speculation?'

Erasmus: 'I would say "deduction". I would be very hard pressed that either Mrs Madikizela-Mandela was giving information to the Security Branch on her own activities or her daughter's [Zindzi Mandela], so the "deduction" was obviously that the third person present would have.'

Richards: 'But when it comes to the identification of the source, on what basis do you make these assertions? You, in your statement, say as much that you had no direct information.'

Erasmus: 'I did not have direct information.'

Richards: 'And if I ask you questions as to who gave you the information you made your so-called "deductions" from, you wouldn't be able to give me the names?'

Erasmus: 'I received verbal information at the time, and I received intelligence reports, but on the intelligence reports one never mentioned the name of the agent anyway. The agents had code numbers to protect their identities from possible leaks within the organisation, and so on.'

Richards: 'Now, by the same token, in that group of 20 or 30 people living at a particular property [Mandela's Soweto residence], it could have been any one of a number of people?'

Erasmus: 'I would agree with that.'

Richards: 'So that means the reliability of the information [relating to this] is extremely low and suspect? In other words, it's only as reliable as your memory is as to matters nine years ago?'

Erasmus: 'This is correct.'

Richards: 'Which is entirely unreliable.'

Semenya: 'I don't think the statement can ever be put like that. As a lawyer ...'

Boraine: 'I am sorry. I must ask you [Semenya] to do exactly what I asked ... If you wish to address the chair, I would be grateful if you would.'

Semenya: 'Chairperson, I think my learned colleague is putting the most untenable proposition, that since the information is nine years old, it's unreliable. At least I remember my age, and I must be many years away from nine years.'

[The question was then concluded.]

Boraine: 'You [Richards] have got many more, though, have you?'

Richards: 'Is it correct that on the 9th of September 1997, you made a press statement to some organisation, the identity of which I don't know?'

Erasmus: "At the request of Mrs Madikizela-Mandela's attorneys, and at the request of Mrs Madikizela-Mandela herself, that is correct."

Richards: 'And on the last page of that statement ... you make the statement, "As regards Stompie Seipei, I heard at the time in official circles that he was murdered by Jerry Richardson after he, Seipei, had found out that Richardson was working for the Security Branch and had threatened to expose him."

'Now, on what basis do you make that allegation?'

Erasmus: 'That was widely held, I think, within the entire Security Branch community within the Witwatersrand and in Soweto.'

[Richards 'concluded' that my evidence was hearsay, and I was then questioned by attorney Peter Jordi.]

Jordi: 'I note that from your affidavit you say that you found it very hard to distribute this kind of information against President Nelson Mandela, and to quote you, "because of his impeccable integrity". Is that right?'

Erasmus: 'Yes. What I mean by that was we had nothing on him personally ... no contentious statements ... like his wife had made, for example with the liberation of the country ...'

Jordi: 'Yes. His wife was in a different category altogether. Is that right?'

Erasmus: 'Different ... she was easy to target because she was controversial ...'

Jordi: 'She was easy to target. [Is that] right?'

Erasmus: 'That's correct.'

Jordi: 'Because there was a lot of factually accurate information in the hands of the Security Police available about her. Is that right?'

Erasmus: 'Well, I wouldn't say "in the hands of the Security Police". I think the media and generally everybody was ...'

Jordi: 'Everybody knew. Is that right?'

Erasmus: 'That's it. That's correct.'

Jordi: 'And even if it was not entirely accurate, you could still have the 70% reliable information which you could mix with the 30% unreliable information. Is that right?'

Erasmus: 'I never consciously, actually, and I don't know of anybody that actually stuck to that point, but that was the ideal formula. Some of the things were total fabrication. Some of them were 100%. Some were half-true.'

Jordi: 'So, in the case of Winnie Mandela, you say there was a lot of information available, I suppose the ratio was much higher than 70:30. Say, 90:10, or a 100%?'

Erasmus: 'I couldn't speculate on figures, but certainly a lot of it was fabrication.'

Jordi: 'A lot of it was fabrication?'

Erasmus: 'Total fabrication.'

Jordi: 'Well, you say here 30:70. A lot of reliable information. You have told me "reliable information" was available. Now you say a lot of it was fabrication.'

Erasmus: 'That is correct. The information, for example, about Mrs Madikizela-Mandela being "a nymphomaniac" was total fabrication. The "dagga-smoking" was total fabrication.'

Jordi: 'You say that as far as Mrs Mandela was concerned, that you could spread information about her that she was "running rampant in the townships" with her Football Club, who were, *inter alia*, "intimidating" the local population. As far as I know, I think you also say something here about her "misusing drugs", and there were also aspects of information related to "marital problems". Was that based on factually accurate information, for example the "drug-running"?'

Erasmus: 'The "drug-running" was a total fabrication on my part.'

Jordi: 'On your part. Well, I put it to you ...'

Erasmus: 'I added, if I may just add on just to what I've said [around] "there was a total fabrication", that the information that I received, factual information, was that the Mandela United Football Club were using dagga or marijuana and it was a logical extension to say that Zindzi and Mrs Mandela were …'

Jordi: 'Okay. Then I have the question for you. Were Stratcom-type activities being carried out in 1995?'

Erasmus: '1995?'

Jordi: 'Ja.'

Erasmus: 'No. Not to my knowledge.'

[After an intervention from the chair, confirming that I was boarded in 1993 and had had very little to no contact with the SB since then, Jordi continued.]

Jordi: 'You say that during the 1980s, Winnie Mandela was monitored on a 24-hour basis, a kind of unprecedented monitoring of her activities. Do you know who were the security policemen responsible for the monitoring of her activities? What are their names?'

[After repeating what I had said earlier, I was again questioned by Jordi, who quoted from my statement, in which I said: 'I was … only given information on an irregular basis, although I did recall that I requested, but never received, detail of, for example, the death of Stompie Seipei.']

Jordi: 'Now it must have been an obvious issue in respect of which to get information. So, you didn't get any detailed information, and we've established that you had a thorough knowledge of misinformation.

'Then there's the press release which is dated the 9th of September 1997, and it deals with Jerry Richardson's involvement in the killing of Stompie, and there's this version here that Stompie Seipei was killed by Jerry Richardson after Richardson found out that Stompie was working for the Security Branch.

'It seems to me that this link between the death of Stompie and the supposed information that was received by Jerry Richardson has no basis in fact. We haven't heard anything about it in the evidence so far. And I put it to you that this is an example of disinformation. What do you have to say about that?'

Erasmus: 'Are you saying that this is an example of disinformation from me?'

Jordi: 'Your press release, yes.'

Erasmus: 'I can only state, chairperson, that I can tell the truth only as I know it, sir, and I am not involved in disinformation [here, at the TRC]. I am totally objective as I sit here today, and I have tried to be objective right through this process.'

Jordi: 'I put it to you further that in the *Weekly Mail* article of the 21st of November 1997, it said that you have "become friendly" with Winnie

Mandela, and that during Winnie Mandela's divorce action, you were in fact called as a witness for her, but that the judge declined to hear your evidence after the President [Nelson Mandela], who we know is a man of great integrity, said that he [Erasmus] would "reveal facts which might damage her image and bring a great deal of pain to my children and grandchildren".

'What do you have to say about that? No further question.'

Erasmus: 'I have met Mrs Madikizela-Mandela on, I believe, about five or six occasions. I am aware that earlier this week an allegation, or somebody alleged, that I have had some sort of relationship with her, which is absolute rubbish and which is in itself a Stratcom attempt, I believe, to discredit me.

'Mrs Madikizela-Mandela has been in contact with me and my family on at least two of the five or six occasions and at other times I have been in contact with her in the presence of her lawyers and bodyguards and other people. I can't think of a time when I have been alone with Mrs Madikizela-Mandela.'

Boraine: 'Thank you. No, wait a minute, no, no, no …'

Jordi: 'I never suggested you were involved in a relationship with her. Thank you very much.'

[The next TRC commissioner to question me was Fazel Randera.]

Randera: 'Mr Erasmus, I just want to come back to your statement … You state there that in October 1990, "I attended a formal Stratcom training course in Johannesburg, and part of that was again the entire issue of destabilising the ANC, the SACP alliance, PAC, right-wing organisations."

'Now, it's related to the question that the Archbishop [Tutu, the TRC chair] asked earlier on to your colleague [Vic McPherson]. We are talking about October 1990, Mr Mandela has been released already. Am I to understand that this was done with the full understanding of the structures in operation, including government, because I think earlier both you and your colleague made the point that there was an annual audit to Cabinet. Or is this part of what we have come to understand of "Third Force" activity?

'Were you acting outside, at that particular time, the ambit of established government structures, or was this part of "Third Force" activities?'

Erasmus: 'It will be hard to distinguish. What I can say is that Stratcom training, as I was aware of it, increased after the release of the President [Mandela]. We were informed on a Stratcom course and in various forums that we had four years, the accent was laid on this statement, we have four years to reduce the ANC to "just another political party".

'A lot of our training was that we had literally laissez-faire to carry on activities and nothing should be turned aside which would hinder us in achieving these aims. The last Stratcom operation that I know of that was implemented was as late as, I believe, about April 1991, which was an operation aimed at SADTU which used terms like "sabotage of the organisation" and which, in documents which I have given to the TRC which are in Cape Town, bore the authorisation of the then Minister of Law and Order.'

[After a brief question from Nkosinathi (Nathi) Mkhize, Advocate Dumisa Ntsebeza, another TRC commissioner, questioned me.]

Ntsebeza: 'Thank you, chair. Mr Erasmus, I sat through the media hearings [at the TRC, in which editors and managers at media companies that operated during apartheid testified] and now I listen to you, and I get the blurring picture of shifting eras the more I listen to people who did the sort of work that you did.

'Now there is just one question that I want you to assist us with in order for us to be able to make a fair assessment of your evidence. When Mr Semenya asked you whether the alleged rumour of a romantic link between the Archbishop and Mrs Madikizela-Mandela was a typical Stratcom operation, you said "yes". That was it.

'Now, in your own admission, you confess to the knowledge of a rumour that links you romantically with Mrs Madikizela-Mandela, and you say that is also a typical Stratcom operation.

'Now the question I want to know from you is, would there be any reason why there should be that sort of Stratcom operation? Why would those who you left be keen to perpetuate disinformation about you because you say that is "total rubbish, absolutely unfounded"?'

Erasmus: 'I can't speculate why people would make allegations like that against me apart from the fact that I find it shocking.'

Ntsebeza: 'In the way it was shocking for you to talk about Mrs Mandela being a "nymphomaniac", Zindzi being a "nymphomaniac", and all those sort of things ...'

Erasmus: 'I have come to realise the horror of what I have participated in.'

Ntsebeza: 'You see, what I am trying to get at, Mr Erasmus ... you had a reason to spread all those rumours, and I just don't know. First it is 70:30 in terms of ratio, then it is 100%. I mean, it's shifting. It's shifting sand now. But whatever it is, you had the reason – you were serving the National Party. You were serving the government of that day.'

Erasmus: 'That's correct.'

Ntsebeza: 'Now you want us to accept and believe that a rumour that links you romantically with Mrs Madikizela-Mandela is a typical Stratcom operation. Two things. Are you saying Stratcom still exists, and that is what it is doing?'

Erasmus: 'No, most definitely not. I merely mention that it's … I cannot but help see the irony in a situation where I spent many years of my life trying to destroy people like Mrs Madikizela-Mandela, the Archbishop and many, many other people that were perceived enemies of the state, and now having to … in front of a Truth Commission, in a forum like the Truth Commission, being accused of something like that. I find very ironic.

'I am not saying at all that Stratcom still exists.'

Ntsebeza: 'And you say it's an attempt to discredit you?'

Erasmus: 'I believe that it's an attempt to discredit me or throw some bad light on the relationship which I have enjoyed with Mrs Mandela, which has been on a friendly, reconciliatory basis of forgiveness and decency.'

Ntsebeza: 'Have you ever gone to her and apologised for all the harm that you had done to her?'

Erasmus: 'I have apologised to her and many other former adversaries of mine in the time of the struggle.'

Boraine: 'Archbishop Tutu?'

Tutu: 'I just have one small question and I think you have already maybe answered it in the course of your answering Dumisa Ntsebeza's question, which is, how did you feel when you were telling the kind of stories that you were telling, when say you say Zindzi or whatever, I mean the kind of stories that you told, when you got back home, what did you say to your wife?

'I mean, I suppose you have a wife. Your family. I mean, what did you say? I have had this or that kind of day in the office, sweetheart? I have told the world that Winnie Mandela is a nymphomaniac and the world has believed me. How did you feel just as a human being?'

Erasmus: 'Chairperson, at the time I saw it, the actions that we carried out and the things that I did [were] as part of a "psychological war". I saw it as justified. My personal conviction was that I was fighting "satanic, godless communism", that people like Mrs Madikizela-Mandela and yourself and many other people were instruments of this totalitarian system which was approaching in South Africa.

'I believed also that we were doing it for many years, and I've since seen the light, that we were doing it, fighting a religious war, almost a "jihad" on behalf of Christianity, to oppose people like yourself and the liberation movements.

'It was only in fact after the release of President Mandela, where the myths that we had grown up with and everything that we had learnt, that the bubble started to burst, and I, and many of my colleagues, started to see the other side of the coin.'

[Boraine then intervened.]

Boraine: 'In your statement, you state that it was after your course in October 1990 and President Mandela was already out of prison – so it took you a while to come to see the light – you actually describe him [Mandela] ... as being senile ... that he had no control over the radical ANC cadres and so on. But that's beside the point ... you [also] state, "Radical elements within the ANC had to be identified as targets ... and others had to be neutralised at all costs and obviously by any means possible." Now those are very strong words, loaded words. "Target." "Neutralised at all costs, obviously by any means." Now, do you mean that?'

Erasmus: 'Most definitely within the context of propaganda, yes, anything went. There were times that I was involved not even in the discrediting of people in the liberation movements, but of a serving member of Parliament for example, for which I was congratulated from above.

'So, it was a matter of striking out at random and using whatever information was available, or whatever means possible, to discredit people, and I was involved in a lot of activities which I can recount involving these people ...'

Chapter Eighteen

Touch-and-Go

Southern Cape, 2001 and 2019

AFTER I MOVED BACK to George in 2001, Winnie Mandela called me.

'Did you see the news, Paul?'

'No, I haven't, ma'am. What has happened? Are you all right?'

'The people in the ANC want me out, led by Thabo [President Mbeki]. Didn't you see what he did to me? He hit me in public in front of the whole world.'

She had arrived a little late at a Youth Day rally at Orlando Stadium and, on her way to take her seat on the stage, bent to greet Mbeki with a kiss. Mbeki shunned her in full view of local and international TV cameras, pushing her away like an annoying insect and knocking her baseball cap off her head. IFP leader Buthelezi picked it up and replaced it on her head. Winnie said she had called me to tell me about that humiliating incident 'because of our friendship'.

Our 'friendship' had really started when I'd been asked to address a press conference at Luthuli House prior to her divorce, to issue a statement setting out the discrediting of herself through the SB and Stratcom. The response from the anti-Winnie media was predictable, and scant attention was given to the content. I was accused of being her apologist, and there were allegations that I was being paid by Winnie to act as some sort of public relations officer for her.

I saw less and less of her when we moved to George. This was to a large extent my fault. I believed I was guilty for having helped to damage her political career through the oxytherapy insanity, and so, apart from interviews or TV documentaries sanctioned by her, I resolved to rather keep quiet and get on with trying to create a life for Dylan.

We were living together without Candice and Linda, from whom I'd got divorced by that time. Candice stayed with Linda while I had custody of Dylan.

Winnie was tremendously kind to my children after my TRC testimony. So much so that I'd plucked up the courage together to show her a poem, 'Angels', which Candice had written when we were in London on the witness protection programme. Winnie was so taken with it that she regularly asked to see Candice.

One weekend when Candice was staying with me, Winnie invited us to a birthday party for one of her grandchildren. After Winnie and Candice had had a long conversation, Winnie took off her wedding ring and gave it to Candice, telling her it was a 'symbol of reconciliation'. Winnie, however, expressly asked that this remain private, but a journalist at the party had captured it, ignored her request and turned it into headline news the following day. I tried to return the ring, but Winnie stood her ground. Few positives emerged from the episode, and the reporting around what was essentially a very special moment between Candice and Winnie was especially vicious.

Winnie was visibly unwell when we had one final meeting not long before her death. Her quick mind and wit were still very much in place, and this remains an extraordinary memory for me.

Not long after she died on 2 April 2018, I received a message from British filmmaker Pascale Lamche, who, Lamche's own PR claimed, had produced 'the definitive' documentary on Winnie. When we spoke, Lamche told me that she had been trying to trace me 'for months' but hadn't been able to get hold of me.

Winnie had apparently told her that I could prove what Stratcom had done – this for the purposes of a film that Lamche was making that would, at last, tell Winnie's story from her own perspective. I had exposed Stratcom dirty tricks before, so I could have done it again, and it might have done Lamche some good had she managed to track me down earlier (which wasn't that difficult) while she was researching *Winnie*, her documentary, which was released in 2018.

I wondered how Winnie would have felt about some of the reviews and reflections about the film in the press. The South African media, which had been wary of Winnie for decades, had only recently taken positive notice of her when she showed up at her eightieth birthday celebrations looking thirty years younger. But even this response proved less than flattering, or even remotely genuine, with many journalists speculating whether she had had a facelift. The supposed 'love' Winnie received from so many was never going to be real.

Lamche's documentary featured some of the testimony McPherson and I had given to the TRC in 2000. She interviewed McPherson on camera in his garden, where he sat with his small dog on his lap, and spoke about Stratcom in completely contradictory terms.

His accounts of the actions against Winnie, in the documentary, didn't entirely surprise me. Many were distortions of what had emerged from all the material he and I had presented to the TRC. McPherson was almost boastful about his 'successes' one minute, and then would move straight on to downplaying the significance of Stratcom.

I've seen this happen regularly over the past 15 years. Gradually, and then rapidly, many ex-colleagues, some politicians and some in the media have sought to make it seem as if the SB's actions and Stratcom were not really *that* serious. After all, they say, those actions had to be seen against the backdrop of a war that South Africa was fighting at the time. Former SAP and SADF commanders, in particular, have tried to diminish the scope of influence of the National Party within Stratcom.

This is just outrageous. Stratcom *was* the National Party. Its influence extended way beyond a simple series of 'tiny operations with little effect on the people', as many would have South Africa now believe.

There is no doubt that Lamche had a powerful story to tell. Winnie was a very serious person. She wasn't frivolous. She rarely gave the media access to her life because she had seen how quickly it could turn on her.

Yet, the responses to *Winnie* revealed plenty about how little this generation of journalists knows – or cares to know – about what really happened in the 1980s and 1990s. All too many were 'shocked' by the Stratcom 'revelations' in Lamche's film.

A simple Google search would have shown the reporters who jumped onto the bandwagon after Winnie's death that the dirty tricks against her had been exposed 18 years earlier at the TRC hearings. There might be some lessons in here about how simple it was for SB operatives in those decades to twist a journalist to our way of thinking – easing our path with a little cash inducement – to make them write what we wanted them to write. In fact, Stratcom works most smoothly when the media is ignorant or, to be more generous, ill informed – it helps political parties and their agents to fuel an ignorance that already exists.

Winnie started referring to Stratcom only at the end of her life, and the word quickly fell into popular (mis)use in 2018 by a new generation of politically expedient people. Four decades after the SB had used it as a torture and controlling mechanism, it was suddenly a catch-all for any real or imagined propaganda-style activities. Now anyone with an axe to grind uses the term 'Stratcom' when they want to attack an enemy.

There's nothing new about Stratcom, and bandying the term about loosely tends to detract from the sheer horror of it all at that time, and fails to encapsulate the full psychological torture that went with it – the kind Winnie Mandela and many others experienced at the hands of the SB. Stratcom was not as straightforward as simply toying with the media to reach an audience, or 'buying' a few journalists. Using the word as loosely as some South Africans do today strips it of its intentional and intimate terror. True, Stratcom was indeed terror; it plotted, always in top secret, using its best and most ruthless resources to unhinge, and render mute by the violence of their own minds, any opposition to it.

The misuse of the word today almost divests it of the pain it caused and the control it was designed to wield. We in Stratcom wanted to annihilate; our intentions were much darker and went far beyond getting the odd positive story into the papers to prop up De Klerk. We were trained to permanently neutralise – ideas or people or institutions – on behalf of the government of the day, using unlimited state resources to do so.

By late 1990, when we finally received formal Stratcom training, it was no longer about race for us. We were sadists looking for targets. Using informers and agents, we studied Winnie and her environment very carefully; we knew her every move, all her weaknesses and vulnerabilities. We exploited each of these to torment her – at first because she was so resistant to our attempts to crush her, then just because we could and, finally, because we knew she symbolised the ANC's worst fear.

Winnie wasn't the ANC's Achilles heel. Although many South Africans wanted her leadership, she was rebellious, and she wasn't what the ANC had in mind as it strategised how it would replace the National Party at the first democratic elections. In fact, Stratcom's campaign against Winnie suited many in the ANC because it ultimately sought to wear her out. She was, after all, the enemy within for many ANC leaders. It came as no surprise, therefore, that some apartheid-era agents and informers, now riding high within the ANC, were among her loudest praise-singers when she died.

It is a fact that the De Klerk government dedicated an entire SB team to Stratcom in the post-1990 period with the intention of destabilising – no, destroying – the hopes of democrats and revolutionaries. That McPherson and I unpicked this at the TRC is also fact.

So when people use the word so carelessly today, I'm tempted to wonder whether it isn't Stratcom behind their use of the term 'Stratcom'. If so, I've been a victim of Stratcom over the past two decades, and not only one Stratcom, but different Stratcoms. This was the suggestion in some of the TRC commissioners' questioning of me – they got it!

You get used to the notion of Stratcom when you're someone like me, or Winnie Mandela, and others who fell to the left or right of the establishment and its baying cohort, or you simply wouldn't survive it.

Amid all the lies, one that affected me more than others is that I had an affair with Winnie. Her former friend and then bitter foe, Xoliswa Falati, told the TRC that she had seen me 'emerging from Winnie's bedroom' during the time Winnie and I had become friends. The dates Falati provided for this coincided with when I was in London preparing evidence for – and 'protected' by – the Goldstone Commission. Nonetheless, this nonsense was eagerly published by *Die Burger*, a turn that hardly slammed the breath out of me, because the paper was essentially toeing the old National Party line. Falati was an informer. The SB paid her and later brushed her off, but Winnie couldn't do that.

It was only later, when I was back in George after the entire witness protection fiasco, that I realised what an impact that story of the supposed affair had had on white people. It drew such a strong reaction in George that people's responses gave me a taste of what it must be like to be treated as a leper. Dylan and I have both taken punches for our stance on Winnie. Significantly, not one person who attacked us ever dared ask whether the allegations were true.

Today I still struggle to come to terms with Ovamboland and the time I spent there. That doesn't go away, even as the years move on. I also still struggle with what happened to Linda and my children, us as a family, as a result of my work.

I can only repeat what I told Jordi and the TRC: that I fully recognise that the work I did for the SB inflicted horrors on many, many people. This cannot be undone. What does one do with this? Say sorry ... again, and again. Live a better life – or at least try. Now I just try to stay the hell off the radar.

In the end, there's only one salvation: I have spent every day with my son since he was 11 years old – some 20 years of being a father. Both to Dylan and Candice.

I nearly lost this too. For a while, it was touch-and-go.

Postscript

I'm sitting with Dylan, who is wearing a suit and looks more like a lawyer than many in Room 8F at the South Gauteng High Court. I'm about to be called into the witness box at the new inquest into the death of Dr Neil Aggett.

Jill Burger is sitting behind me. She's waited 38 years for this chance at justice for her brother. I steal a glance at her and notice she's been watching me. I wish the ground would swallow me. I'm dead tired after an 11-hour statement-writing session with the Aggett family's legal team.

I turn back to looking down at my folded hands while we wait for the presiding judge, Judge Motsamai Makume, to call me to the stand.

It's been happening to me a lot lately, that my mind drifts back to my mother exhorting me when I was a young man to 'not do anything stupid' as I left home for John Vorster Square police station. It was 1978 and it was my first day as a member of the South African Police Security Branch.

I'm now 64 and I've just celebrated my birthday. The way I feel at this moment, the celebration should have been a wake.

National Prosecuting Authority (NPA) advocate Shubnum Singh of the Priority Crimes Unit has been encouraging me. There are a few others. My thoughts are interrupted when Jill Burger thanks me for coming to the court. There's no hostility from her.

Dylan whispers to me that I should 'just tell the truth and you'll be fine'. I close my eyes and offer up a quick prayer. I've got to be as accurate as possible.

When we were preparing for this, Advocate Howard Varney didn't mention that he was going to read the 500 offences that I committed during my time in service. So when I get onto the stand and he does, I think I hear a gasp

253

from the gallery. Later, someone comments that the NPA should have been charging me.

I was given some 13 orders to kill various people while I was at the SB. I wonder if the lie I told my mother, that I would leave the police shortly, might have had something to do with my not committing murders. She died five days after she made that plea to me.

But, yup. Talk is cheap and promises often cheaper.

I had strong feelings at that age. The communists were coming to sow havoc and destroy our Christian nationalism. In terms of my work specifically, white activists were traitors.

In the same way, I have some very strong feelings now, that since no apartheid politician has accepted full political responsibility for the atrocity they sold as a system, F.W. de Klerk and others should be charged or, at the very least, stripped of any awards and privileges. But then again, who am I as a perpetrator to call for this?

As I sit in this courtroom, waiting to testify, it's 23 years since I revealed everything I knew at the TRC. That was the second time I'd been a witness from the inside to the catastrophe that was apartheid. The first was of course as 'Q4' at the secret Goldstone Commission on Third Force activities in Copenhagen, Denmark, in 1994.

I was voluntarily in the box again at the second sitting of the inquest into apartheid activist Ahmed Timol's death at the Pretoria High Court in mid-2017.

Yet, there were years between the immediate post-apartheid testimony I gave and these two inquests. During those decades – which of course flashed past in retrospect, but were often filled with harsher stuff that took longer to handle at the time – I had to do a number of life-altering things in order to be in this courtroom, facing Aggett's family, today.

I had to give up smoking, dry out, try and integrate myself into society with 'normal people', get myself back on my feet financially, raise my son with all his own challenges as a result of the past, repair my relationship with my daughter, look after my failing health and, perhaps most difficult, learn to live with PTSD. Certainly I had high expectations for myself when I started rebuilding my life after the TRC. I also quickly realised that just because I was undergoing a complete turnaround in how I saw history and my role in it didn't mean there wasn't still a lot of antipathy towards me.

When I consider how the whistleblowers of our current political generation suffer, I admire them very much. I wish I could share some warmth, some sympathy, with them, but I realise they occupy a different place from me. Their whistleblowing while corruption was under way and my telling the truth about what happened after the fact are not the same thing.

I will never experience that smooth entry into ordinary new friendships which I hoped I might. For instance, just because I am here in this courtroom testifying for the Aggett family doesn't mean we're all going to have lunch afterwards and share convivial stories about other parts of our lives, and later exchange messages in attempts at creating bonds.

That this isolation, in effect, has affected Dylan so much affects me most. The best I can hope is that my evidence will be irrefutable enough to help secure justice for those who deserve it, and that Dylan may then take something from that into his own, more positive life.

I am pumped up with adrenalin while I wait to testify. In the box, I control it and pace myself. Afterwards, especially in the days and weeks afterwards, a familiar nausea that government may not act on what I and others tell the country in courtrooms like this starts to develop into what amount to the stages of grief.

Disbelief, anger and then a horrible baseline resignation which doesn't leave your mind.

Apart from those whispers of encouragement, Dylan is quiet in the courtroom. I think what he would say if he went into the box would be something along the lines that I, his father, fought back when I realised my former bosses were going to take revenge on our family.

Therein lies a Catch-22 situation. Did I do all of this because I was afraid and believed if I pre-empted the apartheid henchmen from carrying out the inevitable, we, especially I, could be 'spared'? Or did I do it because I genuinely wanted the truth to emerge?

If Candice was in the box, I reckon she would say that she doesn't condone what I did and never will, but that she has come to understand at least something of what motivated me to work for the security police in the first place.

That doesn't wipe out what she experienced. She saw me and her mom go to pieces. She remembers the threats against our family and the pain of being in witness protection when she and Dylan, who were children, couldn't make friends and didn't attend school for more than 18 months. She knows the impact on Dylan, who missed out on essential therapy as we were moved from one dangerous area to another.

I become overwhelmed when I hear my children say they are proud of me after I've been in the witness box at this inquest. Candice says she thinks of me as 'loving and kind'.

Man, in my wildest dreams.

Acknowledgements

WRITING THE ACKNOWLEDGEMENTS for the book was almost as difficult as writing parts of the manuscript, with so many people to thank in such a confined forum. In many instances they were not even aware of the existence of this work but provided inspiration at some crucial times when the pathways became obscured.

So many people have made such a significant contribution to my frequent abandonment of the whole project, but I with much trepidation say that I did work hard to honour promises made to people who really cared. Some just provided the impetus to carry on writing and do much-needed reinvention. MP Dave Dalling, whom I had severely embarrassed with a forged cheque, had referred to my revelations in just one phrase: 'What a wasted life.'

This stung me into making many resolutions and a lot of positives in the latter years.

My heartfelt and eternal thanks are to firstly my beloved children Candice (and Samuel, Tayla and Luke) and Dylan, who have never failed in their love and support for me. I simply don't have the words to convey to them both what their love and ongoing support have meant to me.

During my last visit to an ailing Ma Winnie, which was not long before her passing, she reminded me in a somewhat strict manner of my promise to her to publish this diatribe, not so much because it affected her personally but because Stratcom in particular permeated literally every facet of our lives in South Africa – the National Party's version of state capture.

Winnie believed that my writing would make a significant contribution to what our history is, and we shared many years ago the hope that some may learn and not repeat the mistakes reflected in this writing.

The original manuscript, written after I was tired of writing endless statements, was typed by my former wife Linda, who sat late into the night deciphering my long-hand scrawl ... all 1700 pages of it plus doodlings and beer stains here and there!

My life, and some very difficult times in it, have been made a bit easier by, in no order of priority, Roger Lucey, Dave 'Master Jack' Marks (who has been waiting some 20 years for this!), Ole and Marie Reitov (who've given me much wonderful love and support), Russel and Kathy Galloway, Michael and Barbara Dippenaar, and Corinne Blake.

Back home and close to the soul of this work, I received a lot of kindness, friendship and support from the wonderful Shubnum Singh (NPA), the late Advocate George Bizos and his sage counsel when after the TRC I was being attacked from every quarter imaginable, Jill Burger (sister of the late Dr Neil Aggett), Imtiaz Cajee (nephew of Ahmed Timol and author of *The Murder of Ahmed Timol: My search for the truth*), Piers Pigou (your phrase 'wonderfully disruptive' made my day!) and then Brendon Becket (Mediclinic George), a young medical intern who showed me wisdom far beyond his tender years after recognising me from a TV news insert.

On matters medical, I've survived a few hard times of late and would like to convey thanks and support to Dr Leonie Schoeman (George) and Dr Bilal Bobat and his wonderful team at Wits Donald Gordon, who have glued me (and just maybe some parts of my soul in the process) back together.

All of the above was brought together by Jacana Media, with the incredible Maggie Davey and Bridget Impey and their team, and then renowned author and newspaper editor Janet Smith, who made such a huge contribution and patiently heard my endless ramblings. I was able to further rely on other dear friends like Shannon Ebrahim who, like Janet, also has this endless need to find the truth and who also encouraged and provided input into this effort. Annie Heimerl, another dear friend for many years, helped provide a measure of tranquillity in my sometimes tumultuous existence.

Before I conclude I would like to pay tribute to my former colleagues, many of whom have passed on and for many of whom the road became difficult as we were effectively sold down the river by those who denied the very existence of units such as Stratcom and Vlakplaas. Many served with decency and respect, many were simply posted to the Security Branch and were part of an empire that didn't allow refusal when it came to demands.

Finally to Lord Jesus Christ, who gave me the strength to continue and pray endlessly for forgiveness.

Notes

1　In the late 1970s, the Information Scandal rocked South Africa when it was revealed that Vorster had agreed to Minister of Information Dr Connie Mulder's plan to shift R64 million from the defence budget to undertake secret propaganda projects, which included buying a pro-NP English newspaper, *The Citizen*, and bribing international news agencies to be more favourable to the apartheid government. This culminated in the resignation of both Mulder and Vorster.

2　Abraham Louis 'Bram' Fischer was a South African lawyer of Afrikaner descent, notable for anti-apartheid activism and for the legal defence of anti-apartheid figures, including Nelson Mandela, at the Rivonia Trial. Following the trial, he was himself put on trial, accused of furthering communism.

3　A *gevegsgroep* is a fighting group.

4　The General Law Amendment Act 76 of 1962.

5　Verwoerd, considered by many to be the architect of apartheid, and Prime Minister from 1958 to 1966, explaining his government's policies in 1953. Online at: https://www.sahistory.org.za/archive/soweto-forty-years-black-student-rebellion-1976-professor-noor-nieftagodien (accessed 10 May 2021).

6　Stratcom, also known as Strategic Communications, was a police unit set up to gather information and create and spread falsehoods about 'enemies' of the state.

7　Young people were identified early on and became SB agents at educational institutions where they could study with all fees and costs paid by the SB and, whilst studying, they could spy for the SB. On completion of their studies they were made officers and had to 'pay back' the state's generosity by doing a year or two of service in the police. Some of the top informers/agents were part of this programme. As was usual, the system was open to abuse ... usually senior cops had their kids educated 'free of charge' and many resigned as soon as they were able.

8　Lungile Tabalaza was a young student activist in Port Elizabeth, when he was arrested on 10 July 1978 in connection with arson. The police claimed he committed suicide

(*TRC Report*, Vol. 3, Ch. 2). The words from 'Lungile Tabalaza' include: 'Some men take the hard line and some take none at all. And some just want their freedom and they wind up behind a prison wall. There are cops on every corner and they know what they don't like. And if you're it then you know ... no place for you at night.'

9   J.G. Strydom, *Die Roomse gevaar en hoe om dit te bestry*. Cape Town: Nasionale Pers, 1937.

10 Jann Turner, 'Who shot my dad?' *Mail & Guardian,* 29 August–4 September 1977.

11 Tom Lodge, *Black Politics in South Africa since 1945*. Harlow: Longman, 1983.

12 Solomon Kalushi Mahlangu and Motloung were operatives of uMkhonto we Sizwe (MK), the underground military wing of the ANC. They were involved in a shootout with police in Goch Street, Johannesburg, on 13 June 1977, in which two civilians were killed and two others injured.

13 Schuitema, who was named as a co-conspirator in Breyten Breytenbach's 1975 terrorism trial, was a leading member of the Dutch Anti-Apartheid Movement in the late 1960s. He was involved in an organisation called Okhela, which was a product of Paris-based Breytenbach's Revolutionary Action Groups. Okhela aimed to mobilise white and Afrikaner South Africans. Schuitema returned to South Africa in 1979 and spent 100 days in detention. In February 1980, the SB said Schuitema had been a paid informer since 1978, which he hotly denied, saying the police merely wanted to discredit him.

14 Jay Naidoo was at the forefront of the struggle and served as the founding general secretary of COSATU, the largest trade union federation, from 1985 to 1993. He later served in Nelson Mandela's cabinet.

15 APLA, the military wing of the PAC, was classified as a terrorist organisation and banned. Its members were integrated into the SANDF in 1994.

16 The Harare Declaration was adopted on 21 August 1989 by the Organisation of African Unity (OAU) subcommittee on southern Africa at its summit in Harare, Zimbabwe. The declaration urged the regime to create a climate for negotiations, put an end to apartheid and define a new constitutional order based on democratic principles (listed in the declaration). It also elaborated on the conditions for the negotiations to start.

17 Operation Damocles was a covert campaign of Israel's Mossad in 1962 targeting German scientists and technicians, formerly employed in Nazi Germany's rocket programme, who were developing rockets for Egypt. The chief tactics were letter bombs and abduction. The operation and diplomatic pressure drove the scientists out of Egypt by the end of 1963, but the head of Mossad was forced to resign.

18 André Beaufre (1902–1975), a French military strategist, is the originator of the term 'Total Strategy', a multi-component strategy drawing on other countries' experiences in counter-revolutionary warfare and low-intensity conflict. His theories were refined for the South African context and adopted by the SADF. Virtually every course at the Joint Defence College was based on Beaufre's strategic works.

19 Witdoeke were groups mobilised by a pro-government leader, Johnson Ngxobongwana, into vigilante attacks on UDF-aligned individuals and areas. In May 1986, for instance,

thousands of witdoeke from Crossroads torched and looted squatter camps in Nyanga and Portland Cement while SADF and SAP members were present; no witdoeke were arrested.

20 UNITA (the National Union for the Total Independence of Angola), under Jonas Savimbi, fought alongside the Popular Movement for the Liberation of Angola (MPLA) in the Angolan War of Independence, and then against the MPLA in the ensuing civil war.

21 A referendum on ending apartheid was held on 17 March 1992. The referendum was limited to white voters, who were asked if they supported the reforms begun by De Klerk two years earlier. The result was a 'yes' and universal suffrage was introduced in 1994.

22 The Commission of Enquiry Regarding the Prevention of Public Violence and Intimidation (Goldstone Commission) was appointed by De Klerk in October 1991, under Justice Richard Goldstone, to investigate political violence and intimidation that occurred between July 1991 and 1994. It found no evidence of Third Force involvement until October 1992.

23 The Freedom Front, a party representing Afrikaner interests, led by Constand Viljoen, was registered with the Independent Electoral Commission (IEC) on 4 March 1994 to take part in the April 1994 general elections.

24 Baroness Emma Nicholson, a Conservative MP, fought for the release of Katiza Cebekhulu, the 'missing witness' in the Stompie Seipei case. Cebekhulu, who was going to testify that Winnie Mandela had killed Seipei, was tortured, then kidnapped and taken to Zambia by Winnie's supporters prior to the trial.

25 Winnie Mandela was accused of ordering the murder of a prominent Soweto doctor and family friend, Abu Baker Asvat, who had examined Seipei at her house after his kidnapping from the home of Methodist minister Paul Verryn. Asvat's murderer testified that Winnie had supplied the gun and paid him to kill Asvat on 27 January 1989.

Index

Walsh, M. 212
Ward, Harvey 79–84, 87–88, 105–107,
    109, 212
Washington Star 129
Waspe, Sister Marie 34
Wasserman, Laurence 92
Waterkloof Air Force Base 121
WEA Records 74
Webber Wentzel 94
Weekly Mail 169, 215, 216, 219, 241
Wellman, Peter 18
Western Goals Foundation 80–81, 83
Western Goals Institute 80, 83
Westraad, Clifton 124
White House 86
Whitehead, Stephen 130–144, 155
Wilgespruit Fellowship Centre 126
Williams, Rocklyn 'Rocky' 165–167, 216
Williamson, Craig 116–117

Wit Kommando 46–47
Wit Wolwe 48
Witdoeke 187–188
Wits Great Hall 19
Wits Student Representative Council
    (SRC) 116
World, The 21, 37

Y
Young Christian Workers (YCW) 34, 77
Youth For Peace (YFP) 69

Z
ZANU-PF 79
Zeelie, Charles 165
Zimbabwe 79, 128, 168, 189
Zimbabwe Defence Force 128
Zub Zub Marauders 73
Zuma, Jacob 106